Indigenous North American Drama

SUNY series, Native Traces

Gerald Vizenor and Deborah L. Madsen, editors

Indigenous North American Drama

A Multivocal History

Edited by

Birgit Däwes

Library of Congress Cataloging-in-Publication Data

Indigenous North American drama : a multivocal history / edited by Birgit Däwes.
    p. cm.—(SUNY series, native traces)
    Includes bibliographical references and index.
    ISBN 978-1-4384-4661-5 (hardcover : alk. paper)
    1. American drama—Indian authors—History and criticism.
2. American drama—20th century—History and criticism. 3. American drama—21st century—History and criticism. 4. Canadian drama—Indian authors—History and criticism. 5. Canadian drama—20th century—History and criticism. 6. Canadian drama—21st century—History and criticism. 7. Indian theater—United States—History—20th century.
8. Indian theater—United States—History—21st century. 9. Indian theater—Canada—History—20th century. 10. Indian theater—Canada—History—21st century. 11. Indians of North America—Intellectual life.
12. Indians in literature. 13. Collective memory in literature. I. Däwes, Birgit.

    PS153.I52I56 2013
    812.009'897—dc23   2012023546

10 9 8 7 6 5 4 3 2 1

For my daughter

Juliane Mathilde

Contents

Acknowledgments

According to a Kiswahili proverb, it takes a whole village to raise a child. The production of a good book is no different, and a long-term collaborative project like this one can hardly succeed without the untiring efforts of many more people than can be mentioned here. I would first and foremost like to thank all the contributors for their fine work, and especially Tamara Underiner, Rolland Meinholtz, and Diane Glancy for their insightful comments on this study's structure, outline, and objectives. I owe a great debt of gratitude to Gerald Vizenor for his generous encouragement and his immeasurable contributions to the fields of both Native theatre and Native theory. I thank Tomson Highway for the most amazing Native plays, his kindness and generosity, and for a wonderful German tour in 2009. My colleagues Hartmut Lutz, Klára Kolinská, and Sabrina Hüttner helped me make this tour possible in the first place, and Patricia Cano and Uli Kempendorff—along with Tomson Highway and Drew Hayden Taylor—turned it into the great success that it was.

Furthermore, my mentor, Alfred Hornung, has been a continuing inspiration over the years. Without his theoretical groundwork in the fields of ethnic and transnational American studies, this study would not exist, and I would like to thank him for his unceasing kindness and support. I am grateful to Dana Leonard and the staff at Miami University Press in Ohio for their kind permission to reprint Monique Mojica's "Chocolate Woman Dreams the Milky Way," as well as Katie B. Wade and the staff at Wiley Blackwell for their permission to print an updated and expanded version of Ann Haugo's essay on "Native American Drama." Many thanks are due to the anonymous readers for their suggestions, and to Gary Dunham, James Peltz, Donna Dixon, and the staff and editorial board at SUNY Press for publishing this book.

In the editing process, Maria Elizabeth Frank has been of invaluable assistance with questions of style. Likewise, I would like to thank Daniel Scott Mayfield for his unfailing eye for detail as well as his intellectual and philosophical brilliance. And finally, thanks are due to my wonderful husband Christoph Schubert for his patience, love, and understanding during all kinds of times, especially those of raising children.

—Birgit Däwes
Mainz 2011

Performing Memory, Transforming Time

History and Indigenous North American Drama

Birgit Däwes

It is important to . . . connect our stories of the past to our future. Our future is the generations who will take their stories out into the world of the new millennium and who will create a new legacy for their future generations.

This is the "Persistence of Memory."

—Muriel Miguel, "Director's Notes on Persistence of Memory"

I

Indigenous drama and performance constitute—along with storytelling—the oldest literary genre in the Americas.[1] Ranging from the ancient Kwakiutl mystery plays to the Hopi clown dances, performative traditions have been primary modes of cultural expression all across the continent. In the late nineteenth and twentieth centuries, some of these traditions were transformed into pan-tribal and more secular art forms, such as pow wows, pageants, or scripted plays, which also incorporated European American and Asian theatrical styles. When Lynn Riggs gained mainstream popularity in the 1930s (albeit largely without reference to his Cherokee heritage) and the first pageants were performed at the Six Nations Reserve's Forest

1

Theatre in Ontario, Canada, in the 1940s, the path was paved for a contemporary Native theatre movement. And this movement is well underway. There are currently over 250 published and far over 600 unpublished plays by some 250 Native American and First Nations playwrights and theatre groups on the North American market.[2] Furthermore, the access to an abundance of material is increasingly improving: Mimi Gisolfi D'Aponte's pioneer collection of Native American plays, *Seventh Generation* (1999), was followed by eight other anthologies dedicated exclusively to indigenous plays,[3] and Alexander Street Press's *North American Indian Drama*, a digital full-text collection of more than 200 indigenous plays, is even searchable by semantic parameters. On the other hand, however, this rich and exciting field of American performance is only rarely acknowledged by university curricula, let alone by theatre audiences or the general public.[4] Despite the abundance of primary sources, scholarship in the field is only just beginning to gain momentum. With a few notable exceptions (such as Linda Walsh Jenkins's 1981 article on Native performance art, Jeffrey Huntsman's investigation of traditional ritual drama and contemporary forms in *Ethnic Theater in the United States* [1983], Christopher Bigsby's chapter on "American Indian Theatre" in *A Critical Introduction to Twentieth-Century American Drama* [1985], or Christy Stanlake's *Native American Drama: A Critical Perspective* [2010]), the general practice has been, for the longest time, one of neglect. As Shari Huhndorf diagnoses, "drama remains the most overlooked genre in Native American literatures" (2006, 313).

II

In 1967, a play entitled *A Season for All Things* was published by an Anishinaabe graduate student and community advocate in Minneapolis. This "play of voices, about forty-five minutes" was an inquiry into historical images of Native people, and it "was selected from the writing, speeches, and letters of historical, political, and literary figures in the context of [Minnesota] state history."[5] Unfortunately, the text has been out of print, and the one copy that should be stored at the Minnesota Historical Society's archive is untraceable, much to the astonishment of both the librarian and the author himself. This author is Gerald Vizenor, who explains that

> I wrote and produced *A Season for All Things* while working as a Native advocate in the Native community near Franklin Avenue and Elliot Park in Minneapolis. I encour-

aged several Natives to play the parts of historical figures and to read from what historical figures had written
about Natives. Young Natives were very eager to act, or
rather mock, the voices of historical figures, such as gov-
ernors, missionaries, and others who wrote about their
experiences with the Anishinaabe (Chippewa) Natives in
Minnesota. . . . I think the play was performed several
times in the community, and even the audience seemed
to take part in the rage and irony.[6]

Beside the fact that this play is lost and deserving of additional
detective work, the story of *A Season for All Things* highlights the
interface between history and performance in three crucial ways,
which I would like to use as prolegomena for this book.

First, *A Season for All Things* creatively engages with historical
encounters between people of European American and Native American descent. It thus marks a characteristic feature of the genre:
in response to the long, unfortunate tradition of colonialist image
control and *indian* simulacra[7] that have displaced Native theatre
from North American stages, a large number of indigenous plays
focus on revisions of history. From Columbus's and the Spanish,
French, or English colonizers' arrivals (in LeAnne Howe and Roxy
Gordon's *Indian Radio Days*, Hanay Geiogamah's *Foghorn*, or Floyd
Favel's *Governor of the Dew*) to boarding school experiences (in
Vera Manuel's *Strength of Indian Women*, Shirley Cheechoo's *Path
with No Moccasins*, or N. Scott Momaday's *Indolent Boys*), and from
the Trail of Tears (in Diane Glancy's *Pushing the Bear*) to the silencing or misrepresentation of Native people in history books (such
as Sacajawea in Monique Mojica's *Birdwoman and the Suffragettes*
or the women of the Thompson River Valley in Tomson Highway's
Ernestine Shuswap Gets Her Trout), the history of North America is
continually rewritten on contemporary indigenous stages.

Second, Vizenor's play tells us something about the history
and historiography of Native American drama as a genre. *A Season
for All Things* was written, produced, and published in 1967, and
thus half a decade before what many critics consider the "beginning" of indigenous theatre in the United States—the 1972 New York
premiere of Kiowa playwright Hanay Geiogamah's *Body Indian*.[8] It
thus shows that Geiogamah was not, as critics such as Jeffrey
Huntsman and Christopher Balme have assumed, the first Native
American playwright (see Huntsman 1980, ix, and Balme 1999, 56).
Even before Vizenor, there was an increasing indigenous presence
on stage: Arthur Junaluska (Cherokee) and E. Claude Richards

(Huahotecan) are credited with founding "the first Native American theatre company in the United States" in 1956 (Heath 1995, 147). Rolland Meinholtz (Cherokee) cofounded the performance section at the Institute of American Indian Arts (IAIA) at the University of New Mexico, Santa Fe, in 1966, and Jay Silverheels (Mohawk), George Pierre (Colville), and Noble "Kid" Chissell (Cherokee) formed the Indian Actors Workshop in Los Angeles (see Jenkins and Wapp 1976, 12). Besides Lynn Riggs's plays in the 1920s and 1930s, predecessors to Geiogamah's influential work also include Raven Hail's *The Raven and the Redbird: Sam Houston and His Cherokee Wife* (1965), *To Catch a Never Dream* (1969) by Bruce King (Oneida), *The Dress* (1970) by Nona Benedict (Mohawk), *Yanowis* (1971) by Monica Charles (Klallam), and *Survival in the South* (1971) by Minnie Aodla Freeman (Inuit). As Gerald Vizenor's play demonstrates, many works have been forgotten or lost, so that the historiography of indigenous North American drama requires accurate research and a multiplicity of sources and voices—especially those of the artists and writers themselves.

Furthermore, as is always necessarily the case with artistic work, the increasing visibility of indigenous plays and productions has led to the emergence of a canon: some playwrights and companies are more widely acknowledged or considered more influential than others. In the United States, plays by Hanay Geiogamah, Spiderwoman Theater (Kuna/Rappahannock), William S. Yellow Robe Jr. (Assiniboine), and Diane Glancy (Cherokee) are among the best-known and most frequently anthologized works; in Canada, Native Earth Performing Arts and De-Ba-Jeh-Mu-Jig, Tomson Highway (Cree), Drew Hayden Taylor (Ojibway), Daniel David Moses (Delaware), and Marie Clements (Métis) are usually listed as the most influential contributors to the scene. In this context, *A Season for All Things* serves as a reminder that there is—even in a genre itself long displaced—a struggle over power and recognition. All canons involve hierarchies, and any attempt at literary or cultural historiography involves precarious balancing acts of selection and combination, inclusion and exclusion. The choices and selective processes needed for a framework limited by the realities of publishing are always difficult, and this volume is no exception to the rule.

The impossible project of writing "the" history of this genre would have to include hundreds of individual voices and ignore the rather profane practical aspects of academic publishing (the space between book covers is limited, and so is time: playwrights are busy raising funds, applying for grants, working on new plays, or teaching; some have left the stage or moved on into different fields). As in any anthology or collection of essays, the necessary selection process includes absences, as well. In line with this insight, this collection of voices does not claim to be representative or even just characteristic. It is based on the awareness that canons are there to be continually revised.

Likewise, recent developments in indigenous American studies have rightly shown a turn toward a more inclusive angle, covering the Americas or even the Western hemisphere as a whole. The Kuna notion of *Abya Yala*, or the pan-indigenous "Continent of Life," which Tamara Underiner uses for her approach in this volume, is highly useful in this context. Although the present study also touches upon the francophone parts of Canada (in Henning Schäfer's chapter), and (in more detail) upon Mexico and Central America, the focus is primarily on Canada and the United States. A transhemispheric inquiry into Native American performance remains desired and needed, across barriers of languages and disciplines.

Acknowledging the fact that many voices are needed to begin the story, this study gathers voices both academic and creative, from Europe, the United States, and Canada, and from different disciplines and cultural backgrounds. The contributions collected here are narrative points of departure: they consider themselves work in progress. *Indigenous North American Drama: A Multivocal History* is thus an homage to, rather than a comprehensive assessment of, a rich, diverse, and vibrant genre.

III

"Native theatre," as Drew Hayden Taylor summarizes, "is much older than that scant few years. It is as old as this country, as old as the people who have been here for thousands of years, as old as the stories that are still told today. It is merely the presentation that has changed" (1996b, 51). The history of indigenous theatre, drama, and performance in the Americas is long and complex; and its recording (or narrativization, which history always is) would be the project of a decade, easily filling several volumes. Even though such a comprehensive chronological approach to the genre has not been written, several selective surveys have been attempted. Linda Walsh Jenkins and Ed Wapp Jr. pioneered the research into this field in the 1970s, when they drew attention to Arthur Junaluska's productions in New York in the 1950s (Jenkins and Wapp 1976,

12). In 1983, Jeffrey Huntsman tried to classify traditional dramatic forms according to purpose and listed various twentieth-century initiatives, noting rather generally that "Indians today are continuing, not only to renew traditional dramatic forms and to incorporate outside elements into older dramas, but also to assimilate and adapt the forms of Euro-American drama" (Huntsman 1983, 369). Two years later, Christopher Bigsby saw the influence from the reverse side, emphasizing that "the public ceremony which western theatre worked so hard in the 1960s to foreground, . . . has always been an essential element of Indian life and a vital expression of individual, tribal, and racial identity" (1985, 369). The need for historical orientation within this newly discovered field was obvious, and most publications of the 1990s, while not going into historical detail, mentioned pioneer companies and institutions such as Hanay Geiogamah's American Indian Theater Ensemble,[9] Red Earth Performing Arts (Seattle), the Institute of American Indian Arts (Santa Fe), A-Tu-Mai (Southern Ute, Colorado), Indian Time (Niagara Falls, New York), or Navajoland Outdoor Theatre (Navajo Country). An unpublished dissertation by Sally Ann Heath (1995) was the first attempt at probing more deeply into the genre's practical side by providing research on the twentieth-century development of Native American theatre companies. Annamaria Pinazzi's "The 'Fervent Years' of the American Indian Theatre" provides a survey of exemplary plays from the 1960s to the 1990s, subdividing the dramatic works within this time period roughly into "traditional," "modern," and "historical" plays (1997, 110).[10] In addition to these invaluable collections of data, however, critics also called for a more inclusive understanding of indigenous performative traditions (including ritual, ceremony, pow wows, and dance), and for a better awareness of the problematic "translation of one culture's performance events into another peoples' language" (Jenkins 1975, 66). In 1999, a substantial step toward such a comprehensive understanding was taken by Hanay Geiogamah and Jaye T. Darby's *American Indian Theater in Performance: A Reader*, which collects approaches to Native theatre from various angles. After the turn of the millennium, four more essays—by Christy Stanlake (2001), Ann Haugo (two essays, both in 2005), and Shari Huhndorf (2006)—as well as individual chapters in monographs (in Christy Stanlake's *Native American Drama*, in my own study of *Native North American Theater in a Global Age*, in Günter Beck's *Defending Dreamer's Rock: Geschichte, Geschichtsbewusstsein und Geschichtskultur im Native Drama der USA und Kanadas,* and in Marc Maufort's *Labyrinth of*

Hybridities: Avatars of O'Neillian Realism in Multi-ethnic American Drama [2010]) provided further historical groundwork.

In addition to chronological surveys of the genre's development, the historiography of Native theatre also requires a closer look at the hi/stories of individual playwrights and theatre groups. Lynn Riggs's heritage was revived by Phyllis Cole Braunlich and the University of Oklahoma Press's republication of three of his plays in 2003. Robert Nunn has edited a collection on Drew Hayden Taylor's plays (2008), and it is needless to say that the dramatic works and achievements of Tomson Highway, Diane Glancy, Monique Mojica (Kuna/Rappahannock), LeAnne Howe (Choctaw), Daniel David Moses, Floyd Favel (Cree), Hanay Geiogamah, William S. Yellow Robe Jr., Ian Ross (Ojibway), James Luna (Luiseño/Diegueño), Yvette Nolan (Algonquin), Marie Clements, Margo Kane (Saulteaux/Cree/Blackfoot), and many other playwrights and performance artists active in the Native theatre scene today would deserve similar publications. Some of their stories are beginning to be told in this volume.

The same holds true for theatre companies and groups. Few steps have been taken toward the recording of an impressive history: Jennifer Preston has written a journal article about Native Earth Performing Arts' tenth anniversary in 1992; and the company's twenty-fifth anniversary was celebrated with a memorial video that is available online.[11] Similarly, Spiderwoman Theater, the longest-running women's theatre company in the United States, has been acknowledged by two memorial events: One part of the exhibition *New Tribe, New York: The Urban Vision Quest* showed a thirty-year retrospective of their work at the Smithsonian National Museum of the American Indian's George Gustav Heye Center in New York in 2005, the catalogue of which has been published (McMaster 2005). In 2007, the idea of honoring this legacy was taken up again by the Native American Women Playwrights Archive (NAWPA) at Miami University, Ohio, which hosted a conference dedicated to Spiderwoman Theater, and which also features an online exhibit of the group's history.[12] Furthermore, Shannon Hengen's book *Where Stories Meet: An Oral History of De-Ba-Jeh-Mu-Jig Theatre*—a collection of interviews with former members and current staff of Canada's "longest-running Native theatre [company]" (Hengen 2007, 14)—is a milestone that illustrates how much remains to be done: a similar volume could be envisioned for each of the other most influential theatre companies, festivals, and institutions in Canada and the United States. In this volume, Rolland Meinholtz tells the story of how the Institute of American Indian Arts became one of the nuclei of the Native theatre movement; and complementary hi/stories are needed for Hanay Geiogamah's Native American Theater Ensemble, for Don Matt and Jon Kaufman's Red Earth Performing Arts in Seattle, for the American Indian Theater Company in Tulsa, Oklahoma, and for the highly successful Native Voices Festival hosted every year by the Autry National Center in Los Angeles.

IV

This volume's three sections seek to explore the three central trajectories of historical inquiry: surveys of major developments (in the United States, Canada, and Central America), contributions of individual playwrights to the scene—their experience, their visions, and their perspectives on the genre—and finally, critical analyses of historiography, history, and cultural memory, both as modes of representation and as issues negotiated on stage. The first section, "Indigenous North American Performance: Surveys and Methodologies," addresses the dimension of the history/historiography of indigenous performance cultures from a larger perspective. It clarifies the terminologies and key terms for studying the field, provides surveys of the theatre movements in the United States, Canada, Mexico, and Guatemala, and thus serves as a general introduction. This introduction also offers a fundamental framework of "data" and historical developments without simplifying the genre into narrowly prefabricated temporal or linear categories.

Beginning in the northernmost part of North America, Henning Schäfer gives a survey of the development of contemporary Native theatre in Canada. His summary traces First Nations performance culture chronologically from the tradition of storytelling to contemporary theatre conventions all across the Canadian theatrical landscape. Adding a few methodological stepping stones, Ann Haugo provides a similar framework for Native American theatre and drama in the United States. Like Schäfer, Haugo identifies continuing challenges (funding, training, networking) and exemplarily highlights the interplay between artists and audiences as well as between theatrical and scholarly communities. Focusing on Mexico and Central America, then, Tamara Underiner rounds off the introductory section with a summary of theatrical development south of the U.S. border. Underiner zooms in on three particular issues that arise from any discussion of contemporary Native theatre: history (both theatre as historiography and the history of theatrical forms), languages on stage, and the cultural infrastructure that helps (or fails to help) playwrights to reach their audiences.

The second section, entitled "Individual Hi/stories: Visions, Practice, Experience," is the pivotal and most substantial part of this study. Here, Native American and First Nations playwrights comment on their own contributions to indigenous theatre, their experiences, their audiences, and aspects they consider crucial for the development of the field. From Rolland Meinholtz's memoir on the beginnings of Native American drama at the Institute of American Indian Arts to Daniel David Moses's humorous inquiry into the Shakespearean tradition, and from Diane Glancy's exploration of dramatic writing techniques to Tomson Highway's unique combination of classical music theory and drama, this section illustrates the genre's rich and vibrant mosaic of manifestations.

The engagement with Native companies and playwrights' perspectives on their work is indispensable for the development of methodological approaches to indigenous theatre and drama. Since the late 1980s, there have been heated discussions over critical authority, the problematics of spectatorship and the pitfalls of appropriation. Alan Filewod's claim that non-Native critics can never free themselves from the colonizing gaze ("my watching is an appropriation, even when it is invited" [Filewod 1992, 17]), the discussion over Tomson Highway's alleged misogyny (see Baker 1991 and Schäfer's chapter in this volume), or non-Native critic Susan Bennett's (1993) attack on another non-Native critic, Jennifer Preston, for writing an article about Native Earth Performing Arts, are only three cases in point.[13] Who may speak about the genre? Which angles are appropriate? What ideological backgrounds have to be taken into account? Most importantly, who benefits from the discussion of the genre? Within what Rob Appleford has perceived as a "climate of distrust" (1999, 49), the terminological or methodological frameworks for critical approaches to Native drama are as heavily contested as they are necessary. Christy Stanlake states in her recent study on *Native American Drama* that "in order to read these plays, one must be prepared to read with a perspective that is sensitive to the ways in which Native epistemologies shape the dramaturgy" (2010, 21). Native theatre is informed by a multiplicity of intellectual and cultural traditions, many of them different from European American frameworks of reading. There is thus no history of the genre without indigenous perspectives.

As the second section of this book also reveals, most aboriginal American playwrights agree that the oral tradition is a central aspect of their work. Like Bruce King, who states that "[t]heater and performance are about storytelling" (2000, 167); William S. Yellow Robe Jr., Drew Hayden Taylor, Diane Glancy, and Spiderwoman Theater more or less explicitly consider themselves "contemporary storytellers" (Pulitano 1998, 28). At the same time, many playwrights and groups have developed unique perspectives on their dramatic work and creative processes—both individual and collective. While N. Scott Momaday proclaims that plays "are poems in form and oral tradition in spirit" (Momaday 2007, vii), Choctaw playwright LeAnne Howe emphasizes cross-generational memory in her work. She has coined the term "tribalography" for her process of creating drama:

> As I thought about my identity as a Native writer, as a Choctaw woman, it became clear to me that "everything does matter." When I write . . . I pull the passages of my life, and the lives of my mothers, my mothers' mothers, my uncles, the greater community of *chafachúka* ("family") and *iksa* ("clan"), together to form the basis for critique, interpretation; a moment in the raw world. . . . Then I must be able to render all our collective experiences into a meaningful form. I call this process "tribalography." (Howe 2000, 214–15)

De-Ba-Jeh-Mu-Jig, one of Canada's longest-running Native theatre companies, has developed an improvisational technique called "4D," or "Four Directions," which—as artistic director Ron Berti explains—has become the company's general policy over the years:

> [T]he Four Directions creation process, apart from being a culturally and socially specific method for creating new works, has also become a core principle that applies to everything the company is engaged in. It requires that we adopt a holistic approach to all things, and acknowledge the importance of the relationship between, and the association with each other. It means we recognize that we create with our entire selves—our emotional, our physical, our intellectual, and our spiritual selves. . . . That is why we say, "The artist is the creation, and the performance is the celebration." (Hengen 2007, 67)

Perspectives like these are indispensable for any study of indigenous North American drama, since they shape the methodological groundwork that Diane Glancy calls for: "an expanding theory with various centers of the universe, taking in more than one view, more than one multiplicity" (Glancy 2002, 204). Especially in light of what Ann Haugo calls the "'explosion' of Native theatre" in the twenty-first century (2005b, 347), the history of indigenous American drama and performance has to begin with the artists themselves, their own approaches and critical angles. By collecting the voices and expertise of Rolland Meinholtz, Diane Glancy, Daniel David Moses, Floyd Favel, Monique Mojica, and Tomson Highway, this book's central section provides a dialogue, in printed form, on the creation and perception, the functions and reverberations of Native theatre.

Finally, the contributions to section 3, "Representations of History: Critical Perspectives," approach the topic from the sites of reception. Illuminating in further detail the reverberations of history and historiography on stage, this chapter explores some of the most crucial questions for the study of the field, including language, representation, and the appropriation of historical figures and events.

Marc Maufort opens the section by engaging with the interplay between history and memory in three plays by First Nations writers. Reading Shirley Cheechoo's *Path with No Moccasins*, Tomson Highway's *Ernestine Shuswap Gets Her Trout*, and Marie Clements's *Burning Vision* against the critical backdrop of postcolonialism, Maufort shows a wide range of possibilities for the performance of cultural memory. His analysis identifies alternative methods of approaching the past and demonstrates how, through various manifestations of magic realism, trickster discourse, and cultural hybridity, contemporary indigenous theatre actively resists the "ghettoizing" of "Native historiography."

In a detailed analysis of Monique Mojica's play *Birdwoman and the Suffragettes*, Günter Beck then explores two different modes of historiography in a similar way: the individual process of remembrance and the more formal process of an institutionalized memory. Mojica's play, which centers on the story of Sacajawea, illustrates the ways in which historical figures are exploited for various political purposes, including the male, white discourse of Manifest Destiny and a Western feminist agenda. Both these forms of appropriation, as Beck argues, distort American history and thus silence both Sacajawea's own voice and her hybrid status.

Finally, Klára Kolinská rounds off this section with an outlook at the inter- and transnational reverberations of indigenous North American drama. Having translated six First Nations plays into

Czech, Kolinská elucidates the challenges of making Native theatre more widely available to audiences beyond the United States or Canada, while staying true to the cultural values embedded in the individual works. Whereas elements in Cree, Ojibway, or other indigenous languages undermine the process of appropriating Native plays in an English-speaking context, the translation of these plays into yet another language doubles this problem of representation and poses additional difficulties for the genre's reception.

The issue of cultural transmissibility by which Kolinská concludes this volume seems central to the study of indigenous North American drama, especially in the twenty-first century. Native American and First Nations performance artists such as Drew Hayden Taylor, Spiderwoman Theater, Tomson Highway, or James Luna have become well known in the international contemporary theatre scene. From the beginning of Emily Johnson's and Te Ata's tours to Europe and Latin America, Native theatre artists have reached out across and beyond the Americas to an extraordinary extent, seeing their work staged at the Sydney opera house (Margo Kane) or in Tokyo (Tomson Highway), and touring Asia or Europe. A festival entitled ORIGINS: First Nations Theatre from around the World (organized by Gordon Bronitsky and Michael Walling), was launched in London in September 2007, followed by IndigeNOW, an annual festival of indigenous opera (from North America, Sweden, and Australia) in Australia in 2010. Annamaria Pinazzi is working on a translation of eight Native plays into Italian, and Albert-Reiner Glaap has edited Drew Hayden Taylor's *Toronto at Dreamer's Rock* for German high schools. All of these ventures across different languages and continents show that Native North American drama and performance have a transnational, if not universal appeal, and thus the potential for influencing and enriching theatrical traditions around the globe.

The historical inquiry into indigenous American drama requires many more voices, and many more angles—both theoretical and practical—in the years to come. More work is needed on the interactions between theatrical communities and their audiences, the differences between reservation-based and urban theatre groups, and the local and global arenas that Native playwrights and companies use as sites of creative development. Questions of gender and gender relations in Native plays deserve more attention in future analyses, as do the interrelations between Native theatre and scholarship. In addition to collecting voices from North America and Europe, as this volume does, the transcendence of English-language boundaries is necessary to see indigenous American drama across the hemisphere, as well as in relation to other indigenous cultures worldwide. As Joseph Roach excellently demonstrates in *Cities of the Dead: Circum-Atlantic Performance* (New York: Columbia University Press, 1996), new approaches to indigenous drama tie in most rewardingly with the recent advances into Atlantic, transhemispheric, and transnational American studies. Similarly, the recent collection on *American Indian Performing Arts: Critical Directions*, edited by Hanay Geiogamah and Jaye T. Darby (Los Angeles: UCLA American Indian Studies Center, 2010), combines criticism on contemporary performances with a section on historical stagings, both from international angles. Connecting shared points of reference, and combining analyses of plays by artists such as Tomson Highway, Monique Mojica, or Daniel David Moses with their own perspectives on theatre, the collaborative study presented here furthers the transnational promotion and understanding of indigenous North American drama. As work in progress on a dynamically evolving genre, this book marks an optimistic beginning.

Notes

1. In matters of so-called political correctness, disclaimers about the use of "Indian," "Native American," or other terms precede almost every publication, and breaches of that protocol are reviewers' most popular targets. Aware of these terminological inadequacies, and with respect to indigenous people's sovereignty and inherent right to the North American continent, I am strategically using the hyperonyms "Native," "Native American," "First Nations," "indigenous," and "aboriginal" interchangeably in cases where a comprehensive term is needed. Since these terms are as much a discursive construct as "Western" or "European," and for purposes of differentiation, I am also using distinct cultural affiliations wherever possible.

2. These numbers do not include those published in the monumental digital collection *North American Indian Drama* (Alexandria, VA: Alexander Street Press, 2006).

3. These are, in chronological order: Hanay Geiogamah and Jaye T. Darby's *Stories of Our Way: An Anthology of American Indian Plays* (1999), Margo Kane, Greg Daniels, and Marie Clements's *DraMétis* (2001), Heather Hodgson's *The Great Gift of Tears: Four Aboriginal Plays* (2002), Monique Mojica and Ric Knowles's *Staging Coyote's Dream: An Anthology of First Nations Drama in English* (2003), Jaye T. Darby and Stephanie Fitzgerald's *Keepers of the Morning Star: An Anthology of Native Women's Theater* (2003), Shirley A. Huston-Findley and Rebecca Howard's *Footpaths and Bridges: Voices from the Native American Women Playwrights Archive* (2008), the

second volume of *Staging Coyote's Dream* (2009), and Ann Elizabeth Armstrong, Kelli Lyon Johnson, and William A. Wortman's *Performing Worlds Into Being: Native American Women's Theater* (2009). All of these anthologies contain three or more plays by Native American or First Nations dramatists. In addition to these, Native North American drama has been published in at least twenty-eight more general anthologies, and there are twelve collections of three or more plays by individual playwrights, such as Joseph Bruchac, Hanay Geiogamah, Diane Glancy, Joan Shaddox Isom, Bruce King, N. Scott Momaday, Yvette Nolan, Lynn Riggs, E. Donald Two Rivers, and William S. Yellow Robe Jr. These do not yet include the large number of plays published individually or in journals.

4. As I have argued elsewhere, there are various reasons for this substantial displacement from the canon (see Däwes 2007a, 45–87). Indigenous American theatrical traditions were subject to colonial oppression, prohibition, appropriation, and other forms of exploitative power. Moreover, Native American performance was widely considered in opposition to Western theatrical traditions and thus relegated into the fields of anthropology or religious studies. Beside this methodological diffusion, the genre has been marked by a crucial indistinctness of authorship and authority. From nineteenth-century melodramas to the annual Karl May festival in Bad Segeberg, Germany, plays about, not by, Native American people have been tremendously successful, privileging a practice of identity building that Philip J. Deloria calls "playing Indian" (1998, 1–9). Thus displacing the complexity and political power of actual indigenous performance culture, the practice of "colonial mimicry" (Bhabha 1994, 91) guaranteed European American image control, the dissimulation of historical guilt, and a sense of superior selfhood. In consequence, the Other of Native performance was overwritten by Wild West Show aesthetics: the place of the indigene on American stages had been replaced by the *indian* simulacrum.

5. Gerald Vizenor, "Lost Seasons," e-mail message to the author, July 19, 2004.

6. Gerald Vizenor, "Theater," e-mail message to the author, November 3, 2004.

7. In using the italicized spelling in small letters for the image instead of the actual people, I am following Gerald Vizenor, who marks it as "a simulation with no referent and with the absence of natives; *indians* are the other, the names of sacrifice and victimry" (1998, 27).

8. As McCandlish Phillips noted after the premiere of Hanay Geiogamah's *Body Indian* in 1972: "When the history of the American Indian theater is written in, say, the year 2054, it will probably record that it all began back in 1972 in a narrow loft at 74A East Fourth Street on New York's Lower East Side" (1972, 56).

9. Don B. Wilmeth, for instance, claims that "[o]nly Geiogamah (Kiowa Indian) has gained any real national attention" (2000, 146).

10. Individual studies (like Günter Beck's, and my own) have tried to gain terminological and methodological access to Native North American

performance culture—sometimes within the larger context of postcolonial studies (see Christopher Balme or Helen Gilbert and Joanne Tompkins), and sometimes on its own account (see Christy Stanlake's inquiry into Native dramaturgy, *Native American Drama: A Critical Perspective*). The trend is also exemplified by special issues of academic journals (*Canadian Theatre Review* 68 [Fall 1991], *Aboriginal Voices* 2, no. 7 [September–October 1995], and the *Baylor Journal of Theatre and Performance* 4, no. 1 [Spring 2007]) as well as by collections of essays, edited by Per Brask and William Morgan (1992), Hanay Geiogamah and Jaye T. Darby (2000 and 2009), Rob Appleford, Ann Elizabeth Armstrong, Kelli Lyon Johnson, and William A. Wortman (*Performing Worlds Into Being: Native American Women's Theater*) and, most recently, Steve E. Wilmer (*Native American Performance and Representation*).

11. It can be viewed at http://www.youtube.com/watch?v=bKlTFXugsIY.

12. The conference proceedings are included in *Performing Worlds Into Being* (2009); see especially Murielle Borst's chapter "Spiderwoman Theater's Legacy." For the online exhibit, see http://staff.lib.muohio.edu/nawpa/spdrwmnarchv.html.

13. Bennett particularly accused Preston of subjecting the group "to the tourist gaze of an American and international readership" (Bennett 1993, 12).

Part I

Indigenous North American Performance

Surveys and Methodologies

1

A Short History of Native Canadian Theatre

Henning Schäfer

Prologue

The history of Native theatre is either the shortest or the longest theatrical tradition within the realm of Canada, depending on your point of view. Contemporary Native theatre in Canada can be said to have started roughly forty years ago, but it draws from a tradition of performance that goes back to time beyond memory. With few predecessors, Native theatre began in 1974, had its heyday between 1985 and 1995, and is still growing today despite a few setbacks. The following is only a "short history," because it is impossible to give all the details of this development. For the purpose of this chapter, I will also refrain from discussing terminology, theoretical viewpoints, and the historical background. Instead, I will jump *in medias res* and recount the history of the contemporary Native theatre scene, with the necessary brevity. I am dividing this history into four sections, starting with the predecessors of the contemporary scene, followed by its initiation in the seventies, the breakthrough in the eighties, and the scene's development from the mid-nineties to this day.

Act One: The Predecessors. Time Immemorial to 1974

A variety of rituals and ceremonies could be considered early forms of theatre, such as the Kwakiutl Winter Ceremony, the Shaking Tent ritual, or the Nootka potlatch. Critics have described these ceremonies as ritual drama, mystery, or spirit plays. Others see this interpretation as a devaluation of sacred rituals as simply a pre-form

19

of secular theatre. However, even if they really constitute an early form of theatre, they never had the chance to develop into a distinct secular art form. Thus, the influence on the contemporary theatre scene is minimal. On the other hand, many critics and authors agree that contemporary Native theatre can be seen as a continuation of traditional storytelling. The storytellers have always been performers, rehearsing their performance continuously, taking on different roles, engaging the audience in their stories, and accompanying them by gestures and facial expressions. The similarities between the storytelling tradition and theatre are undeniable, and the beginnings of contemporary Native theatre owe a lot more to this tradition than to elaborate rituals or ceremonies.

The roots of a Native theatre scene can be seen in various developments, such as Wild West Shows, medicine shows, performances of plays by the colonizers that employed Native people as actors, the early cinema, and oratory. One of the first Native artists to establish oratory as an art form was Mohawk poet Emily Pauline Johnson, who performed very dramatic readings of her poetry in the late nineteenth century and thus may be said to be one of the first practitioners of modern Native theatre.

After Johnson, the first Native theatre group on record is the Can-Oos-Sez Skay-loo Drama Group, an Okanagan youth theatre from Inkameep, British Columbia. Under the direction of a non-Native teacher at the Inkameep day school, Anthony Walsh, this group operated from 1939 to 1942. They performed three plays at the opening of Thunderbird Park in Victoria (1940), *Little Chipmunk and the Owl Woman* by Elizabeth Renyi (Okanagan), *The Ants and the Crickets* and *The Partridge Mother*, both by Isabel Christie (Okanagan), and won the "Mohawk Chief Oskenenton Cup" in Oliver, British Columbia four years in a row. The plays were enactments of traditional Okanagan stories, and props and costumes were made by the children themselves (see Osoyoos Museum 2008).

A few years later, in 1949, former school teacher Emily General (Cayuga) established a series of annual pageant plays to be performed at the Great Pine Forest Theatre on the Six Nations Reserve. The pageant consists of several plays about Six Nations history performed in succession, one play per year, and continues to this day (see Krieg 1978). The plays are written by a special committee of the band council and performed entirely by Native people from Six Nations. It is thus the longest-running Native theatre in North America.

An opera called *Tzinquaw: The Thunderbird and the Killer Whale* was on the verge of becoming a similar pageant: It premiered

in Duncan, BC in November 1950 and went on to tour British Columbia. Written and directed by two non-Natives, arts teacher Frank
Morrison and director Cecil West, it was created in collaboration
with the Cowichan Indian Band and performed entirely by Native
people. The performances at the Royal Theatre in Victoria were
sold out five times, and the play was even broadcast on CBC radio.
Although it was revived several times in the sixties and seventies,
the plans to make it a regular event were never realized.

The breakthrough for Canadian theatre, and also one of the
landmarks for Native theatre, were the centennial celebrations in
1967, when James Reaney, John Herbert, and George Ryga were
introduced to the Canadian scene as the first Canadian playwrights
of note. Reaney and Ryga both played their part in the birth of
Native theatre, and George Ryga's play *The Ecstasy of Rita Joe* (1970)
is still seen by many critics as the real beginning of Canadian theatre
in general and also as a trigger for the Native theatre movement. It
was the first play to show the social conditions of contemporary
Native people in a realistic manner, and the performance of Salish
actor Chief Dan George was widely praised.

In the early seventies, three plays were performed that are
often cited as the first Native plays: *The Dress* (1970) by Nona
Benedict (Mohawk), performed in high schools in the seventies;
Survival in the South by Minnie Aodla Freeman (Inuit), performed
at the Dominion Drama Festival in 1971; and *Wasawkachack* by
Duke Redbird (Ojibway), a storytelling piece produced by Pendulum
Theatre in Montreal in 1974. All these examples have to be seen as
predecessors, as they were not part of a general movement, were
not well known in Canada, and thus unable to make much of an
impact.

Act Two: The Creation of a
Native Theatre Scene, 1974–1984

The Cree boxer and opera singer James H. Buller is undeniably the
most influential figure for the whole of the contemporary Native
theatre scene. His goal was the furtherance of Native art and theatre, and for him, the key to the establishment of a theatre scene
was training. Thus, in 1974, he founded the Association for Native
Development in the Performing and Visual Arts (ANDPVA) and the
Native Theatre School (NTS), a summer program for Native theatre artists. The first was held at Carrick Camp near Owen Sound,

Ontario, moving later to Kimbercote Farm near Heathcote. The NTS still continues and has also been exported to the north of Canada.

In 1977, when James Buller was approached to provide a Native play to represent Canada at a theatre festival in Monaco, he asked Cree poet George Kenny whether he could turn his book *Indians Don't Cry* (Kenny 1977) into a play. Together with Cree actor Denis Lacroix, Kenny wrote *October Stranger* (1978), the first full-length Native play about contemporary Native people. They put together an all-Native troupe that called itself Kematewan, including a young Shirley Cheechoo (Cree). *October Stranger* premiered in Monaco in 1977 and in Canada the following year, and although reports about its reception are a bit varied, the play still stands as a prime example of Native theatre, containing many of the qualities of its more famous successors in the mid-eighties.

The scope of Buller's vision, however, was not limited to Ontario or Canada: he wanted to promote indigenous theatre globally. Thus, in 1980, he organized the first Indigenous People's Theatre Celebration in Toronto, with indigenous groups from all over the world. Two years later, a second celebration was held at Trent University in Peterborough, Ontario, because Buller was unsatisfied with the metropolitan setting in Toronto, which gave the celebration the appearance of an exotic tourist event. The celebration opened on the Curve Lake Reserve in August 1982 as part of the annual pow wow.

Also in 1982, Buller again approached Denis Lacroix for a play to be shown at the Centre for Indian Arts' opening at the National Exhibition Centre in Thunder Bay, Ontario. Together with non-Native actress Bunny Sicard, Lacroix wrote and directed a play called *Native Images in Transition*, based on a painting by Odawa artist Daphne Odjig (see Preston 1992, 137). The play was staged as a coproduction with Kam Theatre Lab, and the performers called themselves Native Earth. James Buller did not see the production of the play, nor was he present at the second Indigenous People's Theatre Celebration, for he died in 1982. The celebration was to be the last of its kind.

Around the time of Buller's work with ANDPVA, four companies were founded that carried on his vision. The first was a small touring company called Northern Delights. It emerged from a company founded by James Reaney and Keith Turnbull, NDWT. In 1978, they staged the play *Wacousta!* (Reaney 1979), the first Canadian play to use the Cree language, featuring Graham Greene (Oneida) and Gary Farmer (Cayuga). The young Tomson Highway (Cree) was brought in to help with the dialogue. Later that same year, they toured with the collective creation *Northern Delights*, which focused on contemporary Native and Northern life, and in 1979 with *Radio Free Cree*, written by non-Native journalist Paulette Jiles. Inspired by the play's success in the Northern communities, the company Northern Delights was founded in 1980. They produced another play by Jiles, *Northshore Run* in 1981, and two stage adaptations of Ojibway legends by Jim Morris (Ojibway), *Odess* in 1982 and *Ayash* in 1983, and then disbanded.

In Toronto, Denis Lacroix and Bunny Sicard were inspired by their performance in Thunder Bay to turn Native Earth into a full-fledged theatre company, and in November 1982, they formed Native Earth Performing Arts (NEPA) as a loose group of theatre artists producing collective creations. Their first production, *Wey-Can-Nee-Nah or Who Am I*, opened in 1983 and featured Rosa Sague (later Rosa John) (Tainu/African) and Melvin John (Cree) among others. The musical choreography was done by a Cree classical dancer named René Highway.

After the first production, NEPA was joined by members of Spiderwoman Theater from New York, Muriel and Gloria Miguel, and Gloria's daughter Monique Mojica (all Kuna/Rappahannock). Mojica became Native Earth's artistic director in 1983. The company remained focused on the creation of plays and was not yet producing prescripted plays.

In 1984, De-Ba-Jeh-Mu-Jig Theatre Group (Debaj) was founded on the Westbay reserve on Manitoulin Island, Ontario, by Shirley Cheechoo and Blake Debassige (Ojibway). Their first play, *Respect the Voice of the Child* (1984) was cowritten by Billy Merasty (Cree) and Shirley Cheechoo for the Spirit of Sharing Festival on Manitoulin. The company operated at first as a summer company, producing one play each summer, creating new plays with strong roots in their community.

If the present discussion conveys the impression that Native theatre only happened in Ontario, Margo Kane (Saulteaux/Cree/Blackfoot) proves otherwise. She joined the production of *The Ecstasy of Rita Joe* in 1978 and immediately tried to establish a Native presence in the arts, at first, for instance, by inviting Native dance groups for the preshow. In 1981, she became the first Native Rita Joe, and the tour brought her to Vancouver in 1982, where a non-Native teacher had initiated a summer school for Native drama students. They performed a collectively created play called *Spirit Song*. Kane joined the group as they were preparing for their second

summer term and formed the company Spirit Song, serving also
as its artistic director. Their second production was *Teach Me the
Ways of the Sacred Circle* by Valerie Dudoward (Tshishia). Apart from
Margo Kane, Lynn Phelan (Okanagan), Sadie Worn Staff (Chiricahua
Apache), and Marie Clements (Métis) were associated with Spirit
Song. The company also established a separate theatre school, run
by Worn Staff, and both were operational until 1992.

Apart from these companies, there was an Inuit company
called Nanuksuamiut ("People of the Country") in Nain, Newfoundland, operating roughly from 1983 to 1986. Furthermore, in 1982, a
highly controversial play called *Jessica*, cowritten by Métis writer
Maria Campbell and the non-Native actress Linda Griffiths (1989),
premiered in Saskatoon at 25th Street House Theatre as a coproduction with Toronto's Theatre Passe Muraille. It featured Linda
Griffiths as the lead character, Graham Greene, Tom Hauff, and Tan-
too Cardinal (Cree) under the direction of Passe Muraille's Paul
Thompson. The play was loosely based on Campbell's autobiog-
raphy, *Halfbreed* (1973), but Griffiths' handling of the different versions of the play caused a severe conflict with Maria Campbell. In
the second production in Toronto in 1986, Monique Mojica was cast
as the first Native Jessica, and the play won a Dora Mavor Moore
Award as best new play.

None of these developments until 1985 received widespread
attention, but they heralded the rise of Native theatre, and many
artists involved were to play a major role for years to come.

Act Three: The "Golden Age" of
Native Theatre: 1985–1995

The real breakthrough of Native theatre in Canada came with Cree
playwright Tomson Highway. His involvement with theatre started
as early as 1978, when he was hired as language coach for Reaney's
Wacousta!, and he left his career as a concert pianist around the
same time to do social work. It was not until 1983 that he joined
NEPA, with his brother René and his nephew Billy Merasty, starting
as a musical director and performer.

In 1985, he was asked by De-Ba-Jeh-Mu-Jig to take over as their
artistic director, as Shirley Cheechoo had stepped down in order
to focus on her career as an artist and performer. He stayed for
one year, wrote and directed *A Ridiculous Spectacle in One Act* in
1985, and developed his first major play, *The Rez Sisters*, with Larry

Lewis in February 1986. After offering the play to several non-Native theatres without success, Highway took over as artistic director at Native Earth Performing Arts and produced *The Rez Sisters* himself at the Native Canadian Centre of Toronto later that year. Larry Lewis directed the play, NEPA's first scripted production, and it starred, among others, Monique Mojica, Gloria and Muriel Miguel, as well as René Highway as the Ojibway trickster Nanabush. It became extremely popular, received rave reviews, won the prestigious Dora Mavor Moore Award for Outstanding New Play, was a runner-up for the Floyd S. Chalmers Award, and nominated for the Governor General's Award. At the end of 1987, the play was remounted at Toronto's Factory Theatre, went on a five-month tour through Canada to sold-out audiences, and was invited to the Edinburgh festival in 1988. There is no debate that this play signified a quantum leap for Native theatre, which suddenly received nationwide attention.

Highway wrote and produced several plays over the next few years, but his next great success was the sequel to *The Rez Sisters*, *Dry Lips Oughta Move to Kapuskasing*. The play, inspired by a dream Highway had at his father's deathbed, premiered at Theatre Passe Muraille in 1989, coproduced with NEPA. While *The Rez Sisters* told a humorous story of seven women on a reserve, *Dry Lips* showed the darker side of Native life and focused on seven men from the same reserve. The plays were conceived as the first two of a seven-play cycle about contemporary Native people.

The play was an even greater hit, praised by critics and audiences alike, and it won four Dora Awards, a Chalmers Award, and was a finalist for the Governor General's Award. In 1991, *Dry Lips* was remounted and produced by David Mirvish at the National Arts Centre in Ottawa and Toronto's Royal Alexandra Theatre as the first Native play to be produced on a major commercial stage. As much as this second production was again celebrated, it also brought problems. An article by Marion Botsford Fraser in *The Globe and Mail* about the play's supposed misogyny (Fraser 1991, C1) sparked a heated discussion in the paper. Native women artists like Lenore Keeshig-Tobias (Ojibway) and Marie Annharte Baker (Ojibway) also criticized the play harshly, and Highway became notorious in feminist circles (Baker 1991). As a result of this reaction and his brother René's death of AIDS in 1990, Highway was unable to produce another one of his plays for ten years. The third play of the cycle, *Rose*, has so far only been produced by a non-Native cast of drama students (in 2000). Highway stepped down as NEPA's artistic director in 1992 and returned only briefly in 1993.

After Highway's terms of office as artistic director for both Debaj and NEPA, the scene began to expand widely. Native Earth, Debaj, and the Native Theatre School became the spearhead for a nationwide movement that brought forth many new playwrights and theatre companies.

Ontario

While the scene in Ontario surrounding NEPA, Debaj, and the NTS does not constitute the entire Native theatre movement, companies and artists in other parts of Canada owe a large part of their success to the critical attention that especially Highway generated. Through his success, Native Earth developed into a professional production company that supported emerging playwrights and gave them a forum in their own festival of new plays.

The first to be invited by NEPA as playwrights in residence were Daniel David Moses (Delaware) and Drew Hayden Taylor (Ojibway), who continue to be among the most prolific Native playwrights to this day. Moses's first play, *Coyote City* (1990), premiered at the Native Canadian Centre in 1988 and was a finalist for the Governor General's Award in 1991. It has since then been developed into a four-play cycle about Native life in the city. The play he is best known for, however, is *Almighty Voice and His Wife* (Moses 1992), which premiered at the Great Canadian Theatre Company in 1991, and has been produced twice by NEPA, in 1992 and 2009. It has since been established as one of the most innovative Native plays to date.

Drew Hayden Taylor had his first plays produced by De-Ba-Jeh-Mu-Jig. *Toronto at Dreamer's Rock* opened in 1989, directed by then artistic director Larry Lewis, and won the Floyd S. Chalmers Award in 1992. Among his more important plays from that time are *The Bootlegger Blues*, produced in 1990, and *Someday* in 1991. Taylor is the most widely performed and published Native playwright in Canada, with thirteen plays in print, several of which have been restaged at least once. *The Bootlegger Blues* and *Someday* both sparked their own cycle of plays, and *Toronto at Dreamer's Rock* was also followed by a sequel. In contrast to many dark and depressing plays he saw at the time, he chose a more humorous angle for his writing, even though most of his plays address serious issues. He has been criticized for kowtowing to mainstream tastes but is still commercially the most successful playwright. In 1994, he also took over as artistic director of Native Earth and stayed on until 1997.

In 1989, Native Earth hosted their festival for new Native plays, called Weesageechak Begins to Dance, for the first time, with staged readings and workshops for six plays. This festival continues to this day, and many plays presented there have since been given full productions by NEPA or other companies. Some of the more important plays to emerge from the early years of the festival are Monique Mojica's *Princess Pocahontas and the Blue Spots*, Ben Cardinal's (Cree) *Generic Warriors and No-Name Indians*, Tina Mason's (Ojibway) opera *Diva Ojibway*, Moses's *Almighty Voice*, Beatrice Culleton's (Métis) *Night of the Trickster*, and Margo Kane's *Moonlodge*, all of which were later produced by NEPA. The latter was produced in late 1990, directed by Floyd Favel (Cree), who was artistic director of the Native Theatre School at the time and took over as artistic director of NEPA in 1992. Together with Monique Mojica, Favel turned the Native Theatre School into the Centre for Indigenous Theatre (CIT) in 1994 and expanded its mandate and reach.

Under the artistic direction of Larry Lewis, De-Ba-Jeh-Mu-Jig continued its work on the Wikwemikong reserve, producing plays by Shirley Cheechoo, Drew Hayden Taylor, and Tomson Highway, before they shifted their focus toward traditional stories, sometimes performed entirely in Ojibway. In 1993, after Larry Lewis had died, Alanis King (Ojibway) took over as artistic director. One of her plays, *The Manitoulin Incident* (1994), told the story of Native settlement on the island in a spectacular open-air performance, celebrating De-Ba-Jeh-Mu-Jig's ten-year anniversary. Shirley Cheechoo meanwhile began to tour her autobiographical one-woman show *Path with No Moccasins*, which remains her most famous play.

British Columbia

In British Columbia, the scene was dominated by Margo Kane and other alumni of Spirit Song who had gone on to form their own companies or started careers as playwrights. Margo Kane founded her own theatre company called Full Circle: First Nations Performance in 1992 and continued to develop one-woman performances. The most important ensemble piece of Full Circle is *The River—Home*, which opened in 1994 and is still being performed today. Kane changes and develops all her plays and performances continually, so that they never reach a final stage but are always adapted to the current situation, much in the vein of storytelling.

Two artists who built their careers in Vancouver during the early nineties are Marie Clements, a playwright from a Dene-Métis community in Fort Good Hope, and Mohawk director Dennis Maracle from the Six Nations Reserve. Clements had enrolled in Spirit Song's training program and continued to work with Margo Kane as an actress before she turned to playwriting. Her first play, *Age of Iron* (Clements 2001), was directed by Maracle at the Firehall Arts Centre in Vancouver in 1994. Firehall, formed in 1982, has a multicultural mandate and has brought several Native plays to Vancouver, including Drew Hayden Taylor's *Only Drunks and Children Tell the Truth* (1998). Dennis Maracle has since risen to considerable acclaim as a director. After a sex change, she calls herself Aiyyana Maracle and has directed award-winning restagings of *Dry Lips* and Billy Merasty's *Fireweed*.

Lynn Phelan had already left Spirit Song in 1987 to form Sen'Klip Native Theatre Company on the Okanagan Reserve #1 near Vernon, BC. It had started as a Native Youth Summer Program and evolved into a professional theatre company, performing mostly in the natural environment, sometimes in the wilderness or at an artificial open-air stage called Toom: Tem: (Earth Woman).

Another highly acclaimed production was *NO' XYA' (Our Footprints)* by Headlines Theatre, Vancouver, which premiered in Kisipox, BC in 1987 and toured British Columbia and New Zealand. The play was written by non-Native director David Diamond in close collaboration with the Gitxsan and Wet'suwet'en people of the west coast.

The Prairies

Native theatre on the prairies started to arise shortly after the success of *The Rez Sisters* in Toronto, with theatre companies in Winnipeg and in several smaller communities and reserves. In 1986, Awasikan Theatre was founded in Winnipeg as a puppeteer company, and after 1990 it produced new Native plays, among them Floyd Favel's third play *All My Relations*,[1] *The Land Called Morning* by John and Gordon Selkirk, Tina Mason's *Awena Neena*, and Yvette Nolan's (Métis) *Blade*. The company closed a few years later. Other companies in Winnipeg were Urban Shaman, with Joy and Tina Keeper (Cree), and the Native youth theatre R-Street Vision. Playwrights of note from Winnipeg are Duncan Mercredi (Cree) and Yvette Nolan.

Nolan began her career with *Blade*, which was also produced at Vancouver's Women in View Festival in 1992, meeting with incomprehension because the main character was not Native. Her second play, *Job's Wife*, produced in 1992 at the Theatre Projects Manitoba, overcompensated this perceived shortcoming by featuring a Native version of the Christian God. However, several of her plays do not feature Native characters and she refuses to be reduced to her Native side. Her best-known play is *Annie Mae's Movement*, first performed by Hardly Art, in Whitehorse, 1998 and later remounted by Native Earth.

Floyd Favel relocated to Regina and founded his own theatre company called Takwakin in 1990, focusing on the development of theatre methodologies based on Native culture.

In Alberta, the most prolific company of that time was the Four Winds Theatre Group founded on the Hobbema reserve near Edmonton in 1987 by Darrel and Lori Wildcat (Cree) with Rosa and Melvin John, who had also cofounded Native Earth (see Goffin 1990). Their productions were mainly collective creations revolving around current social issues. The company folded in 1991, but Darrel Wildcat produced a big community play at the village of Fort San in 1993, together with Rachael Van Fossen, called *Ka'Ma'Mo'Pi Cik / The Gathering*. The Johns founded Kehewin Native Performance Resource Network (KNPRN) in 1991 on Melvin's home reserve, Kehewin. KNPRN concentrates on traditional theatre, storytelling, and dance and works with young people, touring all over Canada and internationally.

Other, short-lived companies to mention are SUNTEP Theatre in Prince Albert, Chadi K'asi Dance Theatre in Calgary, the Saskatoon Survival School, and Saskatchewan Native Theatre in Saskatoon.[2]

Québec and the Maritimes

To this day, the only professional company in Québec is Montreal's Ondinnok Mythological Theatre, formed in 1985 by Yves Sioui Durand (Huron-Wendat) and Catherine Joncas. Durand is also the most prolific francophone Native playwright, with *Le porteur des peines du monde*, which premiered at the Festival du Théâtre des Amériques in Montreal in 1985, *Atiskenanddahate—Le voyage au pays des morts* (produced in 1988), and *La conquête de Mexico* (produced in 1991).

There have been a few other playwrights in Québec, such as Ida Labillois-Williams (Micmac) who writes mostly in English. Her play *Beads, Feathers and Highrises* was produced 1985 and *I Hear the Same Drums (Le son du même tambours)* in 1987. Francophone playwrights of note are Bernard Assiniwi (Cree), better known for his *Saga des Béothuks* (2000), with his play *Il n'y a plus d'Indiens* (1983); George Sioui (Huron-Wendat) with *Le compte aux enfants* (1979); Christine Sioui Wawanoloath (Huron-Wendat) with *Femme et Esprit* (1992); and Jean-Marc Niquay (Atikamekw), with *Opitowap* (1995), *Sakipitcikan* (1996), and *Mantokasowin* (1997) (see Gatti 2004; Boudreau 1993).

In the Maritimes there was only one company of note at the time, when Nanuksuamiut from Nain fused with an Innu company of Davis Inlet, Labrador, to form Innuinuit. Together, they performed *Manitou and the People* in 1988, *The Shaman* in 1989, *My Blue Heaven* 1990, *Boneman-Kaiashits* (Byrne 1995) in 1992, and *Happy Valentine's Day* in 1993.

The North

Apart from theatre in the southern provinces, there was also a rich theatre scene in the North developing around the same time. In 1986, Ellen Hamilton and Pakkak Innuksuk (Inuit) founded Tunooniq Theatre in Pond Inlet on Baffin Island. Their best-known plays are *Changes*, performed at the 1986 Expo in Vancouver, and *In Search of a Friend*. In 1989, they also performed two plays at the Arctic Song Festival in Cambridge, UK, *Survival* and *Help* (Killiktee and Arreak 1990).

In Igloolik, an after-school drama club fused with the community's dance club to form the Igloolik Dance and Drama Group, and in Yellowknife, John Blondin (Dene) and others initiated the Yellowknife Native Theatre Group in 1987. Blondin, who had also worked with Ondinnok for a while, passed away in 1996 and the company disbanded.

In Whitehorse, Nakai Theatre continued to bring Native stories to the stage, though most of them were written by non-Native playwrights like Wendy Lill. A notable exception is *Sixty Below*, written by non-Native Patti Flather and her husband Leonard Linklater (Vuntut Gwitch'in) for a play contest at the Yukon Writers' Festival in 1989. It was produced by Nakai 1993 at the Yukon Arts Centre and later was remounted by Native Earth in Toronto, earning seven nominations for the Dora Mavor Moore Award.

Act Four: Consolidating the Scene. 1995 to the Present

Problems of Funding

As successful and celebrated Native theatre was in the late eighties, interest began to wane somewhat by the mid-nineties, and it became obvious that maintaining a long-term theatre company was a lot more difficult than starting one. Established companies and organizations like Native Earth, De-Ba-Jeh-Mu-Jig, CIT, and Full Circle encountered unforeseen problems, while others, like Sen'Klip, Four Winds, or Awasikan, vanished completely. Although new companies were founded to fill the gap, these also often were short-lived. Several reasons for these problems could be named: 1. While the scene expanded considerably, the amount of funding did not. 2. Some of the initiators of Native theatre's breakthrough, like Margo Kane, were under a lot of pressure, as their companies depended too much on their enthusiasm, or fell out of favor, as is the case with Tomson Highway. 3. The media seemed to be looking elsewhere, as Native theatre was no longer new. 4. For a while the scene seemed to stagnate artistically, as many new plays only repeated the patterns of their predecessors. Most of the plays were underdeveloped, performed after a short workshop and never restaged or published. Many promising playwrights thus never got beyond their first successful play.

The problem of funding is not only a question of the amount of money. There are quite a few possibilities of being funded. Some Native organizations and provincial arts councils give out grants for Native theatre companies, the Department of Canadian Heritage has started to support Native theatre training programs, and the Canada Council for the Arts has established a special program called Developmental Support to Aboriginal Theatre Organizations, with a Native program officer, Métis actor and playwright Bruce Sinclair. However, it is especially the governmental programs which are often criticized for being overly bureaucratic and not tailored to the needs of Native companies. Some, like Kehewin, have decided to do completely without funding from the government to keep their independence.

Other common points of criticism are that these special Native programs further a ghettoization and hinder the professional development of Native theatre, because the organizations are not judged by the same standards as non-Native artists. Floyd Favel claims that between 1992 and 2002, productions of Native plays by professional theatres had decreased by 50 to 90 percent (Favel 2002b). On the other hand, these special programs could be seen as a temporary measure to even the scales that would work toward their own abolition.

Lack of funding, personal pressure, and artistic differences meanwhile led several theatre companies into crisis. Native Earth

Performing Arts especially has been a revolving door for artistic directors between 1997 and 2002, with three in 2002 alone, one of them only staying for two weeks. Their importance and innovative force shrank to the point that several voices from longtime supporters were heard that one should let NEPA die in peace. Also, tensions had arisen between NEPA and the Toronto scene on the one hand, and theatre artists in the rest of Canada on the other, who sometimes felt as if they were looked down upon and found NEPA's work too close to the mainstream. However, in 2003, Yvette Nolan took over as artistic director and did good work with the company until only recently, when Tara Beagan (Thompson River Salish) took the helm.

In Vancouver, Margo Kane was on the verge of quitting as artistic director of Full Circle because of exhaustion, until in 2003 she received a grant by Canadian Heritage and stayed on to develop a training program and the annual Talking Stick Festival. De-Ba-Jeh-Mu-Jig and the Centre for Indigenous Theatre encountered similar problems but also finally weathered the crisis. Floyd Favel's company Takwakin was developed into a performance laboratory and continued to produce innovative theatre, but recently Favel has taken a leave from theatre altogether. Kehewin and Ondinnok, however, seem to be unaffected by this general crisis and continue their work to this day.

New Companies

While the established companies suffered setbacks or folded and playwrights vanished from the scene after their first production, many new companies and artists arose all over Canada. Not all of them could maintain their work for long, but they left a definite mark. Two examples of companies that endured are Red Sky Performance in Toronto, founded by Sandra Laronde (Teme-Augama Anishinaabe) in 2000, and Saskatchewan Native Theatre Company (SNTC), founded by Kennetch Charlette (Cree) and Donna Heimbecker (Métis) in 1999.

Red Sky has made a name for itself with innovative, genre-bending performances that include classical and traditional dance, sometimes a big orchestra, storytelling, and theatre. They have adapted a children's book by Tomson Highway, *Caribou Song*, and traditional stories like "Raven Stole the Sun," written by Drew Hayden Taylor. They have performed in great concert halls and toured all over Canada.

Saskatchewan Native Theatre Company (SNTC), in contrast, is more community based, working with young Native people and developing them into theatre artists and professionals. SNTC has a very holistic concept that involves all generations: apart from their Youth Ensemble, also producing issue-centered plays-for-hire, they produce professional main-stage productions and employ an elder's ensemble. In 2008, Alanis King took over as artistic director, followed by Curtis Peteetuce (Cree).

Apart from these success stories, several companies were started and vanished again or changed direction. In Vancouver, Marie Clements founded her own theatre company called Urban Ink in 2001, producing a celebrated performance of her play *Burning Vision* in 2002. But since she has stepped down as artistic director, the company's mandate has become more intercultural, and no Native plays are currently in development.

In Penticton, BC, the Rainbow Productions Society was founded in 1998 around the Kwim'cxen' Theatre Players, who had their first performance in 1996, with Cree actress Marlena Dolan as artistic director. For a while, they produced innovative, youth-based theatre with strong dance elements, but the company disbanded in the mid-2000s.

In Calgary, Robin Melting Tallow (Cree/Métis) and others founded Crazy Horse Theatre in 1999. They opened in January 2000 with Drew Hayden Taylor's *Only Drunks and Children Tell the Truth* and housed the Crazy Horse Aboriginal Playwrights Festival in 2001, which showed new, unproduced work by Native playwrights. Some of the plays shown have gone on to full productions, like *Misty Lake* by Darrell Racine (Métis) and Dale Lakevold and *Time Stands Still* by Terry Ivins (2003), but the company folded shortly afterward.

Other companies of note were Big Sky Theatre in Edmonton, founded by Anna Marie Sewell (Micmac/Ojibway) in 1998; Red Roots Community Theatre in Winnipeg, founded by Dennis Saddleman (Thompson/Okanagan) 1997, later led by Michael Lawrenchuck (Cree); and Pawei' Nation in Halifax, a youth program initiated by Garnet Hirst in 2003. None of these companies are still in existence.

Canonizing Native Theatre

Despite the aforementioned time of crisis between 1995 and 2002, Native theatre continues to grow and is slowly being included into the canon of Canadian literature. Plays by Tomson Highway, Drew Hayden Taylor, Daniel David Moses, Marie Clements, and others have found their ways into university curricula, and the sheer amount of publications alone speaks for the scene's continuing popularity and critical success. Three monographs have been published about the Native North American theatre scene in general, and several other full-length studies, dissertations, and collections of essays have been devoted to the subject. More than a hundred Native Canadian plays have been published in some form or other and several of them have been anthologized more than once. A number of anthologies exclusively collecting Native theatre have been published, most notably the two collections by Monique Mojica and Ric Knowles, *Staging Coyote's Dream*, Volumes 1 (2003) and 2 (2009). Native theatre artists have won prestigious awards, a variety of plays have been produced internationally and in mainstream theatres, and some of them have even been turned into movies: Taylor's *In a World Created by a Drunken God*, Clements's *Unnatural and Accidental Women*, as well as a play by Métis singer and actress Andrea Menard, *The Velvet Devil*.

The vast majority of publications on Native theatre are focusing on Tomson Highway, with Drew Hayden Taylor, Daniel David Moses, Monique Mojica, and Marie Clements following in respectful distance. Highway has finally found his way back onto the stage, with plays for Western Canada Theatre (*Ernestine Shuswap Gets Her Trout*, 2004), De-Ba-Jeh-Mu-Jig (*A Trickster's Tale*, 2003), and Red Sky (*Caribou Song*, 2000), and at the moment he is planning a large-scale Native opera.

Apart from Highway, Clements, Taylor, and Moses continue to be the most prolific and productive playwrights. Apart from *Almighty Voice*, the most highly acclaimed work by Daniel David Moses is the double-bill *The Indian Medicine Shows* (Moses 1995), which was produced by Theatre Passe Muraille in 1996. Marie Clements's most celebrated works are *The Unnatural and Accidental Women*, which premiered at the Firehall Arts Centre in Vancouver in 2000 and was restaged by Native Earth in 2004; *Copper Thunderbird*, about the Ojibway painter Norval Morrisseau, commissioned by Ondinnok and produced 2007 at the National Arts Centre in Ottawa; and *Burning Vision*. Drew Hayden Taylor won his most critical acclaim for the controversial *alterNatives*, which opened in Kincardine, Ontario 1999 and was later produced in Vancouver, where it received a bomb threat due to supposedly racist content, and *In a World Created by a Drunken God*, which premiered at Persephone Theatre, Saskatoon in 2004.

Plays by Taylor, Highway, and Moses have been performed internationally. *Burning Vision* by Clements and *In a World Created by a Drunken God* have both been nominated for the prestigious Governor General's Award, but the first Native playwright to win this award is Ian Ross (Ojibway) from Winnipeg with *fareWel*, in 1997. Also, his play *Bereav'd of Light* (2005) was the first Native play to be produced at the Stratford Festival in Stratford, Ontario in 2002. Another important award, Canada Council's John Hirsch Prize for emerging theatre directors, was awarded to Aiyyana Maracle in 1997 as the first and only Native director.

Other promising playwrights who have emerged over the last ten years are Joseph Dandurand (Salish/Nooksack) (*Please Do Not Touch the Indians*, 2004), Darrel Dennis (Shuswap) (*The Trickster of Third Avenue East, Tales of an Urban Indian*, 2005), Tara Beagan (*Dreary and Izzie*, 2006), Darrell Racine with Dale Lakevold (*Misty Lake*, 2000; *Stretching Hide*, 2007), Sheldon Elter (Métis) (*Métis Mutt*, 2006), and Kevin Loring (Thompson River Salish) (*Where the Blood Mixes*, Governor General's Award Winner in 2009).

Training and Networking

Part of James Buller's plan for a new Native theatre scene was to provide ample training. His Native Theatre School summer program has continued since its installation, but as a summer program, its possibilities are limited. Since then, several organizations have taken up the task and now provide training to aspiring Native actors or playwrights.

The most important institution in this respect remains the Centre for Indigenous Theatre, which still runs the NTS and has since established the Indigenous Theatre School (ITS) as a full-time two-year program. Carol Greyeyes (Cree) initiated the ITS in 1996. Its program is the most comprehensive, encompassing classical and culturally specific training. The Banff Centre has an aboriginal dance program, and the En'Owkin Centre in Penticton, BC includes a writing school. Several theatre companies also have their own training programs, most importantly Saskatchewan Native Theatre Company, De-Ba-Jeh-Mu-Jig, and Full Circle. These programs are strongly rooted in Native culture and also include a social aspect, educating young Native people to become role models for others. Michael Lawrenchuck and Yves Sioui Durand, on the other hand, have cooperated with regular theatre training programs at the University of Winnipeg and the National Theatre School in Montreal instead.

Besides training, another aspect of Buller's vision was networking. He wanted to establish an international network of indigenous theatre artists and even had plans for a global Indigenous People's

Theatre Association. Although these plans were never realized, at the beginning of the twenty-first century a similar network was formed on a national scale.

Instrumental in the establishment of a network were CIT and Native Earth. In 1998, Native Earth was housing the first National Native Theatre Symposium at the University of Toronto, with Native theatre artists from all over Canada. At this symposium, the idea to organize a National Aboriginal Theatre Alliance was born. A second conference was held at the En'Owkin Centre in Penticton, BC in 2000, called Coyote's Roundup: The National Aboriginal Theatre Gathering. At this conference, a committee of nine key figures in Native theatre was formed to continue the work of the two conferences. The Centre for Indigenous Theatre worked as a base for the new network and began to create a database of Native theatre artists. Another follow-up meeting took place in Montreal 2001, and in 2003, Native Earth housed a Native Playwrights' Summit. After the initial enthusiasm, the alliance has progressed only slowly. It has been renamed the Indigenous Performing Arts Alliance, and holds annual meetings, but to what extent the Native theatre scene can benefit from it remains to be seen.

Epilogue

Even though Native theatre is a relatively recent phenomenon in Canada, it is by now an integral part of the Canadian cultural landscape. It takes on many forms and draws from various traditions like storytelling, European theatre, traditional dance, and multimedia. It resists any clear-cut definition and is constantly exploring new forms of expression. That is not to say that the scene is without problems. There is still a form of tension between the very urban scene in Toronto and Native theatre artists in the rest of the country. The question whether the scene should be opened to the mainstream by accepting non-Native actors in Native roles or non-Native theatres producing Native plays, and by abolishing special aboriginal arts programs, remains unsolved. However, the potential to establish a Native voice on Canada's stages in the long term exists, and slowly, Native theatre thus also contributes to the ongoing process of healing the wounds of colonization. James Buller may be dead, but his vision has come alive in the Native theatre scene today.

Notes

1. Published as *All My Relatives* in 2002 (Favel 2002).
2. This company is not connected to the later company of the same name.

Native American Drama

A Historical Survey

Ann Haugo

During the last quarter of the twentieth century, important changes occurred for American Indian people and cultures in American theatre, both on the stages and in scholarship. The Native Theater Movement, which was begun in the early 1970s by Kiowa/Delaware playwright Hanay Geiogamah with the formation of the American Indian Theater Ensemble, was sustained through the formation of several other companies in the next few years, most notably the 1974 founding of the Thunderbird Theatre company at Haskell Indian Nations University and the 1975 founding of Spiderwoman Theater. As a result of these theatres, as well as others, there are now Native theatres throughout the United States and Canada, with dozens of playwrights from many different Native nations publishing and producing their works. This chapter will provide a survey of the Native Theater Movement, shedding light on key artists, plays, and scholarly publications in the field.

Colonialism, Theatre, and American Indian Identity

During the 1960s and 1970s, examinations of American Indian drama would have focused on dramas written by non-Native authors about Native subjects. Plays like Arthur Kopit's *Indians* are examples, but his drama is hardly the first of its kind. Some of the most famous early American dramas, such as John Augustus Stone's *Metamora: or, The Last of the Wampanoags* in 1829 created Native characters (or rather, caricatures) in their dramas. In addition, some of the first theatre publications on American Indian subjects examined this body of plays by non-Native authors. Eugene Jones's book *Native Americans as Shown on the Stage, 1753–1916* (1988) studies Indian "character types" by non-Native playwrights. The consequences of Jones's work inspired a series of scholarly books that examine the representation of Native Americans during the nineteenth and twentieth centuries. Don Wilmeth's 1989 essay "Noble or Ruthless Savage? The American Indian on Stage and in the Drama" also focuses on dramatic stereotypes of Indian men—the "noble savage" and "red villain," for instance—from early American drama to the plays of the late twentieth century. Wilmeth draws attention to Native playwrights, such as Monica Charles (Klallam), Robert Shorty (Navajo), Bruce King (Oneida), and Hanay Geiogamah (Kiowa/Delaware), in the later portion of his essay. He briefly discusses Geiogamah's *Body Indian* and *Foghorn*, noting that Geiogamah's characters "avoid, for the most part, the stereotypic image of the usual stage Indian, although he is not above using stereotypes for his own purposes" (2000, 146). Wilmeth closes his essay by observing:

> The majority of plays about American Indians, certainly those that have gained some popularity or critical attention, have been written by white authors with little knowledge of real Native Americans. For the most part plays with Indian characters have only created stereotypical Indians, dominated by the noble savage, the villainous red devil, and the Indian princess or pathetic maiden, with few of these types portrayed as real people having distinctive personalities. (2000, 150)

Wilmeth's statement still resonates. A few additional American Indian characterizations appearing to portray Native Americans "as real people having distinctive personalities" have surfaced onstage in the late twentieth century. Yet these productions—Christopher Sergel's adaptation of *Black Elk Speaks*, or Robert Schenkkan's *The Kentucky Cycle*, for example—fail to escape the unfortunate shortcomings of American Indian representations on the stage. Perhaps the most egregious fault lies in the fact that these plays, as well as others, tend to depict American Indians in the past tense (as if they no longer exist) rather than as contemporary, living people with families, homes, jobs, and dreams.

An examination of Native theatre should acknowledge the inheritance of these misrepresentations in American theatre, because that

inheritance establishes what I have referred to elsewhere as a particularly hostile representational context for Native playwrights and
actors (Haugo 2005a). The problem is hardly a theatrical one, but
rather a problem endemic to American popular culture in general.
The equivalent of minstrel shows, with their stereotypic depiction
of African Americans, still occurs for Native America, most notably
in the performances of sports team mascots like the Cleveland Indians' Chief Wahoo or the University of Illinois at Urbana-Champaign's
Chief Illiniwek.[1] America cultivates the obsession with what Cherokee author Rayna Green has dubbed "Playing Indian": non-Native
people pretending to be Indian. Green describes this desire to perform Indianness as "one of the oldest and most pervasive forms of
American cultural expression," a practice that has its roots in the
"establishment of a distinctive American culture," implicated in the
growth of American national identity (1988, 31). Philip Deloria's book
Playing Indian (1998) also documents and explicates some of these
performative traditions, from the carnivalesque masquerade of the
Boston Tea Party to the Tammany Society, the Boy Scouts, and the
Grateful Dead.[2]

Postcolonial critics have noted that a colonizing culture tends
to speak for the colonized, and in doing so tends to reinterpret
the colonized people's identity. In America, this has meant defining Native cultures as "primitive," passing legislation that defines
who can and cannot be recognized as Indian by the government,
or replacing tribal groups' names. Thus, the Anishinaabe became
the "Chippewa" and the Ho-Chunk were given the name Winnebago.
Colonial cultures obsessively control the identity of the colonized
subject, and in a rather ironic way, the obsession is sometimes
enacted in masquerade.[3]

Frantz Fanon has argued that the colonial project completes its
final act of domination when the colonized people see themselves
through the eyes of the colonizer. In America, following Fanon's
assertion, if Native people accept misrepresentations on the screen,
stage, in the classroom, or in the sports arena, the American colonial project succeeds. However, resistance to these images and innu-
endoes emerges. While there are undoubtedly social and political
problems in Native communities (as in all communities), Native
people are far from a defeated nation and still actively resist colonization. Native theatre is one of many venues through which the
resistance happens. Some Native theatre artists resist consciously
and overtly, in politically charged theatre creations that challenge
stereotypical, colonial policies and their aftermath. Other artists,

whose work is not overtly political or confrontational, challenge ongoing colonialism indirectly; for example, some theatres employ Native languages, using the stage as a way to teach and preserve Indigenous languages that are endangered. Some Native theatres or projects focus primarily on helping Native people recover from the effects of colonialism, aiding in the recovery of spiritual identities as indigenous people. One such play is *Strength of Indian Women* by Vera Manuel (Secwepemc/Ktunaxa), which draws on the stories of women who survive abuses of the residential school system in Canada. The play is frequently performed at conferences for survivors, providing a catalyst for dialogue about the experiences of being taken from their families, all too often physically and sexually abused, and taught to be ashamed of their Native identity and families. Native theatre draws on oral traditions, dramatizing trickster stories or creation stories. The importance of these works is political as well as aesthetic. Muriel Miguel of Spiderwoman Theater notes, "just the fact that you're on stage telling these stories is political. Just the fact that you're there" (Haugo 2002, 227). In a society that would have eradicated their languages (and in some cases succeeded in doing so), taken their children, and eliminated as much Native culture as possible, the mere public act of claiming one's Native identity is a political act.

In an illuminating illustration of the power of Native theatre to resist colonial attitudes, Gloria Miguel of Spiderwoman Theater stands onstage toward the end of their play *Winnetou's Snake Oil Show from Wigwam City*. Arms extended from her sides, she turns slightly so that the entire audience can see her. "See me. I'm talking, loving, hating, drinking too much, creating, performing, my stories, my songs, my dances, my ideas. Now, I telling you [*sic*], step back, move aside, sit down, hold your breath, save your own culture. Discover your own spirituality." The other performers then join her, each speaking their own words of survival: "I'm alive. I'm not defeated." "My stories, my songs. My culture." "All our bones are not in museums. We are not defeated. We are still here" (Spiderwoman Theater 2003, 262).

The Native American Theater Ensemble

In the late 1960s, a literary movement began that scholars now refer to as the Native American Literary Renaissance. Its initial moments are marked by the 1968 publication of *House Made of Dawn*, a novel by Kiowa author N. Scott Momaday. That novel would win the 1969 Pulitzer Prize for Literature, the first time for a Native American author to win that prize. While Native Americans had been publishing literature since the eighteenth century, it took until the 1970s for a new level of attention to be paid to Native writers. Presses began programs specializing in Native literature; universities began teaching courses on Native literature; and Native writers were included in "survey" courses of American literature. Authors such as Momaday, James Welch (Blackfeet / Gros Ventre), Leslie Marmon Silko (Laguna Pueblo), Paula Gunn Allen (Laguna Pueblo), and others, became a rising presence in the literary scene.

Parallel to the literary movement and certainly influencing it was the "Red Power Movement," the term used to describe the civil rights movement for American Indians. Organizations whose activities gave initial strength to the movement were the National Indian Youth Council (founded 1961), the Native American Rights Fund (1964), and the Indian Historical Society (1964), but the organization that became the best known in the Red Power Movement was AIM, the American Indian Movement, founded in Minneapolis in 1966. These new pan-Indian organizations fought for the improvement of American Indians' lives throughout the United States and Canada.[4]

It was during the activity of the Red Power Movement and the Native American Literary Renaissance that Hanay Geiogamah ventured to New York City to start an American Indian theatre company. American Indians had been working in the entertainment industry—theatre, film, television—for decades, but few Native artists had creative control. The founding of the American Indian Theater Ensemble (later known as the Native American Theater Ensemble or NATE) marks a moment when Native theatre artists began to have a greater degree of control over their own work by running companies, writing plays, and directing productions.

At the time a youth barely out of college, Geiogamah started examining the possibility of an American Indian theatre company in the summer of 1970. At that time, there were plenty of models of minority theatres, but very few models of professional Native theatres. Geiogamah was aware of companies like Arthur Junaluska's American Indian Repertory Company, but very little information was available about them. The Institute of American Indian Arts in Santa Fe, New Mexico, had started a Native theatre training program, but it did not have a professional theatre company.[5] As a result, it was to other minority theatres that Geiogamah turned for guidance, examining how theatres like El Teatro Campesino worked in its community, or how the theatres of the Black Arts Movement incorporated social, cultural, and identity issues in their works. From the outset, Geiogamah's vision for a Native theatre was not simply to bring Native artists together to do theatre, but to do theatre that would relate to the lives of the artists and the audiences, performing stories that came from Native cultures and examining issues relevant to Native audiences.

When Geiogamah met with National Endowment for the Arts representatives in Washington, D.C., they recommended that he talk to people at New York City theatres that could serve as models for him, such as the New Lafayette, a black theatre in Harlem, or La MaMa Experimental Theatre Club on New York's Lower East Side. Geiogamah began by contacting them, recalling that "they were intrigued, puzzled, happily bemused that here's an Indian person trying to do this."[6] From those initial phone calls came in-person consultations with many of the most significant theatre leaders off Broadway. Geiogamah found himself traveling between Washington, D.C., and New York City for most of that summer, making plans for the launch of the company. By the end of the summer, Ellen Stewart of La MaMa had become Geiogamah's staunchest advocate and adviser. Geiogamah credits both her and La MaMa artistic director Wilford Leach with helping him define the company's scope.

With Stewart, he worked out a one-year budget for a sixteen-person company that would be housed at La MaMa. The plan was to bring together a group of ten to twelve actors, as well as designers, playwrights, a director, possibly a choreographer, and a musician/composer. According to Geiogamah, his plan from the outset was for a pan-tribal company, a company made up of artists from many different Native nations. Although some sources have since argued that the purpose of making the company pan-tribal was to deconstruct stereotypes, Geiogamah states that it was based on the logistics of pulling a company together; if that conquers stereotypes, it is more an effect than a cause. Geiogamah remarks:

> Pan-tribal reality had very little, if anything, to do with countering stereotypes. Pan-tribal reality was that you couldn't get twelve Siouxs [sic] together to do theatre, twelve Navajos together to do it. At IAIA [Institute of American Indian Arts], they had people from all over. Pan-tribalism was politically prevalent at the time, not something we just invented, just part of our reality, that became the necessary ethos. The reality was that it was

just about impossible to get one tribal unit together in a company, although I'm sure somebody would strongly disagree.

Pan-tribalism lent itself to the social issues, the political issues. All tribes were impacted by poverty, by alcoholism, by loss of spiritual strength. The issues applied to everybody. At least in those days the plays could present a form that could be applicable to all Indians. *Body Indian* is a pan-tribal play because the things it addresses applied at that time to everybody, not to just one tribe.[7]

Geiogamah had already been in contact with Lloyd Kiva New (Cherokee), who was then director of the institute. About half of the theatre artists who Geiogamah would bring together in the American Indian Theater Ensemble would be IAIA-trained artists.

The institute had begun developing its theatre coursework in 1964 when New was art director. Drama instructor Rolland Meinholtz, music instructor Louis Ballard, and dance instructor Rosalie Jones all helped to build the theatre program. The theatre curriculum was well developed when New composed his "Credo for an American Indian Theatre" (1969), which outlined how an American Indian theatre, as a distinct form of American theatre, could be created. New was careful to point out that an American Indian theatre should grow from "the most sensitive approaches imaginable" to "the framework of Indian traditions." Ceremonies, pow wow, and even dramatic representations of American Indian people New referred to as "raw material" (qtd. in Traditional Elders' Circle 1980). An American Indian theatre would be a new form of American drama, one that would demand from its artists an emphasis on both rigorous training in Euro-American methods and knowledge of American Indian cultural traditions, combining these interpretive skills to bring cultural traditions to the stage.

Geiogamah's approach was not unlike New's: emphasize training, draw from indigenous traditions, and find methods that would marry Euro-American and American Indian elements while remaining true to what was uniquely indigenous. The company first assembled in New York City in March of 1972. They set their target date for an opening production as October of 1972—seven months to go through a massive training program that Stewart and Geiogamah had conceived, and to write and rehearse the material. They met their deadline and presented two pieces for their premiere performance in October 1972: *Body Indian* and *Na Haaz Zan*. *Body Indian* is a short play that Geiogamah wrote for the opening. The play was eventually turned over to the company members to essentially workshop the piece during their rehearsals; Geiogamah suggested changes that were significant to the play's success.[8] They also presented *Na Haaz Zan*, an adaptation of the Navajo creation story that company members Geraldine Keams, Robert Shorty, and Timothy Clashin had shaped and rehearsed with the help of Lee Breuer, then director of Mabou Mines (Brown 2000).

Their premiere performance was reviewed positively, and NATE continued to perform regularly through 1976, including a tour to Europe, although some company members did depart for other opportunities. Three plays that Geiogamah wrote for the company—*Body Indian, Foghorn,* and *49*—were published in 1980, becoming the first collection of Native plays published in either the United States or Canada. Several NATE members went on to form other companies and to long careers in the performing arts, including Geiogamah himself. When asked what he feels NATE's greatest contributions have been, Geiogamah's answer is twofold. First, NATE demonstrated that it was possible to form and sustain an American Indian theatre, even with minimal funding. And second—what Geiogamah describes as NATE's primary legacy—NATE offered a model for establishing theatres in tribal communities, a goal that Geiogamah had in mind from the outset, and that he would pursue throughout his career. From New York City, NATE had relocated to Oklahoma. Following their success, several other companies formed in tribal communities or towns near reservation communities.[9]

Spiderwoman Theater

When Joseph Chaikin and Peter Feldman founded the Open Theater in 1963 in New York City, one of their original company members was twenty-something modern dancer and choreographer Muriel Miguel, who was raised in a Native family in New York City. Her mother was Rappahannock (American Indian) and her father was Kuna, an indigenous tribe from the San Blas Islands off the coast of Panama. An experimental artist, Miguel appeared in some of the edgiest performances of the time, including Megan Terry's *Viet Rock*, the first major play to protest the war in Vietnam. By the first years of the 1970s, the feminist theatre movement had emerged partly out of the experimental theatres of the 1960s, and woman-focused theatres were surfacing in major cities around the country. In New York City, Miguel began to bring women together to perform their own stories, and by 1975 she had secured a grant to gather a company of five women, including her two sisters, Lisa Mayo and Gloria Miguel, as well as Lois Weaver and Brandy Penn. Mayo and Gloria Miguel also came from performance backgrounds. All three sisters had actually performed as children with their parents in "snake oil shows": performances for largely white audiences in which Native people played, quite literally, popular stereotypes. But as adults, each sister pursued different avenues for professional performance training. Muriel Miguel had studied dance. Lisa Mayo was a classically trained mezzo-soprano who began studying acting for her work in opera, then began to focus more heavily on the-atre performance, studying with masters like Charles Nelson Reilly and Uta Hagen. Gloria Miguel majored in theatre at Oberlin College, where she had studied with Bill Irwin and others.

The original members named the company Spiderwoman The-ater after the Hopi goddess who taught her people to weave. Muriel Miguel's close friend Josephine Mofsie (Hopi) had performed with Miguel and Lois Weaver in an earlier performance about women's spirituality. Mofsie had told the Spiderwoman creation story while finger-weaving. Just a few months later, and before the new compa-ny premiered, Mofsie died tragically in a car accident; the company took the name of Spiderwoman to honor her work and her memory. The name also helped the company define and describe their pro-cess; the concept of "weaving" would become important in their method of performance creation. Spiderwoman created their own performances, on their feet, without writing scripts. In programs, they described their "storyweaving" technique as "creating designs and weaving stories with words and movement."

> We work onstage as an ensemble, basing our productions on life experiences. We translate our personal stories, dreams and images into movement, and refine them into the essential threads of human experience. In seeking out, exploring, and weaving our own patterns, we reflect the human tapestry, the web of our common humanity. Finding, loving and transcending our own flaws, as in the flaw in the goddess' tapestry, provide the means for our spirits to find their way out, to be free. (Chinoy and Jenkins 1981, 303–04)

Spiderwoman Theater's performances throughout the 1970s and into the 1980s were always about women's issues: exploring the effects of violence in women's lives, deconstructing popular images of women, satirizing popular ideas about sexuality, and so on. The company was multi-ethnic, and perhaps because of that, unlike most feminist theatres of the period, Spiderwoman's performances always investigated racial issues and racism. The company performed throughout the 1970s with a fairly elastic group, some members leaving, others joining (some for several years), and some working together for just one or two productions. The most significant member change occurred in 1980. The Spiderwoman group developed two separate performance pieces. The Mayo and Miguel sisters created *Sun, Moon, and Feather*, inspired by their childhood in the Red Hook section of Brooklyn. Weaver and Peggy Shaw developed *Split Britches* about Weaver's female relatives in the Blue Ridge Mountains. The process of working independently convinced the two groups to make their way as separate companies. Weaver and Shaw left the company to form the lesbian company Split Britches, and Spiderwoman's core members were now the three Kuna-Rappahannock sisters from Brooklyn.[10]

It would be seamless, perhaps, to suggest that the transition in 1981 marks the moment when Spiderwoman "became" a Native theatre. The reasonable truth, however, is more complicated. As company members, the sisters had always contributed stories to Spiderwoman performances, and Native issues were part of Spiderwoman pieces from the beginning. Their first piece, *Women in Violence*, contains vignettes offered by every company member, including two scenes that were inspired by the Miguel sisters' personal experiences as part of the American Indian Movement. In the first scene, Muriel sits at a table with an unidentified (and in performance, invisible) man across from her. She flirts, makes jokes, and is suddenly and abruptly hit in the face twice. She protests, "Hey, I was just fooling," and she gets hit again. Through her protests, she gets hit again, and again, until finally she lands on the floor. She stands up and addresses him: "I know about genocide. I'm your mother, I'm your sister, I'm your cousin" (1976, n.p.). When the unidentified man continues to come at her, she calls for the help of other women surrounding her, protect her from the abuse, and with her, face the audience, all repeating: "In a revolution, a woman is equal." The women move forward and describe being second-class citizens within their own civil rights movement, and then merge to the words spoken at the 1973 occupation of Wounded Knee, South

Dakota, by Wallace Black Elk, a Lakota elder and descendant of Nicholas Black Elk. Black Elk describes the tree of life of the Lakota, symbolically linking them with all other human beings, different branches growing from the same root.

As early as 1976, with the premiere of *Women in Violence*, Spiderwoman was performing stories within their works that came from a Native perspective and emphasized Native issues. Starting a feminist company with women from different backgrounds and different ethnicities meant that Miguel and the other women had to wrestle with race issues, and as Native women, the sisters had to confront the mainstream face of feminism that often, if not always, ignored Native American issues. As Spiderwoman grew and as its membership changed, the philosophy of its feminism and its relationship to Native issues also evolved.

> So we started to define ourselves. We were not White people. We were women of color. We were women. And that is the reason why it eventually turned into a Native theatre, because we had all these things happening to us. We didn't look like anyone else. We didn't look like the ones in our group, so we were pulled out because they wanted to take pictures of us. (Qtd. in Haugo 2002, 228)

According to Miguel, by the time the company performed *The Three Sisters from Here to There* (1982), a retelling of Chekhov's *The Three Sisters* in which the sisters' dreams are not of Moscow but of crossing the Brooklyn Bridge to Manhattan, all Spiderwoman pieces tended to deal heavily with racism, though not necessarily just from the perspective of Native people. Several members throughout its history had been women of color: Chicana, Asian American, and African American. During the 1980s, Spiderwoman's membership continued to shift, as did the emphasis of their productions. "We were changing. We kept adding more and more Indian-themed things" (Haugo 2002, 229). By the time the company developed *Winnetou's Snake Oil Show from Wigwam City* (1988), the focus was on Native politics, though always also from a feminist perspective. For this performance, they were joined by fellow Native performer Hortensia Colorado (Chichimec/Otomi), who helped to develop the performance and would perform the piece with Spiderwoman whenever possible.

Winnetou's Snake Oil Show from Wigwam City premiered in the Netherlands at the Stage Door Festival, with its United States premiere following in 1989 at New York's Theater for the New City. The Traditional Elders' Circle had asked Spiderwoman to create a play that would address the increasing problem of spiritual exploitation: the "selling" of Native American spirituality. As early as 1980, the Traditional Elders' Circle issued a warning to Native and non-Native people to be vigilant, to inquire about the backgrounds of people who purported to be medicine people and to understand the seriousness of the problem.

> These individuals are gathering non-Indian people as followers who believe they are receiving instructions of the original people. We, the Elders and our representatives sitting in Council, give warning to these non-Indian followers that it is our understanding this is not a proper process, that the authority to carry these sacred objects is given by the people, and the purpose and procedure is specific to time and the needs of the people. (Traditional Elders' Circle 1980)

The name that quickly attached itself to those practicing this spiritual fakery was "plastic shamans." *Winnetou's Snake Oil Show from Wigwam City* takes on plastic shamanism and Indian fakery more generally, trampling on centuries of stereotypes of American Indians that include the late twentieth-century trend to adopt Indian identity and spirituality, often in partial and questionable ways. The title and a good portion of the play refer to the German novel *Winnetou* by Karl May, a novel whose hero is the noble savage Winnetou. May wrote the novel without ever meeting a Native person or visiting the United States, and despite this, the novel was wildly popular and influenced what generations of Germans—and other Europeans—believed to be "real" about American Indians. In creating the performance, Spiderwoman's method was, as always, as much autobiographical as it was research-oriented, delving into their own pasts, however painful that might be, recognizing their own and their family's part in the exploitation, and their responsibility to help curb it.

> We've been a part of that circus. We've been a part of sideshows. We've been in Wild West Shows. When we did *Winnetou's Snake Oil Show*, all of that stuff came from our backgrounds. The whip. The sharpshooter. The horseback rider. All of that. All of what we've seen. So we

just kept on layering it. Like my naugahyde (a costume
piece), when I said, "You know how many nagahydes I
killed for this?" (laughter) Well, people think that that's
the way you look. All of those old movies. That's the way
they looked, with fake braids. (Qtd. in Haugo 2002, 227)

Spiderwoman created several other performances that drew on contemporary Native issues and the authors' experiences as Native
women. *Reverb-ber-ber-rations* (1991) explored the gifts of spirituality. After critiquing exploitations of Native spirituality in *Winnetou*,
Spiderwoman had stories to tell about their own spirituality, in a
more positive sense about what it means to be spiritual Native
women and to value that spirituality. *Power Pipes* (1992) brought
the Colorado sisters back to work with Spiderwoman; both Elvira
and Hortensia Colorado had worked with Spiderwoman previously,
in between developing their own work. Also joining the company
was Gloria's daughter Monique Mojica, a playwright and actor. In
recreations of the play, Muriel's daughter, Murielle Borst (also a
playwright and actor), joined the company. In 2001, the company began to work on *Persistence of Memory*, a play reflecting on
what Spiderwoman has accomplished and how it has influenced
the future. In a revealing scene, the three sisters weave actions on
stage with fractured, repeated phrases: "I understand now, but I
didn't understand then," and "I understand. No, I don't understand."
Gloria, in increments, begins to tell a story about her great-niece
Josie, Muriel's granddaughter. As Gloria steps forward, she mimes
holding a picture in one arm and speaks as Josie addressing her
Auntie, asking her about the picture in which one child's brown
face appears out of a sea of white children's faces in a classroom.

"Is that you, Aunt Gloria?" Yes, that's me. Looking up at
me she said, "Then you know how I feel." Our eyes met
for a moment. Yes, Josie, I know how you feel. Three
generations, three generations and that knowing feeling
is still present. (Spiderwoman Theater 2009, 54)

In the young Josie's recognition of her place and her ability at the
age of six to articulate it to an Auntie, Spiderwoman assert their
influence and hopes. As young girls themselves, they "didn't understand" how to value themselves as Native women, how to survive,
intact, amid a sea of whiteness—in a classroom or in the world.
For them, being proud, perhaps defiant, and certainly rooted in

their identities as Native women, has been a process of becoming, a process sometimes painful and arduous. Gloria's final line bridges to a film clip of Josie singing the *Persistence of Memory* song: "She understands now" (2009, 54).

Like their other works, this Spiderwoman play emerged from the intersection of all aspects of the sisters' identities: gender, ethnicity, class, and sexuality. At the end of *Reverb-ber-ber-rations*, Muriel Miguel addresses the audience simply and directly, with words that speak to the healing power of performing their own stories, not simply for their generation, but for the next:

> I am an Indian woman.
> I am proud of the women that came before me.
> I am a woman with two daughters.
> I am a woman with a woman lover.
> I am a woman whose knowledge is the wisdom of the
>   women in the family.
> I am here now.
> I say this now because to deny these events
> About me and my life
> Would be denying my children. (Spiderwoman Theater
>   1992, 212)

The Canada Connection: Native Earth Performing Arts

In the fall of 1986, Muriel Miguel, Gloria Miguel, and Monique Mojica created three roles in the Toronto premiere of the play *The Rez Sisters* by Tomson Highway. A Cree playwright from Manitoba, Highway was then artistic director of a Native theatre company in Toronto titled Native Earth Performing Arts (NEPA). Native Earth had started in 1982 as a performance collective, and Mojica had been active in its development, including a stint as its artistic director. This was one of many times that the Spiderwoman sisters or other Native artists would cross the border—Canadian Native artists working in the United States or American Indian artists working in Canada. It is important to treat the two performance worlds as connected, since there may be more cross-fertilization between the United States and Canada in Native theatre than in any other drama and theatre.

The Rez Sisters went on to win the Dora Mavor Moore Award for Best New Play in Toronto's 1986–1987 season, as well as the 1986 Floyd S. Chalmers Award for Outstanding Canadian Play. Other

Native companies had been producing theatre as well,[11] but the success of Native Earth's first scripted piece, *The Rez Sisters*, catapulted Native theatre into the Canadian spotlight and earned Highway and Native Earth international recognition. Native Earth continued to earn nominations for Dora Mavor Moore awards over the next few years, and then, with a coproduction with Toronto's Theatre Passe Muraille in the spring of 1989, Highway and NEPA earned six Dora nominations and claimed four for *Dry Lips Oughta Move to Kapuskasing*, a sequel to *The Rez Sisters*.

It is important to note that mainstream success is only one measure of value in a minority theatre movement. Any narrative that privileges awards and mainstream recognition over the reception of Highway's plays by Native people should be suspect unless balanced by an analysis that included Native American reception. Geiogamah offers a lesson in how to evaluate Native plays:

> In judging an Indian play, readers and viewers should keep in mind that the most important function of the Indian dramatist is to communicate with his own people. The major questions are: Does the play speak effectively to Indians? Can Indians understand what is happening on stage? If there is a message, is it communicated clearly and effectively in Indian terms? Are the characters and dialogue culturally authentic? (2000, 163)

Geiogamah adds that even when all these parameters are met, a Native play can still be accessible to a non-Native audience. Highway's plays seem to be examples of Native plays that do speak to divergent audiences; to Native audiences yet still accessible to non-Native audiences (providing that mainstream recognition serves as an example of broad accessibility). Both plays, *Rez Sisters* and *Dry Lips*, draw on Cree and Ojibway traditions in their creation of the central trickster character, Nanabush, and both liberally drew on indigenous languages (Cree and Ojibway) in the writing. *Dry Lips* earned its share of controversy among Native people, as some women critics questioned its gender politics, but the published arguments were not about the effectiveness of the representation of Cree or Ojibway cultures and characters onstage.[12]

In the same season that *Dry Lips* premiered, Native Earth began a festival of new plays called Weesageechak Begins to Dance, a festival that continues to sponsor Native dramas in the twentieth-first century. Festivals like this have become important in both the

United States and Canada as a means for Native artists—accomplished or new on the scene—to develop their work among other Native artists. In the United States, the Native Voices Festival, started by Randy Reinholz and Jean Bruce Scott in 1994 at Illinois State University and now located at the Autry Museum of Western History in Los Angeles, offers a similar opportunity, and Native community venues like the American Indian Community House in New York City often serve as locales for workshop performances.

Into the New Millennium

With the work of companies like NATE, Spiderwoman, and NEPA, and the development of new generations of artists at IAIA, Haskell's Thunderbird Theatre, and Toronto's Native Theatre School, the Native Theatre Movement had taken root in the 1970s and 1980s. By the 1990s, the movement was energized, with several resident Native American companies throughout the United States and Canada, and an increasing number of Native-authored plays in publication.

IAIA continued its theatre program in the early 1990s, with playwrights Bruce King (Oneida) and William Yellow Robe Jr. (Assiniboine) teaching in the Creative Writing and Theater programs, respectively. Under their instruction, students produced and wrote several plays, and, for several consecutive years, published their plays in collections printed by the institute. IAIA and Haskell Indian Nations University fulfilled important roles throughout the last three decades of the twentieth century, training Native theatre artists in all aspects of theatre. Both institutions, however, survive on federal funding, and in 1996 Congress cut roughly one-third of IAIA's budget, forcing the institute to reduce its faculty from twenty-seven instructors to eleven. The Performing Arts program, which had played such an important part in the Native Theatre Movement since New and Rolland Meinholtz's work, was cut, and both King and Yellow Robe sought opportunities elsewhere.

Yellow Robe had studied under Meinholtz at the University of Montana and worked in regional theatres around the country, including as literary manager for the Seattle Group Theatre. While several of his plays had been produced and published in the 1980s and 1990s, a collection of his plays, *Where the Pavement Ends*, was published in 2000. Many of the plays included in it had been produced by the pan-tribal company he founded in Albuquerque in 1997, Wakiknabe, drawing its name from an Assiniboine word meaning "we return home" and envisioning a place for artists to gather, develop their craft, and share their talents (Wakiknabe Theatre Company n.d.).[13]

King had attended IAIA and studied under Meinholtz as well, writing his first play, *To Catch a Never Dream*, and publishing it in the late 1960s, before the founding of NATE. He continued to write, and his play *Evening at the Warbonnet* became a popular play for Native companies in the late 1990s. After putting his plays in the hands of a non-Native, off-Broadway producer and finding himself less than pleased with the result, he decided it would be much better to "pilot my own ship," and still early in his career, King cofounded Indian Time Theater in Buffalo, New York (qtd. in Rathbun 2000a, 316). Like Geiogamah, King saw the potential for theatre to bring Native communities together. Since the 1970s, King has developed several community-authored pieces in which he removed his name from the program. In a 1993 interview with *Native Playwrights' Newsletter* editor Paul Rathbun, King explained what it takes to create a community-based, Native theatre:

> To succeed, you have to find some equilibrium for those people to come together to work. Well, Shakespeare does not cut it. The reality is that I have to go by what's going to work in that community, and which everybody will agree to. Most of the time what they agree to comes out of the middle of them, where they can all invest their ideas and invest their opinions. They invest something that they have to say that affects them all, and that they agree on. Then it starts working. (2000a, 307)

The communities that King works together with might be a reservation community like the Menominee reservation in Wisconsin, or a group of urban teenagers, using theatre as a way to "change their interests from gang-banging to staying alive" (2000a, 307) and creating performances from their lives, about substance abuse or other issues that affect their survival, for example.

Several other playwrights saw their work published and produced as the twentieth gave way to the twenty-first century. E. Donald Two Rivers (Anishinaabe) published *Briefcase Warriors* in 2001. Two volumes of Cherokee playwright Diane Glancy's plays appeared: *War Cries* in 1997 and *American Gypsy* in 2003. A prolific playwright, poet, and author, Glancy, like many other Native playwrights, tended to find it easier to publish her work than get it produced, and that is a significant challenge that playwrights are taking into the twenty-first century. Yellow Robe and Two Rivers addressed the challenge in one way, by starting their own companies, but for many playwrights, founding a company is not an effective answer.[14]

Several important multi-author collections have appeared, all selecting a balance of work by playwrights relatively new on the scene as well as those who have figured importantly in the development of Native theatre. *Seventh Generation: An Anthology of Native American Plays* (1999), edited by Mimi Gisolfi D'Aponte, was one of the first collections published. It contains plays by Native writers from the continental United States, Canada, and Hawaii, including arguably William Yellow Robe's most popular play, *The Independence of Eddie Rose*. In the same year, *Stories of Our Way: An Anthology of American Indian Plays* was coedited by Hanay Geiogamah and Jaye T. Darby as part of a new initiative Geiogamah founded in 1997, Project HOOP (Honoring Our Origins and People through Native Theatre, Education, and Community Development). The anthology appeared with a companion volume of essays and other resources, *American Indian Theater in Performance: A Reader* (2000), designed for use in college classrooms. Geiogamah's vision for a Native theatre in tribal communities was further advanced through Project HOOP, as one of the primary goals of the program was to develop theatre curricula at tribal colleges, piloting the project at Sinte Gleska University on the Rosebud Reservation in South Dakota, and then partnering with Haskell Indian Nations University.

Darby coedited another volume of plays published through Project HOOP, this volume with Stephanie Fitzgerald (Cree). *Keepers of the Morning Star: An Anthology of Native Women's Theater* (2003) collected eight plays and performance pieces by Native women from the United States and Canada, including some of the most innovative artists working today. Marie Clements's one-woman piece *Urban Tattoo* was developed through Native Earth's Weesageechak Begins to Dance Festival in 1995 and grew through several supported workshops and festivals, including a tech-supported staged reading at the Native Voices Festival. A Vancouver-based Métis performer, Clements worked with some of the most influential artists in Canadian Native theatre, including Margo Kane (Cree/Saulteaux), founder and artistic director of Full Circle: First Nations Performance. Melding storytelling and biography with detailed multimedia presentations, *Urban Tattoo* tells the story of Rosemarie, a Métis girl displaced from her history and identity. Through her memories, encounters that she replays to herself, Rosemarie reconnects herself, her "memories getting caught on my skin," gathering tattoos as emblems as she does so, until in the final moments of the play she stands facing the audience, "tall":

> As if those tattoos had come from me.
> As if we had an understanding that in going past I know my place
> And in going forward I have I become bigger than you can Imagine.
> Amen.
> Ho. (Darby and Fitzgerald 2003, 228)

A coedited volume by Monique Mojica and Ric Knowles, *Staging Coyote's Dream: An Anthology of First Nations Drama in English* (2003), was the first multi-author collection of Native plays to be published in Canada by a large press. It presents plays by ten Native playwrights and companies from the United States and Canada, including Mojica's *Princess Pocahontas and the Blue Spots*, the first time that this play has been republished since its 1991 first publication. It contains Highway's previously unpublished *Aria* and works by Drew Hayden Taylor, Floyd Favel, and Daniel David Moses, arguably the most popular and influential Native playwrights working in Canada at the time of the volume's publication. Mojica and Knowles followed this with volume 2 of *Staging Coyote's Dream* in 2009. Volume 2 offers another ten plays, collecting important Canadian titles from the 1990s, such as De-Ba-Jeh-Mu-Jig founder Shirley Cheechoo's *Path with No Moccasins* or Yvette Nolan's *Annie Mae's Movement*, inspired by the life of Anna Mae Aquash. Daniel David Moses and Floyd Favel are again published in this volume; Muriel Miguel's solo piece, *Trail of the Otter*, appears, as does daughter Murielle Borst's performance piece *More Than Feathers and Beads*. Newer titles in this volume include *The Scrubbing Project* by the Toronto-based Turtle Gals Performance Ensemble, whose original members included Mojica, Jani Lauzon, and Michelle St. John, and Marie Clements's *Burning Vision*. Nominated for six Jessie Awards— Vancouver's award for excellence in professional theatre—*Burning Vision* won two: for best original script and best production. When published by Talonbooks, *Burning Vision* was nominated for the Governor General's Literary Award for drama in 2003 and received the Canada Council's Canada-Japan Literary Award in 2004, a prize awarded to Canadian authors whose work is about Japan or promotes greater understanding between Canada and Japan. Robin Whittaker opens an analysis of the play by observing that it "operates by way of premise more than plot" (2009, 130), which could be an apt description of much of Clements's dramaturgy. Embracing complexity rather than reducing it, Clements crafts nonlinear, multilayered plots that defy easy categorization. *Burning Vision*'s premise or core rests with the journey of uranium, from the ore mined on Dene land by Dene laborers, through the tests of the bombs in the American Southwest, to the dropping of Little Boy on Hiroshima. Rather than depict that journey in linear fashion, however, Clements's drama explores thematic connections of exploitation, loss, and disregard for life and the land.

Two volumes associated with the Native American Women Playwrights Archive were published in the first years of the twenty-first century. Founded in 1996 at Miami University of Ohio's King Library, the Native American Women Playwrights Archive (NAWPA) functions as an "archive" in the traditional sense of that word—a repository for scripts, notes, programs, and the like—and exceeds that definition. Since its inception, NAWPA has assisted with the promotion and development of Native women's theatre in the United States and Canada. Thus, while it holds all of Spiderwoman Theater's official papers, it has also sponsored numerous performances, readings, and lectures by Native artists. The two volumes associated with NAWPA illustrate this sense of purpose. Edited by Rebecca Howard and Shirley Huston-Findlay, *Footpaths and Bridges: Voices from the Native American Women Playwrights Archive* publishes representative works from the archive along with Monique Mojica's dramatic essay "ETHNOSTRESS: Women's Voices in Native American Theatre," which she presented at the first conference sponsored by the archive in 1997. The 2009 volume *Performing Worlds Into Being: Native American Women's Theater* collects papers presented at the 2007 NAWPA conference held in honor of Spiderwoman Theater, including addresses given by daughters of Spiderwoman members—Murielle Borst, daughter of Muriel Miguel, and Monique Mojica, daughter of Gloria Miguel—both of whom are writers and performers. The volume also contains Spiderwoman's most recent collectively created piece, *Persistence of Memory*, and an onsite interview with members of the company.

While the availability of plays in publication is a wonderful thing, most playwrights write for the stage, not the page; the goal is to see one's work produced, that is, not necessarily to see it published. Throughout the 1990s and the beginning of the twenty-first century, a central subject of conversation and action among Native theatre artists and allies has been the need to locate and develop venues for the production of Native theatre. Unlike Canada, the United States has not had a history of stable resident Native theatre companies that assist the development of young writers (such as Toronto's Native Earth Performing Arts and its Weesageechak Begins to Dance Festival of New Works) or institutions whose mission is to train new Native theatre artists (such as Toronto's Centre for Indigenous Theatre). In the first years of the twenty-first century, more production opportunities became available to Native playwrights and, in turn, made Native theatre more accessible for audiences.

Randy Reinholz (Choctaw) and Jean Bruce Scott have continued developing outreach programs at Native Voices at the Autry. Native Voices' annual Playwrights' Retreat brings four playwrights to their Los Angeles location to workshop new scripts with directors, dramaturges, and actors—the script development model that Native Voices started with in its infancy at Illinois State University in 1994 and 1995. In addition, their Young Native Voices project brings Native youth together with professional artists, devising scripts and performance projects. Now quite secure in its partnership with the Autry Museum of Western Heritage, Native Voices commissions one new play and stages two full Equity productions each year.

Beginning in 2007, New York City's Public Theater under the leadership of Artist Director Oskar Eustis began to enthusiastically support Native theatre. Eustis had collaborated with Native theatre artists before taking the reins at the Public, developing its "Theatre from the Four Directions" staged reading series as artistic director of Trinity Repertory Company and producing works by several Native artists through it. In 2005, Eustis as artistic director of Trinity Repertory Company and Lou Bellamy of Penumbra coproduced a complete production of William Yellow Robe's *Grandchildren of the Buffalo Soldiers* that performed at both theatres and then toured to several sites. At the Public, Eustis continued this productive energy by obtaining Ford Foundation funding to establish the Native Theatre Initiative, whose goals are "to support the work of Native theatre artists across North America; to create a forum for field discussion among Native theatre artists and professionals; and to further raise visibility and awareness of Native theatre artists for New York audiences and the greater field of American Theatre" (Native Theater Festival 2009). The Public sponsored Native Theater Festivals in 2007 and 2008 that brought artists from across the United States and Canada together for a series of staged readings and related programs and discussion. In 2009, as their Ford Foundation funding ended, the Public announced plans for Ford Foundation officer Elizabeth Theobald Richards (Cherokee) to spend a year in residence at the Public, helping to create a sustainable future for the Native Theatre Initiative.

Establishing professional Native theatre companies and networks of support in large cities is one means of creating more production opportunities for Native plays. Urban productions, however, do not reach a majority of tribal audiences. One challenge that Native artists are embracing is how to get their works staged for tribal audiences, on reservations or in rural areas. The 2006 premiere of JudyLee Oliva's (Chickasaw) *Te Ata* provides one example of how playwrights could meet this challenge, as the production of Oliva's play in Chickasha, Oklahoma, may be the first production in the United States to be substantially supported by a tribe, in this case by the Chickasaw Nation. *Te Ata* tells the story of Chickasaw actress and storyteller Te Ata Fisher, whose performing career spanned seventy years and included performances for the Roosevelts' White House and English royalty (see *Te Ata* World Premiere). The production of *Te Ata* played to roughly 3,300 audience members and was staged for the Oklahoma centennial, signaling another potential production venue for Native theatre, as tribal governments and organizations may find reason to support plays with stories and themes relevant to their histories and cultures.

The paradigm of "success" as recognition in the professional theatre world is seductive, and worth questioning. If this is the primary measure of quality and success for contemporary indigenous theatre, what work might get lost in the margins? Some of the strongest roots of U.S.-based Native theatre have been in community-responsive theatre—Native artists traveling to Native communities, urban or reservation, working from the community's stories, and developing work that might only be staged once or twice. This is work that rarely gets national notice, but it addresses the needs of a specific tribal community and speaks to that community, while at the same time it perhaps builds an interest in theatre in that community as well. That vision is closer to the vision that some of the movement's founders—Geiogamah, for example—articulated for Native theatre: in the communities, for the communities, by the communities. In fact, different answers about the health of the Native theatre movement might emerge if it was assessed not only by its national visibility or by its professional footprint, but also by the vigor and quality of community-responsive, grassroots, and experimental performance—the artistic and political ground that sustained much of this work prior to the 1990s.

Notes

1. See King and Springwood (2001) for a collection of writing on the mascot controversy.

2. See Bird (1996) and Huhndorf (2001) for more scholarship on the numerous manifestations of "playing Indian" in America.

3. A useful introduction to postcolonial studies with an excellent bibliography and references to primary sources is Ashcroft et al. (2000).

4. See Johnson, Nagel, and Champagne (1997) and Smith and Warrior (1997).

5. See Rolland Meinholtz's chapter in this volume (chapter 4) for details.

6. Hanay Geiogamah, interview with the author, March 14, 2003.

7. Ibid.

8. Ibid.

9. Ibid.

10. Several sources document Spiderwoman's history. See Canning (1996), Haugo (2002), and Schneider (1997).

11. See Henning Schäfer's article in this volume.

12. See Baker (1991).

13. For more information about Yellow Robe's work, see Rathbun (2000b) and Pulitano (1998).

14. For further discussion on this issue, see NAWPA Authors' Roundtable (1999).

3

Burning Texts

Indigenous Dramaturgy on the Continent of Life

Tamara Underiner

The weather that evening in mid-July was hot and humid, the saturated air unleavened by even the memory of a breeze. But the crowd of Mayan men, women, and children gathered in the town center of Maní, deep inland on the Yucatán Peninsula, seemed not to notice its oppressive weight. Something much more pressing was happening in front of them. In front of the colonial church, a fire was burning and a priest was praying, in Spanish:

> En el nombre de Jesucristo y de los reyes de mi patria ordeno que se quemen esos ídolos y todos estos vestigios que son obras del demonio y que no quede nada de ellos, ya que constituyen una vergüenza para las civilizaciones avanzadas de esta época. Y que toda persona de estos lugares, sea cual fuere el rango que tenga, se le castigue severamente como escarmiento, y que se entienda que la única religión válida será la católica y que se pondrán en uso las costumbres de Castilla.

> [In the name of Jesus Christ, and the king and queen of my homeland, I order that these idols and relics—works of the devil—be burned so that nothing remains of them; they're a disgrace to the advanced civilizations of our time. And any person from these lands, of no matter what rank, will be severely punished as a lesson. Let it be

understood that the only valid religion is Catholicism,
and that the customs of Castilla will go into effect.]

As his appointed executioner suited the action to the word, moans
and cries of protest in the local language rose up, only to be brutally
repressed by the weapons of the Spaniards. By the end of the day,
thousands of idols and sacred texts would be destroyed.

The year was 2009. And this time, it was "only" a play.

I use quotes around "only" for two reasons. One is that,
although they occurred close to half a millennium ago, the true
events represented in this play have had enduring consequences
for the descendants of indigenous peoples in this hemisphere, and
for the non-indigenous people who care to know more about them.[1]
The second is that, as a contemporary practice of local historiography, the performance of this play (which was written between 1988
and 1991) makes it more than a simple reenactment of these past
events. It is also a latter-day enactment of presence and prophecy,
as much political as it is artistic, for the final words of the Mayan
leader, Tutul Xiú, confronting the priest are:

> Jaa, jach jaa, ts'o'ok a ts'áancha'tko'one'ex, chéemba'le'
> bíin líi-ko'on ka'a k-tóoch'ba, tumén to'one'ka'a
> sijone' beyo'on le ik'o, beyo'on le ch'íich'obo' u pajtal
> k-popokxik'e'le káan k'uchke k'iin je'elo' k-yum k'u to'on
> kun antko'on. (Dzul Ek 2007, 103)

> [It may now seem like you have conquered us. Howev-
> er, some day you will suffer the consequences, because
> we were born free—free like the air we breathe, free
> like the birds that fly; and our gods will protect us and
> we will reclaim our pathway. (Trans. Montemayor and
> Frischmann 2007, 109)]

As an "episodic reconstructing of the past in the present to impact
the future,"[2] this play registers several key issues facing indigenous
dramaturgy in *Abya Yala* (a Kuna term that means "Continent of
Life," preferred by many organizations and coalitions working for
pan-indigenous solidarity across the Americas[3]). In this essay, I will
focus on three of these important and interrelated issues: historiography, or the relationship between theatre, history, and the writing
of and about both; the politics of language in indigenous dramaturgy
in this hemisphere; and finally, the question of access and circula-

tion as factors in the development and craft of indigenous playwrights, and in the conditions through which their work becomes visible outside of local contexts.

Historiography

In its original Yucatecan Mayan, the title of this play by Oxkutzcaban playwright Carlos Armando Dzul Ek is *Bix úuchik u bo'ot ku'si'ip'il "Manilo'ob" tu ja'abil 1562*. In Spanish: *El auto de fe de Maní o Choque de dos culturas*. In English: *The Maní Inquisition or the Colliding of Two Cultures*. As the title suggests, it is based on events that took place on July 12, 1562, when Fray Diego de Landa Calderón, the Franciscan monk serving as Bishop of the Archdiocese of Yucatán charged with bringing the Catholic faith to the Mayan peoples, conducted this ceremonial burning of religious icons and pictographic codices numbering in the thousands. De Landa has served as an icon for an ontological, epistemological, and historiographical dilemma: he and other men like him, in the interest of eradicating idolatry and converting souls to Christianity in what many of them took to be the end times, systematically set about destroying local customs and local historiography. At the same time, and in a similarly systematic fashion, he and other men like him carefully recorded the practices they were determined to eliminate, frequently manifesting a kind of admiration for the skill and talent brought to indigenous work. Their reports have been principal sources of information from the time before, during, and immediately after encounter and conquest. Thus, what has been knowable about the peoples' history, literature, and performance traditions at the time of the Spaniards' arrival has been largely filtered through Spanish eyes, ears, and tongues. Or, it remains almost impenetrably coded in stone, whose silence over long centuries is only beginning to be broken, thanks to the work of archaeologists and linguists.[4] In reports and dictionaries compiled in the early days of colonization by both religious and military men, the Spanish described a vibrant existing theatrical tradition in which

> we find references to "farces," "comedies," and "tragedies," "magicians," "acrobats," "jesters," "jongleurs," and "puppeteers." They inform us of spectacles both aristocratic and popular, religious and profane; of schools for dancers and singers and their priestly supervisors;

of performance rehearsals and the use of masks, wigs,
facial makeup, and elaborate natural scenery. (Montemay-
or and Frischmann 2007, 22)

While it is tempting to see in these reports a close correspon-
dence with theatre as we know it in Anglo-American theatre history,
researchers like Diana Taylor, Adam Versényi, Stephen D. Houston,
and Dennis Tedlock caution against assuming too much similarity,
since ancient performance practices in the Americas often featured
actors who *became* rather than represented the divine or ancestral
characters they assumed, for audiences comprising the living, the
dead, and the divine. The *Rabinal Achi* offers an instructive example. Still performed in what is today Guatemala, this performance
tradition has long been considered to provide evidence for pre-
Columbian performance practice. In his lengthy study and translation of the text of this dance drama (from the original K'iche' into
English), linguistic ethnographer Dennis Tedlock reports that the
actors consider themselves to be impersonating the ghosts of the
historical figures in the play, not these figures while they were alive.
As these ghosts still live in a cave outside the town of Rabinal,
the contemporary performers must ask their permission "to make
their memories visible and audible in the waking world." When it is
performed on the feast day of the town's patron, St. Paul, Tedlock
writes, it will draw its largest audience—"its largest visible audience, that is" (Tedlock 2003, 14–15).

So what the Spanish witnessed of "teatro" when they arrived
not only featured non-Christian content, but also participated in a
performative economy that was as much transubstantiation as it
was representation. The problem for the Spaniards was that transubstantiation was reserved for the person of Christ within the
Christian Mass. Thus, where there was a Native text or a codex
to burn, it was burned. Where there was a performance practice
connected to deeply held belief systems, it was banned. And, as
Church records show, banned time and time again, suggesting the
persistence of such practices long after Conquest, despite the best
efforts of Spanish authorities.

Indeed, from colonial times forward, these practices have continued, often in ostensibly Christian fashion. Staged during feast
days of the Catholic liturgical year, they may nevertheless bear what
James Scott (1992) calls "hidden transcripts" of pre-Hispanic beliefs
and stories, and/or contemporary political critique. The underlying
message is often veiled to outsiders but visible to the community.

In his study of Moors' and Christians' dance dramas in Mexico and New Mexico, for example, Max Harris uses the notion of hidden transcripts to suggest that "the sanctioned narrative of Catholic triumph masks a subtext that invokes the world of the Aztecs in order to challenge current power structures" (2000, 19). Victoria Reifler Bricker's studies on Mayan *carnaval* in the state of Chiapas similarly show how Tzotzil-speaking Maya use the Easter story as a loose structure upon which to perform their own origin stories and political history of ethnic conflict (Bricker 1981). In countries where official history often ignores the particularity of local knowledges, indigenous peoples use performance as a form of alternative historiography. Sometimes that historiography is overt, as in the case of the Maní performance, but draws on oral traditions as well as official accounts and adopts local perspectives as well. In other cases, the historiography may be more difficult to unpack. Studies like Harris's and Brickler's, the result of painstaking on-site ethnography, lend support to Diana Taylor's proposal that performance, far from being a "disappearing act," serves agendas of cultural preservation as "acts of transfer" of cultural memory (Taylor 2003).

Questions of Language

To approach the study of indigenous performance in *Abya Yala*, scholars need more than English, Spanish, Portuguese, or French— which puts us at a disadvantage to most of the participants and audiences for this work. *Bix úuchik u bo'ot ku'si'ip'il "Manilo'ob" tu ja'abil 1562*, for example, is written and staged in a mixture of Yucatecan Mayan and Spanish (with some Latin as well for portions of the Catholic priest's prayers). It is performed for audiences who are themselves bi- and, increasingly in the context of hemispheric migration, trilingual (in this case, in Mayan, Spanish, and English). As such, Dzul Ek's work partakes in a "continent-wide emergence of literature in indigenous languages . . . that were scheduled to disappear with globalization, and that had long been marginalized by imperial Spanish" (Franco 2009, 24). Jean Franco credits the start of the movement in the quincentennial year of 1992, when, during a meeting in Quito of 120 representatives of indigenous communities from across the hemisphere, participants asserted that "the subordination of native languages to Spanish ratified the long-standing oppression of the originary inhabitants of the continent" (24). In Mexico alone, some 55 local languages in addition to

Spanish are spoken, and at least one of them—Náhuatl—has been incorporated into university courses, while others are often used in officially supported workshops for writing and social programs. This is somewhat rare and radical, for most education in indigenous communities takes place exclusively in Spanish, despite the fact that another language is spoken at home. As Franco adds, "One cannot write in an indigenous language without calling up the whole history of colonialism, given the power relations that dictated the first and many subsequent transcriptions of Native American texts into phonic writing" (25).

In fact, drama in indigenous languages is not new to the hemisphere—the same sixteenth- and seventeenth-century missionaries who worked so hard to eradicate the content of local performance traditions were quite happy to co-opt the talents of local performers to produce plays in indigenous languages that taught Christian doctrine and Bible stories. Later, at least in Mexico, the context with which I am most familiar, that missionary impulse would be channeled into "cultural missions" in service to the Revolution, whose aims would be demonstrated in didactic plays and puppet shows in local languages throughout the countryside (Underiner 2004). Coincident with these aims was a definition of a European-inflected modernity in which indigenous language and culture would have no place except, perhaps, as "local color." This generated new anthropological interest both within and outside Mexico, among researchers interested in documenting such culture and its languages before they disappeared. But of course, they have not. The very means by which the promoters of a post-Revolutionary modern Mexico advanced their own aims, as well as the interest anthropologists have shown in these communities, have been appropriated locally as a way to preserve and advance language and tradition (although it must be said that the pervasive economic hardship compelling migration north and to Europe is rapidly changing community demographics throughout Mexico and Central America).

What is new about this era of indigenous-language theatre (which actually predates the 1992 Quito conference) is the question of authorship, theme, and point of view, with indigenous people themselves writing about their vital experiences for audiences who are also (but not always exclusively) indigenous. At times, plays are written by individual authors who have been involved in school or community theatre, or who themselves are educators who have seen the value of theatre in teaching and preserving the local language. Such is the case with Dzul Ek, who majored in history and was trained as a middle school teacher; he formed the theatre and dance group Sac Nicté (Plumeria Flower) in 1978 in Maní in conjunction with a new bilingual school, as a means of extending the school's valorization of local language and culture. For similar reasons in east-central Mexico, Nahua playwright Ildefonso Maya founded the Hidalgo Huastecan Cultural Center, which often sponsors the staging of one of his nearly 300 theatrical works (Montemayor and Frischmann 2007, 27). Other playwrights who write in Yucatecan Mayan include (but certainly are not limited to) Feliciano Sánchez Chan and María Luisa Góngora Pacheco, who have been part of a long-standing tradition of *teatro comunitario* in the region. Other theatre groups operate more collectively, as do the celebrated Chiapan troupes of Lo'il Maxil (Monkey Business) and FOMMA (an acronym for Fortaleza de la mujer maya, or Strength of the Mayan Woman), both of which have also nurtured individual authors like Petrona de la Cruz Cruz, Rogelio Hernández Cruz, and Isabel Juárez Espinosa. These latter two organizations, whose histories have been amply documented elsewhere, are examples of how theatre developed out of anthropological interest in the region, but was quickly reclaimed for local purposes.[5]

The repertory of indigenous-language theatre is as extensive and varied as any vibrant theatre tradition anywhere, encompassing all genres, forms, and subjects. As might be expected, many include the dramatization of local legends and tales, and as I have already suggested, a substantial body of work is being developed that treats local history in a politicized key. A quite recent example of this is a 2009 work by the aforementioned María Luisa Góngora Pacheco, *La fuerza del pueblo maya en la voz de la mujer indígena* (The Strength of the Mayan People in the Voice of the Indigenous Woman). This bilingual work treats the life of Felipa Poot Tzuc, a Mayan woman who worked on behalf of indigenous and women's rights in the region and was murdered by political enemies in 1936. Góngora utilized published accounts of her life, oral histories from the region, and her own imagination to explore the gendered roots of the violence against this important but understudied figure. Significantly, her play ends with a parade of placards featuring the latter-day demands of the same village, suggesting that the indigenous rights Poot fought for are still far from guaranteed.

For every historico-political drama or drama of cultural recuperation there is a romantic comedy, or a farce, or a dramatization of a story, poem, novel, or play from local and European sources. My experience studying such theatre over the past two decades tells me Dzul Ek is not alone in his belief "that through theatre everything, absolutely everything, can be performed" (qtd. in Montemayor and Frischmann 2007, 26).

Access and Circulation

It is one thing to write in indigenous languages; it is another to be heard, and seen, and read in them. This "other thing" proves devilishly difficult to achieve. The collusion among post-Enlightenment rationality, military and spiritual conquest, and global capitalism has institutionalized and commodified both culture and knowledge about culture to such a degree that the ability to speak one's truth in one's mother tongue in every place that it should matter requires both strategic labor and well-placed friends.[6] (The English-only nature of this anthology is itself a manifestation of this difficulty.) Festivals that bring indigenous theatre groups together have enriched the work, but often they must first be translated into Spanish, Portuguese, English, or French so that they can travel to other communities and to cities where a European language is dominant. This increases knowledge about the work, as well as its reach, but of course much can be lost in the translation. Yucatán once again provides a recent and fascinating exception, which possibly signals an important new direction for indigenous-language dramaturgy in Mexico. A new play by Juan de la Rosa and Socorro Loeza, working in the capital city of Mérida, was selected for travel to the prestigious Muestra Nacional de Teatro (National Theatre Festival) in Ciudad Juárez in the fall of 2008, where it was the only play to have been staged almost entirely in an indigenous tongue. It then traveled on to my own university (Arizona State), where it was also performed without translation.[7]

Ma'ti na'a ti kech / No te entiendo / I Don't Understand You tells the story of a Mayan family in which the daughter has not received the benefit of a ceremony that would prepare her for life in her community. Bereft of its benefits, she has grown up without the ability to speak or understand her native tongue and her family members who speak it, and although she speaks only Spanish and attempts to acculturate to a non-Mayan way of life, she still faces rejection and denigration in the world outside her community, simply for having been born into it. The play explores and exposes that dilemma without resolving it, but in the course of the exposition suggests that, far from being a backward tradition, the ceremony in question can prepare Mayan children to face the difficulties posed by movements between village and city and the pressures they bring. I was fortunate to see this play when it was staged at my university, and to witness its compelling power even for audiences who had little Spanish, let alone Yucatecan Mayan. Presented in a realistic form, exquisitely acted and impeccably presented within a proscenium frame, the play offered us a privileged glimpse into Mayan family life.

For readers of English and Spanish who wish to experience something of this work less directly but more accessibly, we are fortunate that some of it is now available in translation. A collection of Lo'il Maxil's plays has been translated by anthropologist Robert M. Laughlin (2008); FOMMA's *The Demon's Nun* appears in a new anthology, *Stages of Conflict*, edited by Diana Taylor and Sarah J. Townsend (2008, 318–25); Petrona de la Cruz Cruz's early *A Desperate Woman* appears in Taylor and Costantino's *Holy Terrors* (2003, 291–310). Perhaps the most ambitious undertaking in publishing has been Carlos Montemayor and Donald Frischmann's three-volume and trilingual *Words of the True Peoples* (2007), which comprises the work of dozens of Mexican indigenous-language writers. Volume 3 is devoted entirely to theatre, and includes many of the works mentioned here, including the full text of Dzul Ek's *Auto de fe*. Excerpts of FOMMA's work in performance can be found on the website of the Hemispheric Institute for Performance and Politics, which has been instrumental in bringing together artists, scholars, and activists together for *encuentros* in which new work can be shared. Finally, as Birgit Däwes mentions in her introduction to this volume, Gordon Bronitsky's international ORIGINS festival of First Nations Theatre is currently expanding to include Latin American indigenous performance for the first time.

Although in this essay I have focused mostly on Mexico and Guatemala, I believe many of the issues of history, historiography, language politics, and access have resonance for work elsewhere on the Continent of Life. Every day brings news of indigenous resistance to neoliberal economic policies in places like Mexico, Bolivia, Peru, and Ecuador, in which it is clear that indigenous peoples are seeing themselves as new political and social actors in Latin America and are being seen as such by powerful people. As Fabiola Escárzaga and Raquel Gutiérrez point out, their strategies encompass everything from peaceful protest to dialogue and negotiation to violent confrontation with the various states, as they defend their collective rights against exploitive economic and environmental practices (2005). In my own state of Arizona, increasing numbers of indigenous migrants from Mexico and Central America encounter violent reactions from U.S. "nativists" aligned with vigilante groups like the Minute Men. At stake is a new definition of citizenship that, for indigenous peoples, often transcends geopolitical borders. Indeed, it is worth recalling that both southern and northern U.S. borders were drawn up without input from tribal communities along them, even when doing so effectively divided intact communities along national lines, as was the case with the Tohono O'odham in Arizona/Mexico, and the Blackfeet/Blood in Montana/Canada (Luna-Firebaugh 2002). Chicana/o theatre has long registered the indigenous component of Mexican American subjectivity as it articulates within a post-Treaty of Guadalupe-Hidalgo United States; examples are Luis Valdez's *Mummified Deer* (2005) and even a key scene in his classic *Zoot Suit* (published in 1992), as well as Cherrie Moraga's *The Hungry Woman* (2001). Groups like the Colorado sisters' Coatlicue Theater Company make such multiple identifications a key focus of their work. The latter have also begun to bring theatre workshops to indigenous communities in Chiapas in support of women's rights in Zapatista territory, manifesting a transnational indigenous subjectivity and solidarity through performance (Underiner 2007). Such theatre has shown itself to be a powerful tool for making demands for the recognition of indigenous subjectivity visible and audible. The texts that result still burn, but now as beacons to the pathway Tutul Xiú invoked half a millennium ago.

Notes

1. As elsewhere in the hemisphere, the term "indigenous" in and of itself is not quite sufficient to encompass the complexity of cultural identifications within and apart from nation-state identifications in Mexico, Central and South America. For the purposes of this essay, it will refer to descendants of the peoples present on the continent at the time of the arrival of the Spaniards, whose first and/or preferred language is similarly descended from one of the languages spoken at that time.

2. I am indebted to Nestor Bravo-Goldsmith, a doctoral student in Theatre and Performance of the Americas at Arizona State University, for this phrase, which is a lovely way to describe these and other kinds of performances in the hemisphere. (He uses it in his dissertation in progress, to describe the Chilean military parade.)

3. According to the website NativeWeb, "[t]he Aymara leader Takir Mamani suggested the selection of this name (which the Kuna use to

denominate the American continents in their entirety), and proposed that all Indigenous peoples in the Americas utilize it in their documents and oral declarations. 'Placing foreign names on our cities, towns and continents,' he argued, 'is equal to subjecting our identity to the will of our invaders and to that of their heirs.' The proposal of Takir Mamani has found a favorable reception in various sectors" (Becker 1994–2002). It should be noted, however, that a true "pan-indigenous solidarity" remains elusive and utopic, as internecine conflicts do exist.

4. An abridged copy of De Landa's *Relación de las cosas de Yucatán* survives and can be found at the Royal Academy of History in Madrid; for a translation, see Tozzer (1941). For Spanish historiography, also see Durán (trans. Heyden 1994). For work on Meso-American archaeology and linguistics, see Schele and Mathews (1998); Houston, Chinchilla Mazariegos, and Stuart (2000); Tedlock (2003); Inomata and Coben (2006); and León Portilla (trans. Kemp, 2006).

5. In addition to Underiner (2004) and Montemayor and Frischmann (2007), see Laughlin and Sna Jzi'ibajom (2008); Taylor and Townsend (2008); and Taylor and Costantino (2003).

6. For an extended critique of this collusion, see Walter D. Mignolo's *The Idea of Latin America* (2005).

7. This play was staged as part of a "Readings in Mexican Theatre" Symposium, cofacilitated by myself and my colleague Israel Franco of the Centro de Investigación Teatral Rodolfo Usigli of Mexico City, in November of 2008. Franco and I provided Spanish- and English-language summaries in the program.

Part II

Individual Hi/stories

Visions, Practice, Experience

4

Coyote Transforming

Visions of Native American Theatre

Rolland Meinholtz

From 1964 until the fall of 1970, this author was instructor and artistic director of drama and dance at the Institute of American Indian Arts, Santa Fe, New Mexico. Working with Louis Ballard (music) and Rosalie Jones (dance), together we spearheaded a search for the roots of American Indian theatre. The institute's overarching educational principle during the sixties was that the traditional culture of the young high schoolers coming to us was their greatest strength. Many of them, if not most, had lost touch with that culture. The genocide of the Native peoples of America had been cultural as well as physical and was still ongoing.[1] If our students were truly to be themselves, to become people of strength, they needed to be reintroduced to the centuries of artistic achievement that was the gift from their ancestors. They needed to know it, understand it, deal with it, struggle with it, hopefully integrate it, and lastly, build upon it. To create not really a "new," but more accurately, a "now" response; a thoroughly contemporary American Indian Art, informed by the past, living and reflecting the present. Art to feed the souls of living Indian people. The Now People.

One warning: what follows is not a history. It is accurate as far as memory can be accurate, remembering events that transpired forty-four years ago. But a history of drama at the institute is not the purpose of this memoir. That has already been attempted elsewhere. This is a memoir, or even more accurately, a mosaic; a seemly random collection of bits and pieces worked into a whole. I wish to recall, discuss, and illustrate the principles of the Indian theatre artistry our students and faculty discovered and were guided

by during the sixties. It is an artistic statement I hope might have
surprising validity to Indian theatre artists of today, both in considering what they have already achieved, and more importantly,
what they may hope to achieve in the future.

Our work began with two significant challenges.

I. One Visionary Man

"Should Indian theatre look and sound like Neil Simon? What kind
of theatre could come out of a tribal myth? Can you imagine what
it would be like: an American Indian theatre? Its look? How would
the actors move? What would Indian theatre do to a contemporary
audience that Broadway productions would not?"

The myth referred to was from the fabulous Navajo epic, "Diné
bahane,"[2] telling of the meeting of Sun God and Changing Woman.
The questioner was Lloyd Kiva New, arts director of the Institute of
American Indian Arts at Santa Fe, New Mexico. I was a prospective
candidate for the position of drama instructor. The time was August
of 1964. During the next few hours and on into the next day, Lloyd
New and I envisioned possibilities that excited both of us, and I got
the job. "We believe," Lloyd New wrote in 1969,

> that young Indian people must be trained in the fullest
> degree regarding all aspects of theatre: the history of
> universal forms, the technical aspects, acting, speech and
> movement. Against this understanding they must then be
> led to examine Indian culture for that which is theatrical,
> and then find ways to interpret those unique aspects for
> contemporary audiences in true theatre settings. Indian
> theatre ultimately will be born from this group of sophis-
> ticated Indian artists. Until their statement is made and
> a heretofore new theatrical form is evolved we can only
> view present dramatic manifestations of Indian life, the
> religious ceremony, the grandstand performance, the
> Indian pow wow as the raw material from which Indian
> theatre will evolve. (New [1969] 2000, 3)[3]

Our project, as I understood it from Lloyd, was to develop an American Indian theatre that would be thoroughly contemporary, but, if
informed by the entire historical performing culture of America's

Natives, one that would also be strikingly unique; as recognizable in its way as Japanese Kabuki, Indian Kathakali, or Italian Opera.

The institute had a quality library to support my work. Further, being situated in New Mexico, we were sited in the middle of Pueblo, Apache, Navajo, Ute, Zuni, Hopi, Havasupai, and Pima/Papago lands. Most of these tribes conducted active ceremonials. Our Southwestern site also offered a rich tapestry of ancient Native places: Chaco Canyon, Aztec National Monument, and the lands of the Mimbres culture. Together with the copious petroglyph and pictograph sites strewn all over, the Southwest was a gigantic outdoor museum of places to investigate, play in, and dream of possible implications for a contemporary Indian theatre.

Our drama group received a momentous challenge right from the start. We were invited to perform a full-length piece for the Scottsdale Arts Festival at Scottsdale, Arizona. We accepted, of course; how could one say no to such an opportunity? I had just stumbled across a Northwest Tsimshian myth of a chief called Moqwina, whose story bore an uncanny resemblance to Shakespeare's *Macbeth*. Perfect! A Northwest Indian Macbeth! My students were galvanized. Something from their culture that could hold its own with one of the highest expressions of European culture? The Wow factor was irresistible.

Moqwina's methods were the fruit of early piecemeal research. Putting that research immediately on stage proved to be a tremendous guide as to what did and did not work in view of our overall objectives.

For example:

1. *Moqwina* used dance sparingly. The little it had demonstrated immediately the necessity of dance to all future projects.

2. Our script was in verse. We quickly realized that verse and open staging reinforce each other in wonderful ways. We began investigating Native American poetry for guidance and inspiration.

3. We instinctively used drums for transitions and often as support throughout scenes. Thus we came to a nontheoretical appreciation of how the drum is, to this day, truly the pulse of Native life.

4. We used face painting for characters not wearing actual masks. The painting was based upon both totems
   and mask design. It was bold. But face painting made
   it extremely difficult for the audience to know what
   the actor's expression was from moment to moment.
   Face painting seemed wrong in performance, at least
   when applied generally to everybody.

5. Actual masks used were what we found in the Northwest. Though initially striking in performance, these
   near copies either created a sense of woodenness or
   raised questions about transgressing the sacredness
   of the original mask.

6. Performance helped us realize that a copy of a traditional mask was not wise. Traditional masks needed to
   be digested, redesigned—transformed by one of our
   gifted sculptors back home. For us masks needed to
   be a contemporary interpretation of the mask's spirit
   for people living in the present.

7. Lastly we came away with the strong suspicion that
   one long drama, cast in the tragic mode, was not an
   accurate expression of Native culture. Further the
   mythological Moqwina escaped Macbeth's hubris, ex-
   iled from his tribe, living in shame. We did not have
   the courage to stick with mythology's truth and kept
   Shakespeare's ending of tragic murder, reasoning that
   it was more theatrical, and more satisfying. After a
   series of performances of this work, we knew our ending was wrong. We knew we had to find another way
   of creating theatre.

Interlude: Musings Looking Backward
through the Spectacles of 2008

Native Americans all across our continent have reveled in Trickster
stories. For much of the country, the Trickster was Coyote.

His tales are set at the dawn of the world. Animals and humans
were in flux, talking to themselves and each other. Trickster spirits,
like Coyote, had the ability to transform themselves into almost anything that suited them, animal or human. Coyote's transformative
abilities were protean, but his overweening appetites often got him,

as young people say today, into "deep doo-doo"; literally, scatologi-
cally. But in addition to the fun of impossible, dirty situations, Coyote was a poignant expression of the will to survive by a resourceful
and intelligent creature who often was his own worst enemy.

One of the most fascinating covert transformations Coyote
made was at the hands of his storytellers. As misadventures for
Coyote gained in scope, they could not resist humanizing him, slowly allowing Coyote to change, first, into a bumbling hero, and later
a noble one. Thus it is Coyote who became emblematic of the core
nature of American Indian theatre: transformation. However, these
transformations were not accomplished without rampant backslid-
ing; one moment noble, the next animalistic: the steady march of
progress was never Coyote's drumbeat. Coyote is deeply encoded
with the secular playfulness of the people who gave him life: a
playfulness that explodes into theatre.

Because of this transforming messiness, Coyote also best epit-
omizes another principle of Native drama: for Indian theatre, there
is no clear division of comedy and tragedy as found, for example,
in ancient Greek drama. Comedy and tragedy are one: one extreme
transforming into the other. Everything humans perceive as fixed is
actually transitory and subject to transformation.

Transformation is a power, a gift, finally, implicit in being alive.
It is to be used to honor Mother Earth as well as the ineffable Male
Spirit. If transformation is misused, it leads to impossible complications—some wayward, some harmful, even dangerous; many all-of-
the-above and quite funny. Death, itself, is not a tragedy in Native
drama: it is a transition—as long as, that is, one can, like Coyote,
hang on to the tip of one's own tail, one's essence. To die is simply
to go away. Tragedy has a little "t" and occurs only within a life: it
always has an element of comedy embedded within it.

There actually are one or two tales in which Coyote is forced
to give up the tip of his tail. He then is nothing. Zilch. But—the
Great Spirit remembers Coyote and in remembering him transforms
his memory into, once again—a living thing. He does this because
the people simply cannot get along without Coyote. He makes them
weep with laughter.

II. Traveling Around[4]

During our first year, my playwriting seminar was not producing
scripts. Two students wanted to create a play about their grandparents. All the material was before us. Their grandparents all but

came and actually sat with us every time we met. But the kind of dramatic event we could engage them in was maddeningly evading us. We could intuit what it was we were after but could not actually write it. At that time my ineptitude as a playwriting teacher was a big part of the problem, but also the conviction that we didn't want a standard European drama featuring statement of problem, development of conflict, crisis, climax, and denouement. We knew what we did not want, but could not yet envision an alternative.

I looked into Japanese Noh dramas. We knew that our play would be about a spiritual struggle. Noh theatre was one of the few world dramatic forms that emphasized such struggles. One play in particular caught my imagination. In it, a woman, recently dead, struggled with whether to remain as a ghost haunting a living man she intensely loved, or to pass over to the realm of spirit and relinquish her lover. Remaining, she would be a tortured ghost. In the play, a simple freestanding archway wrapped in white cloth represents the boundary between this world and the next. At the heart of the play, the woman places one foot in the arch, but quickly draws it back, unwilling and unable to complete her action because of her tremendous attachment. She repeats this action many times. A chanting chorus, sitting at the side of the stage, reveals her struggle to the audience. Finally her urge for peace strengthens her will. Poignantly, she passes through the arch.

Further research led to vision-quest material of the Nez Perce. One of the grandchildren in our class was a Nez Perce student. He had shared with our class that his grandmother had been his guide for a vision quest. With these two bodies of material and chock-full of all the stories my students had told me, though I could not teach them how, I felt I could get a play down on paper. So I began writing. My students became my first readers, guides, and critics.

The play we created together was *Black Butterflies*. In it an aged grandmother, who knows she is dying, valiantly hangs on long enough to guide her grandson through his vision quest. Once he has danced his vision, his grandma can let go and leave this life, safe in the knowledge that her spirit and the ancient spirit of their people will live in him.

This drama used the discoveries of our latest research: a bare stage, the underpinning of the drum, elevated speech (i.e., verse), the use of a chorus to comment upon the action and give the play timelessness, a climax of achievement (in this case, achievement that was translated to the audience via dance). I hoped and believed that with this play the logjam would be released and student works would follow. And that is exactly what happened.

A terribly shy young woman approached me, mumbling that she thought, since she had seen *Moqwina* and *Black Butterflies*, she should be writing plays instead of poetry. Her name was Monica Charles. She was of the Klallam tribe from close to Port Angeles, Washington. Monica was to become a vital resident spirit and playwright in our program over the next couple of years. I soon learned that beneath her unprepossessing exterior lay bands of the truest steel, called honesty, courage, perceptiveness, and like Coyote, an indomitable will to survive. Monica and I began work on a play she had started calling *Mowitch*.

Perhaps the most important issue for us that had to be met head on and resolved, at least in principle, was the question of the relationship between sacred ceremonials and a nascent drama. The received scholarly wisdom at the time we began our project was that the Native peoples of this country did not develop a formal theatre, even though they had had thousands of years in which to do so.[5] Even my students and I were making the same assumption, tinted by a faint pall of derogatory bias, by becoming excited at the wonder of something from Native culture appearing to be Shakespearean. Further complicating our creative work, we were both encouraged and warned to keep our hands off sacred materials. Considering IAIA's guiding goal of using traditional culture to produce contemporary art, where did that leave us?

My training in theatre history taught me where to look and what to look for: impersonation, someone pretending to be someone or something they are not, fictive storytelling, and the depiction of an opposition and/or struggle.

A later development of almost all drama is the technique of dialogue used in dramatic address. Its presence demonstrates well-advanced, more sophisticated methods in the presentation of dramas. Dialogue is terribly useful because it is such a reliable earmark for the transition of pure ritual / ceremony firmly into theatre.

Through research I began to discover that assumptions that seemed self-evident about Indians and theatre were not true. One of the earliest breakthroughs for my students and me came while observing a deer ceremony at a local pueblo. Encouraged by Pueblo students at IAIA, we got ourselves up a 4:30 a.m. to drive for half an hour in darkness and arrive at 5:00 a.m. We had been told this was a ceremony we would not want to miss. Why? What were we to see?!

Observation: At a Pueblo Near Santa Fe, mid-1960s

ONE: Prologue and Introductory Dance

The Hunters left the pueblo before first light. As the sun rises and the hand pats that had shaped the brown adobe walls of the pueblo come out of hiding, the Hunters return leading a long line of Deer.

The dancing regalia of the Deer glows with quiet resplendence in the flat morning light. Deer and Hunters are greeted by a men's chorus. They raise joyful songs of welcome. Made to feel at home in the world of the People of the Pueblo, the Deer begin dancing to the songs of the chorus. Their delicate stick front feet bless the earth of the plaza as they trod upon it. Morning blossoms into day.

TWO: A Drama

Close on to midday, the Deer dancers quietly disappear and the People gather at the main plaza of the pueblo. In their midst appear the Hunters with their guns. They sit and mime a nonexistent campfire. A young boy has joined them. He is old enough to be safely taken hunting, but not old enough yet to be dreaming of girls.

From their dialogue, Tewa speakers learn that men and boy have been chosen by the People to hunt Deer for the pueblo, so that all might have meat for the winter. The boy has never been hunting before. He must suffer teasing from the men, though they also tease and play tricks on each other. After a time, they bestir themselves, and by their actions, we know they are stalking Deer. They see tracks, they examine and smell sign. They don't seem especially serious about their enterprise. In fact, they give the impression of being buffoons. Their audience, sitting and standing around them, are amused by their antics as they "travel" about the plaza.

Several Deer appear. They are nervous and skittish. Their quarry in sight, the Hunters' activity is intensified, but they literally are the "gang that can't shoot straight." It is the boy that, at last, brings down a Deer by running and jumping on one Deer's back. This action is an embrace rather than a death grip. As one of the Hunters fires a shot into the air, the Deer sinks to the earth, offering itself to the People.

THREE: A Semiprivate Ritual

The now limp Deer is carried to the home of the young boy's family. The body of the Deer is elaborately welcomed and honored.

The boy is praised and asked to tell his story. Later, as the Deer is being "cleaned," wonder of wonders—a man is discovered within the Deer's body. The family rejoices. They formally adopt this man as their own son.

FOUR: Final Dance and Recessional

The remaining Deer are escorted to the edge of the pueblo as the shadows of dusk tint the mountains in pale blue greens and purples. Songs of praise and statements of the Elders assure them that this is exactly how they will always be treated. The Deer are peaceful and sure-footed as they delicately leave the pueblo and return to the hills, whose paps are now touched by the softest of alpine glows.

The Deer are, of course, men from the village impersonating deer complete with costume, headdresses, and the unforgettable front feet, played by sticks held in the hands of the dancers/performers. This impersonation is a step toward theatre compared with, for example, the Catholic mass in which the priests are actually priests and the choirboys truly choirboys. It was the introduction of the Hunters and their boy companion later in the day that was revelatory for us. Here we had impersonation, storytelling, a depiction of a struggle, and even dialogue.

Moreover, the Deer now appeared in a new mode, taking part in the drama by pretending to be somewhere they were not (the hills beyond the plaza) in a condition they were not (nervous and skittish), participating in an activity that was playfully imaginative (that they were being hunted and that one of them would be caught and die). The fact that the Hunters were buffoons suggested a completely different take on drama, comic or serious. It was the very first time I saw Coyote's yellow eyes peering at me from around the corner of the walls of the plaza. The mystical moment of a man being discovered in the Deer was also inspiring and instructive. It was so elegantly simple!

Later on in our voyage of discovery I was privileged to witness how Mud Head and Koshare kachinas sparked dramatic situations within the ceremonies of the Zuni, Hopi, and Pueblo people. Both are dramatic encapsulations of the spirit of Coyote. Wherever they wander through a ceremonial, always running free, irrepressible, the quintessential "loose cannon ball," they invariably pull out stories, short comic scenes, and tricks they play upon each other (and sometimes unwary audience members).

My students and I saw Koshares at one pueblo engage in a lengthy improvisation while attempting to climb a twenty-foot-high greased pole to get food that was placed at the top. The action, skits, dialogue, and pratfalls were all furious in tempo and frequently outrageously funny. Yet they could not hide the fact that the pole really was heavily greased and extremely difficult to climb. If the Koshares failed to reach the top and throw down the food to the crowd watching, the people of that pueblo believed that they would be facing famine throughout the coming year. This kind of comedy in the midst of seriousness illustrated the wellsprings of Indian theatre.

But how far does this sophistication go? Some authorities, especially back in the sixties, will argue that the events I am describing are examples of what might be called "protodrama." And they are right, in that key hallmarks of formal theatre, items such as physical structures, scripts, and noted authors at first glance seem to be nonexistent. American Indians, to the best of our knowledge, were nonliterate until the time of the Cherokee and Sequoia. Earlier scripts were developed orally, the authors never known or forgotten in the mists of time. But what about physical theatre structures? Have Indian peoples always danced out of doors around a fire? One answer to that question lies in Northwest New Mexico and takes us back to approximately the time of Christ.

Interlude: A Visit to Aztec National Monument

Lloyd New wanted me to have the experience of knowing Chaco Canyon and Aztec National Monument firsthand. During the second summer we finally were able to clear schedules and make the trip to Northwest New Mexico.

Chaco Canyon has a mysterious presence that is as powerful as any other ancient site I know. The sheer size of the place and the massive, intricately beautiful stonework of Pueblo Bonito are awe-inspiring. But for a theatre person, it is the Great Kivas that rivet one's attention. These ceremonial/performance centers of the Anasazi, the ancient ones, are circular in shape and two-thirds buried beneath the earth. Their diameters can stretch as wide as sixty-five feet. To the east, is a fire pit and altar. Before the altar is an open space that could easily accommodate twenty or more performers. There is a seat-high bench completely round the wall of the Kiva, yet one can speculate that many of the audience would have sat on the floor. Citing contemporary Pueblo practice, one can guess that the bench probably would have been for performers, elders, and officials of the ceremony.

In some of the Kivas there is a narrow tunnel entrance coming up to the floor of the Kiva from below the altar. These peoples' desire to have regular subterranean entrances fires the imagination. Coupled with the ladder through the smoke hole of the Kiva's roof (down which would come all the adult male audience of the community as well as the performers); the verticality of these peoples' worldview is quite striking.

The Great Kiva at Aztec National Monument, about sixty miles north of Chaco, has been restored, including the massive roof needed to span such a huge chamber. Lloyd and I made a surprising discovery as the result of being in this roofed Great Kiva. I was drawn to a series of offstage little rooms that were at ground level all around the circumference of the Aztec Kiva, each about eight by eight feet. Each had a doorway and ladder built into the wall of the Kiva that would allow a person in the small room to enter into the great circle of the Kiva itself. Crouching in the "wings," so to speak, while Lloyd relaxed down below, I began intoning the mumbling practice-type of chant I had often heard Indian performers use as a rehearsal technique before making their entrance. As I entered the great space singing and speaking on the floor of the Kiva, Lloyd became quite excited. "That's amazing," he burst out. He ran over to me and pulling my arm said, "Here, let me do it for you. Sit! Listen!" He went through a truncated version of my preparation and entrance while I sat on the back bench. Depending on his position, Lloyd was demonstrating anywhere from thirty to sixty feet away, immediately I got it. No matter where he was, in the little room or down stage center, the sound of his speaking and chanting was as though he were sitting right beside me, speaking in a normal conversational tone. All sounds made in the building, offstage and on, were meant to be heard. Not only had these people developed a magnificent, subtle, and complete theatre structure, but like the Mormons in Salt Lake City, or the Greeks at Epidaurus, they had command of perfect acoustics!

III. Shakin' Things Up

In our second year, for the first time, we had a performance space; a remodeled chapel designed for the style of theatre we were ever more strongly envisioning. It featured natural materials, largely wood, with a thrust stage partially surrounded by a raised (raked) audience. It was a presentational stage. The only thing it lacked, in my mind, was a fire pit shared by actors and audience. Fire codes could not be negotiated in time for our completion date.

That fall, Rosalie Jones had joined our faculty as dance instructor. She immediately began working on a project that became important to us all, a modern realization of the Lakota Sun Dance. This work was a gorgeously symbolic and spare heightening of the Sun Dance Ceremony. The central pole around which the dancer makes his sacrifice became an Earth Mother spirit, danced by a woman in white buckskin. A long thong, held between dancer and spirit, created connection and tension between them. Rosalie kept much of the dance monotonous, avoiding the temptations of her modern dance training that could have led her to feature visual novelty. But at the same time, she used the expressiveness of modern dance to mark the stages of selfless sacrifice being made by the dancer/worshiper. This treatment, trusting monotony as an artistic tool that we could use to our advantage, was one of many gifts that Rosalie's artistic partnership brought to us.

During our third winter our program produced the first "Evening of Indian Theatre." It featured *Black Butterflies*, *Sly Old Bag* (another play I authored), and *Mowitch*. *Sly Old Bag* is a comedy telling of a silly old grandmother (played by a male actor), who tricks Coyote into believing her bag of bones actually contains meat.

Our student play, *Mowitch*, was an energetic piece depicting the cleansing of troubled spirits within an Indian Shaker church, and was by Monica Charles. It featured a large battle scene that was entirely danced. The warriors wore fringed capes inspired by Tlingit dancing blankets, whose foot-long fringes whipped through the air, sculpting movement as each parry and thrust leaped across the stage. The "Evening" ended with a Rosalie Jones-choreographed "Mystical Dance," which prominently used handheld screens with Northwestern box drum designs adapted by faculty member Neil Parsons. The dancers themselves wore headdresses also designed by Neil and inspired by Northwest Kwakiutl examples. This dance sought to deepen and stabilize the mystical high points of both *Black Butterflies* and *Mowitch*.

IV. Results of the Experiment: A New Feather Robe

1. Indian theatre in performance would present a series of short events. A single unified dramatic piece is not representative of Indian ceremonial performances now or in the past. These events might be connected thematically but would not complete each other as in

one story told from start to finish. The events would be grouped to total an even number, four or six being the most suggestive as they represent the four partial or six complete directions recognized by Native peoples. These events are offertory to the spirits with whom we share this world.

2. Our theatre would use masks to represent unusual or mystical characters; persons who have genuine spiritual power. The mask is one of the chief opportunities for literal and physical transformation in our theatre.

3. Every event in Indian theatre, whether called a "dance" or a "play," would be permeated with dance.

4. Our theatre would be overwhelmingly non-naturalistic and non-scenic. Principle scenic elements used are costumes and properties. Both should be elaborate and richly suggestive.

5. Whereas Bertolt Brecht's theatre seeks to inform and mobilize, George Bernard Shaw's theatre to get people to think, Noel Coward's to entertain, Anton Chekhov's to empathize, Indian theatre wishes to spiritually and emotionally transform its audience. This is achieved through mutual involvement in a ceremony.

6. The arc of a dramatic climax in our theatre is flatter and is of longer duration than in Western theatre. Whereas a climax in European theatre might be imaged as mountain climbing to a great height with a very quick trip back down (the so-called peak experience); Indian theatre's image would be that of a clear glass tumbler being filled with translucent but strongly colored liquid. When the glass is full it is held and contemplated. (Many persons have experienced such a response as a result of living through the all-day and all-night dance/dramas of, for example, the Shalako Ceremonies at Zuni pueblo, or the Deer Ceremony described earlier.)

7. Soul time or Heart time would be the operative measure in Indian theatre. Linear time especially, but indeed, all time is in flux and always susceptible to transformation.

8. Chanting and singing, especially by a chorus, is an undergirding practice of our theatre. As IAIA composer Louis Ballard and many others have shown time and again, the music and chanting of Indian performance is incredibly rich and pervasive.

9. The chief characteristics of Indian dance are:

- Repetition of movement, often to the point of monotony.

- Ritualistic character.

- The notion that the earth/ground the dancer dances upon is the origin of the power in the dancer. By setting his/her feet in rhythmic patterns upon the ground, dancers draw spiritual power from the earth, which they transform with their bodies.

- The importance of floor pattern. Chief patterns are the circle, the line, both horizontal and diagonal, and the square or rectangle (less common). Often the dance is oriented around something, for example, a fire or a design, laid or painted on the floor.

- Elegant simplicity. It stems from the artistic economy of means and not from "primitivism" or lack of development.

- An ingrained sense of the angular: the crouch, arms held at right angles to the body with elbows akimbo, the head held in opposition to the slant of the body. Against this sharpness are often set large sweeping circular movements. These are often accentuated by long fringe or other hanging pieces of costume or stick-like props, such as coup sticks, rattles, or staffs.

- The throb of the drum that has saturated every moment of Indian dance. All movement, no matter what else it may be, is in reaction to the pulsation of a drum, whether a drum is present or not. (Often a pow-wow dancer away from the arena will demonstrate moves he has seen by a mark-through demonstration that he accompanies by singing. His voice provides the drum's rhythmic pulse.)

- Addendum: Our last extensive experiment with the nature of dance in Indian theatre concerned the use of dance to forward dramatic action. The focus of our attention was upon the mystical elements of our plays. Rosalie and I felt that it should be possible for the climax of a play to be achieved through dance. Hints of what might be possible were to be found in the narrative dramas of Martha Graham, the courting dances of Kathakali, and the slow-motion mimes/dances of Noh theatre. Several healing dances of the Pacific Northwest or the struggle dances of Mud Heads and Shalako at Zuni, to name two, gave us encouragement from traditional sources.

Observation: Summer of 1968, on Tour in the Pacific Northwest

We had arrived at Port Angeles, Washington, the home of our chief playwright, Monica Charles. It was a night of great excitement. Our host theatre facility was lovely, the design of its proscenium quite soft, and the acoustics good. Our audience proved to be easily 50 percent Native and buzzing with anticipation. They all knew Monica and via "Indian telegraph" knew that their Klallam life was her subject.

Just before the evening began, Monica, already suffering many fears and doubts, drew in a sharp breath. Her eyes became huge. "It's my Uncle," she whispered. It was her uncle joining the audience and sitting dead center and about thirty feet back. He was the main character of our first play. As *Yanowis* began, the audience slowly came to acute attention. Many of them recognized Monica's uncle on stage. They knew the actual man was sitting in their midst. Our auditorium's atmosphere was now electric. Our actors, sensing something was up, met the challenge by giving a first-rate performance.

Having seen the work of one of their own, our audience left elated. What they had seen had the smack of truth and relevance; a new experience for them. Monica had called a spade a spade, but had done so with perceptiveness, balance, and understanding.

Backstage, real Uncle approached the actor who had portrayed him, who was still holding the mask he had worn as stage uncle. It had been carved by a Navajo student sculptor who had listened to

Monica's many stories of her beloved uncle but had never met him
or seen a photograph of him. Now Uncle asked if he could hold the
mask. He gazed at it at arm's length, gingerly tilting it one way and
then the other, his eyes blinking with the rhythm of a slowly beating
drum. "Eh, it looks like me," at last he breathed. Suddenly cast and
crew realized the truth of his statement. Then with a tragicomedy
frown, Uncle held the mask close to his face and lightly shaking
it as though it were a raggedy doll, chuckled. "You!" he said with
merry eyes, "you drink too much."

Interlude: An E-mail Thought from Monica Charles

> In real Indian life the Spiritual and mundane mix. . . . The
> Spirit world and our world coexist in the same time and
> space. I think that is what Indian theatre should show.
> We are Tribal people. That is unique in this country. We
> are a part of a whole. . . . Everything we do affects the
> whole. (E-mail to the author, November 8, 2008)

V. Getting Physical, Part I: Other Theatres

The Great Kivas were not the only examples of theatrical structures among Native Americans. The Zuni people build specifically
designed rooms onto their houses in which to house the annual
Shalako Ceremony. Iroquoian tribal groups developed large and
elaborate lodges in which winter ceremonies were held. Indians
of the Northwest also developed large cedar structures to house
events social and theatrical. Northwest culture was especially notable for the unending bounty of costumes, wigs, masks, properties,
magic tricks, and other regalia: inventive creative abandon with
which to dress up these performances. What do we learn from all
these physical examples? What do they have in common?

VI. Getting Physical, Part II:
More from "Indian Theatre, an Artistic Experiment"

10. The physical setting for our theatre features:

  • Placing the actors in space, partially or completely
    surrounded by the audience.

- Awareness that offstage space is often just as important as onstage space. Preparation and Arrival are quite important in Indian theatre. They are intrinsic to Ceremony.

- A space sized according to the amount of symbolism desired in the drama. The less symbolism, the more expanse is needed.

- A fire pit with live embers shared by actors and audience.

- Provisions for the audience that comfortably squeeze them into the performing space. They should be able to see not only the stage but most of the auditorium as well. Actors will be ranging throughout the entire area. Lighting for the auditorium seldom goes completely dark.

- Musicians, singers, drummers accommodated on stage with the actors/dancers.

Observation: Winter of 1967 in Hopi Lands

We had sat through forty-five minutes of actors and singers preparing for the main events of the evening. Outside it was crisp: six degrees of frost. Here, within, the fire pit coals glowed, slowly blinking cats' eyes, warming us until our bones sang. So much was going on. Costumes were being donned. Elders were coaching the young men who were this evening's performers. The beats of large and small drums were all around us, both without and within. Performers softly practiced their songs in guttural mutterings.

At a signal we were not able to distinguish, a back door opened and women and children quickly entered and took their places as audience. The children's black eyes sparkled reflecting the coals of the fire pit above their smiling ruby lips. Anticipation was a jug wine everyone shared. The very air was transforming. Reality had an unreassuring edge made bearable by the coziness of the fire. Gradually from far off we heard powerful male singing. It came closer, ever closer. Voices called to each other in high-pitched falsetto mountain-to-mountain tones. In a burst of drumming, masked performers tumbled down the ladder through the entrance in the roof that was

suspended over the fire pit. Drum and chorus music settled around
us like the folds of a point blanket. Behind the dancers came a line
of costumed performers. All depicted one kind or another of Florida
or Hawaii Anglo-Tourist. They sported loud shirts, shades, bikinis,
miniskirts, polka-dot shorts, beach towels, umbrellas; all danced
with spastic urgency. Some paraded and spouted silly lines. Others were grouped in twos or threes and produced short-scripted
skits to different parts of the room in rapid succession. But many
other scenes were mimed. All were terribly funny, but also, to this
Anglo-Indian, ruefully spiced.

It was then I realized one of the most basic tests for essential
American Indian theatre. The event before us was entirely peopled
by non-Indian characters. Instead of being about Indians, it was
solely about white tourists. Nevertheless, there could be absolutely
no question whose theatre we were witnessing. The spare setting,
the drumming, the chanting and singing, the dancing, its episodic
nature, and its wry point of view all proudly proclaimed this was
Indian theatre. Coyote dancing! Coyote transforming! Indian theatre,
making us weep with joy.

VII. From *Black Butterflies*: A Beginning

Grandmother: Lean forward, my son. (He does so, and Grand-
               mother places a bone whistle, which is on a leath-
               er thong, around his neck. Grandmother holds the
               whistle as she talks about it.) This once belonged
               to Chief Hahots Ilpilp. Use it only in time of peril. In
               such a time, blow it softly and your spirit power will
               come to you. This bone is from a blue heron killed
               by a mountain eagle. Treasure it in your medicine
               bundle.

Chorus: Dim eyes flashing,
               That hawk mind reached
               Far back through shadowy
               Mists of many departed
               Spirits: her heart throbbing
               To the rumble of an ancient
               Drum.

Grandmother: It was the custom of the Nimipu
               To meet once every year on the

Wieppi prairie. Every man who was
Able would come to the place and
Pitch camp. The smoke of a thousand
Camp fires would filter through the
Evergreens and cottonwoods into the
Face of almighty God, our Sun Father.
The aspen would quake with joy
At our return and it is said
Even Grandfather elk was drawn
To this place by the pleasant
Echoes of our laughter. The prairie
Thundered like a war drum as
Our braves raced their sweat-streaked
Appaloosas in gay abandon. Or perhaps
The air was charged with the silence
Of the hunt, as our men stealthily stalked
The silent deer, the disdainful mountain sheep,
With huge crowns of horns, or the
Shy, skittish Antelope. Little children
Romped and rolled through bushes and hid
Behind secret rocks. All sun long they played
As naked as the shallow streams into which
They tumbled. Giggling they rose from the water
Shimmering in rays of light and hungry
They squealed as they searched for huckleberries.
Women dug roots: wild carrot, cow parsnip,
Or the blue lake camas; or else wove
Tule and rushes into mats or baskets.
At night, wrapped in warm buffalo skin,
Our people thrilled to the rhythms of the stick game.
Behind us our shadows rollicked and spun
On a backdrop of white birches. This
Was the joyous time of the Nimipu;
And it was near the end of this period
That the spirit dance was held.
It is now that time! My son,
What would you do?

Auskewush: I would dance the song of my protector.

Grandmother: My son, what would you do?

Auskewush: I would dance the song of my protector.

Grandmother: My son, what would you do?

Auskewush: I would dance the song of my protector.

Grandmother: My son, what would you do?

Auskewush: I will dance the song of my protector.

Grandmother: It is good. He will dance.

Notes

1. During the 1960s, the continuation of genocide among Native Americans is an inconvenient truth that the dominant European culture of the United States would like to sweep under the nearest rug. 1) Political: the struggle over a reservoir on the Seneca Reservation in New York State; the appalling misuse of funds set aside for Native people by the federal government; treaty terms still being broken every day between the tribes and the federal government every day. 2) Medical: the ghastly condition of the Indian Health Service; inferiorly trained doctors, inferior service and in many situations extremely poor, or no recognition of the need for superior alcohol abuse treatment systems. Tuberculosis is raging anew among many Native populations. 3) Societal: the lack of crime enforcement on reservations because of unclear jurisdiction that has lasted for years. Lack of a professional class among Native Americans and very few opportunities for there ever to be one because of poor education from grade 1 on to poor access to colleges. Many reservations were third-world countries within the United States. The life expectancy of Native peoples was and is today a fraction of that of the dominant culture with early deaths and suicides being triple that of the rest of the country. It was announced on *Native American News* (PBS) in September 2009 that the Navajo Reservation had just finally obtained running water for a large portion of their people! These examples, while not "genocide" in the sense of Darfur or Rwanda, are, especially taken as a whole, affective genocide.

2. Washington Matthews, *Navaho Legends* (Salt Lake City: University of Utah Press, 2002, rpt. [orig. 1897]). Since the 1960s, a complete version of this great work has been translated by Paul G. Zolbrod, University of New Mexico Press, 1984.

3. A full version of New's statement along with an older and incomplete version of the artistic principles of the theatre program at the institute later appeared in Hanay Geiogamah and Jaye T. Darby, eds., *American Indian Theater in Performance: A Reader* (Los Angeles: UCLA American Indian Studies Center), 3–4.

4. "Traveling around" is a phrase used to indicate Coyote on the prowl. Other titles in this essay also reflect the Coyote tradition and stories.

5. The discipline of Native American studies in the arts and humanities during the early 1960s was unknown. All that was available were ethnological studies that investigated Indians as scientific objects for study. No one I know of other than Lloyd New had entertained the idea that Indian performance might be considered worth study for any other reason than scientific. There were a few pioneers crying out in the wilderness, Vera Lasky, Oliver LaFarge, Frank Waters, Edward S. Curtis through his photographs, and a few others; but they struggled with what they perceived as the sacred nature of their discoveries on one side and their feelings that their discovered material had the look and shape of a great drama. Quite a few Indian people themselves were frequently too close to their ceremonials and the profound meaning they have/had for them. They could not conceive of the idea that there might be an evolution toward "theatre." Almost none were trained theatre people and had no idea what to do with what they had learned or knew except to present it as accurately and sensitively as possible in the context of ceremony. In other words, the basis of today's view of "Native theatre" had not been thought of yet. One exception was Arthur S. Junaluska, a professional actor who had appeared with Katherine Cornell on Broadway and dreamed and worked toward a professional Indian Theatre. He was certainly one of the first persons, if not the first, to grapple with the concept of "Indian Theatre." But his vision, as he communicated it to me, had no great interest in Native traditions equaling theatre; in the late fifties and early sixties he sought a theatre "about" Indians largely no different than the professional practice of his day, much like the current Negro Ensemble in New York City (author interview with Junaluska in winter of 1965, IAIA, Santa Fe, NM; see also Däwes 2007a, 23).

5

From SALVAGE to Selvage

The Restoration of What Is Left

Diane Glancy

Salvage, fr., to save as in the rescue of a ship at sea, or the utilization of any sort of damaged or waste material.

Selvage is a specially woven edge which prevents cloth from raveling.

I

Salvage/selvage is a technique I use for the understanding of Native dramatic writing. It uses the wreckage and loss of the past, and weaves it with a selvage, which is the act of preservation by its presentation on stage. Native writing is a combination of retrieval, restoration, and preservation of the culture in all its layers, from the stereotypical Plains Indian imagery, to the tribal-centered movement, back to a pan-Indian *generalness* of what *Indianness* is about, and how it can be presented on stage, a vehicle that it does not fit because Native writing is round, or circular, and a stage is usually rectangular. Native theatre is nonlinear. All events do not lead to a final dramatic end. Native theatre takes migration and places it on a stage, which it works against.

A lot of my work comes from traveling on the prairie. The open plains of America are a stage for storms—ice storms in winter, called white-outs, and wind or rain storms in spring. Sometimes, in passing through terrible wind and rain on the prairie, I find ideas or feelings to write about. It was where I found *Salvage*, the third play on which I am now working with Native Voices at the Autry.

I was driving on Highway 2 in Montana, researching the voice of Sacajawea who traveled with the Lewis and Clark Expedition, 1804–1806. The research became *Stone Heart*, the second play of mine that Native Voices produced. Somehow I remember the edge of the highway, a dirt lot, and a corrugated fence. I think the play entered my car at that time, and I didn't even know it yet. I remember taking note of the white crosses along the highway from traffic deaths. I remember the wide curve of the highway into Browning, Montana. I remember the land felt elevated. It felt like it was right up under the sky. Somehow I had found another voice.

As I said, I was researching one play when another one came. I must have picked it up hitchhiking there on the road. You don't have to stop for a story to get in the car. It can even ride with you for years before you know it is there.

II

In November, 2007, I left for Los Angeles from Kansas City, Missouri; a trip of 1,600 miles in a time of wildfires in California fueled by high winds and drought, to continue work on the development of *Salvage*, a play I had worked on in an earlier developmental workshop. Writing a play is a solitary act in its preliminary stage. Then comes the director, the actors, and the dramaturge, who read it. Then there is the rewriting stage when I see how far I still have to go. It usually takes about three years to finish a play.

The basic plot of *Salvage* is upheaval: A Blackfeet man in Montana has a car accident. The man he hits stalks him, and events escalate that unravel their lives. It is about the sudden and irrevocable change in a way of life that encapsulates the history of Native life. The collision is a reminder of the first contact with the cavalry. Then the railroad. The slaughter of the buffalo, wagon trains, settlers, boarding school.

After the first idea of the play came, I had to write the play containing the conflict and resolution that the dramatic form demands. During that process, the play lost some of its early magic. Later, I worked back toward that first unraveling when there was no border between past and present, physical and abstract, seen and unseen, making it seem as though darkness was as important as light.

The staged play will mix old Blackfeet photos with a contemporary, animated, Indian action figure video by Ian Skorodin. Who knows as yet what will work. Writing a Native play is like stepping onto the prairie in the midst of flying arrows. Who knows where they are aimed. It is now June, 2008, and I am returning to Los Angeles for more work on the play.

I remember during the last workshopping process, waking in the night with a dream toward the end of the week. Maybe it was more of a question, or questions. What was this play about? Whose play was this? I decided it was Mrs. Stover's play. It was her voice seeking an answer. She is the woman whose car the main character hit, injuring her family and eventually killing her. She was seeking forgiveness in the afterworld. Her conclusion: Forgiveness can come through the understanding of the one who harmed you. The play was about understanding the family that hurt her family. It was about putting rest to some of the wars in Indian community.

III

I got involved in Native theatre long ago through an American Indian Theater Company in Tulsa, Oklahoma, and the Five Civilized Tribes Playwriting Competitions. Then Native Voices came along, and I found the venue for development I needed. I was teaching and writing in other genres. But a play has a way of making itself known.

I began my writing career with poetry, then drama. The plays became the silenced voices, or those voices that did not have a chance to speak, that I heard.

I think what is important to me about my work is working to tell the story.

When the audience leaves the show, the first thought I always want when I leave a play: "That was a good play!" Meaning it was a cohesive unit. "All parts drove the play toward its conclusion. I enjoyed it on the level of its accomplished presence on stage. It made me enter it and forget where I was. It was a pleasure to watch, even when it was about the discomfort of the characters." I want the audience feeling sympathy for the characters, maybe understanding the family, even though they are from a different culture. I want the audience to be moved, to be excited about the thoughts and the dramatic events presented. I want to give acknowledgment to the spirits along the road, and acknowledgment to the land.

IV

Over the years, I have returned to many of the same issues: loss, acculturation, how to live in this world while remembering the old.

But I hope the issues change, deepen, see with a wider scope to
the under-issues, the complications of Native life.

I hope my audiences are Native people and also those of European descent. I am interested in the left-out voices of history. I hope
my work is for those who want the full history of our country and
our world. At one time, I traveled for the United States Information
Service before it was put out of commission. I had lovely trips to
Germany, Italy, Syria, Jordan. I had audiences there when I read.

V

In an article for the *Baylor Journal of Theatre and Performance*, I
wrote:

> In the beginning of the writing process, I always struggle
> with the shadow of oral tradition, which is one person
> talking while others listen, then later, others can talk,
> can tell the story, building on it with their own voice.
> I often begin writing in separate monologues. I like the
> isolation of characters. The isolation of the Native and
> white worlds that are not able to communicate. I like the
> intra-tribal conflicts such as the magic of the conjuring
> world and its tension with Christianity. I like non-chron-
> ological order. The aesthetic that defies logic. But in the
> end, in the tradition of Western theatre built on reason
> and progression, the characters must interact with dia-
> logue. The play must communicate with the audience in
> a way that the audience understands. It must tell a story.
> I think communicating the Native world to a non-Native
> audience is vital. Education also is a part of theatre along
> with entertainment and the tightly-knit construct of art
> in the conflict / resolution / epiphany / character change
> / and all the other interwoven elements of theatre such
> as style and voice and the arc of the dramatic structure.
> (Glancy 2007, 95)

In Western theatre, storytelling is a group project. Yet when I am
in the first stages of telling a story with one person talking, my
voice is not alone. There are other voices, old voices, riding upon
the voice of my voice and then the voices of the characters in the
play. Even though the play is original, and something outside the

actual history of what was there, that I was not there to know, the history of Native life is there, even if a facsimile, which is running far ahead and I am unable to catch it.

VI

I have been listening to a tape of Bill Bryson's *A Short History of Nearly Everything*: "We live in a universe whose age we can't quite compute, surrounded by stars whose distances we don't altogether know, filled with matter we can't identify, operating in conformance with physical laws we don't truly understand."

How much like that is starting into a play.

I borrow another term from physics: recessional velocity, which is the outward movement of the universe, the acceleration of it, especially the outermost edges. I feel the edges of the Native past moving quickly away. I want to capture it on stage before it is gone. This for me is the exploration of the structure or construct of Native theatre. It is like an atom, an empty space that the stage is, with the dense nucleus of a drama at the core.

Though I am drawn to discussing the logical and reasonable way through a play, I want to return to theory. The turned-upside-down disconnect that Native playwriting is because it connects two worlds that do not connect. It shows a world written in a language that does not belong to that world, yet must convey it anyway. There are immense difficulties and pitfalls that are not easy to work around, for me anyway. I want to write a play for the Western theatre because that's where the world is, yet I want it to be an agency for the Native universe, the mixed-blood universe I know, caught between past-and-present, tradition and assimilation, preservation of a way-of-life that has all but vanished while forging a contemporary worldview in the process of being created.

It seems to me there are two main issues in the translation of Native American work: external and internal. The external translation is the translation of one culture into the understanding of another. How do I communicate the Native world to the non-Native, while maintaining a Native aesthetic and perspective? How do I translate the Native experience without losing the spirit of the Native experience in the translation? I want Native work to be Native. It is a world that is often circular, nonlinear, not necessarily chronological. There is not always one central narrator. It is not always plot-driven. There is not always a recognizable conflict,

resolution, and epiphany, so central to Western literature. The outcome often is not as important as the process of the journey. All
this is antithetical to Western thought and expectation. So how do I
let "the other" know the Native mindset, when there is no stage or
garage or receiving dock in the Western mind on which that mindset
can be communicated, accepted, and understood?

The internal translation is one within the Native aesthetic. How
do I translate oral tradition into a written text? The voice or spoken
word is a living energy. A force field. A creator. It has spirit, mind,
and heart. When a story is written, it suddenly is trapped by written letters on a static page. The voice is killed, or at least caged. I
always begin a rough draft from the stance of oral tradition—one
person telling a story—other voices and other stories riding on that
voice. There is so much "gathering" in the process of telling a story,
meaning, so much goes on that we do not at first recognize. The
whole history and past of a tribe is there in oral tradition. There is
a slow evolving or unfolding of the story into the one who hears.
The hearer hearing the words of a story knows it becomes a living
text within their spirit. Then when various circumstances arise, that
living story is translated for that particular circumstance. It is as if
the story transmutes to meet whatever the person is facing: This is
what you do in a time of hunger. This is how you call buffalo to your
arrow. This is what the snow means. This is what the wind says.
This is what to do when you are lost. This is how you wait on the
Maker. This is where you find blueberries. This is what happened
in the past. This is our history. This is the fabric of our survival.

Thus, the external and internal, or outward and inward aspects
of cultural translation.

VII

In my collection of plays, *American Gypsy*, I have an afterword called
"Further (Farther)," about creating dialogue to talk about Native
American plays. "There has been conversation toward making a
literary theory for Native American plays in which often the unseen
world intrudes as though it were seen. The parts not connecting
until the play as a whole is seen and sometimes it (the meaning)
still trails" (Glancy 2002, 200).

The afterword is an experimental essay written in three scenes
with a denouement. "A Native play is often orbiculate. . . . realized improbabilities probably describes the network of possi-

bilities for the unlikely elements of the topography of the Native stage. The improbable happenings . . . , the acceptable improbabilities . . . , cold and heat, thunderstorm . . . , humor and bleakness . . . , all the other upheavals of Native theatre" (2002, 204). As I was writing, I misspelled the storm as thundrestorm, which I suppose is what a staged storm would be. Native drama tries to catch the play on words, the misrepresentations, the humor, the happenstance of Native life. The trick is getting the Trickster language of oral tradition into written form. Though I rely on *play* in my work, it often runs on the serious side: Sacajawea's long trail with the 1804–1806 Lewis & Clark Corps of Discovery in *Stone Heart: Everybody Loves a Journey West*, the 1838–1839 Cherokee Trail of Tears in *Pushing the Bear*, the seventeenth-century smallpox epidemic among the Mohawk in *The Reason for Crows*, and the swift and irrevocable loss of a way of life in the contemporary *Salvage*.

The difficulty in Native theatre, for me, is bridging the disparate parts—or joining the dislocations—in other words, structuring the dis-structure of the Native mindset or aesthetic in an act of restoration and preservation while circling the expectations of dramatic structure—these things that do not mix.

I want to weave a selvage with performance. It is an abstraction that can't be held like a book.

6

"Shakes Spear" Isn't an Indian Name?

Daniel David Moses

"Who do you think you are? That's the question. And how dare you invoke The Playwright's name for a joke?"

I

I'm a playwright, too, I think, one of those who's inherited or, to tell more truth, been saddled, through the histories and decisions of my families, with English and some of its traditions, one who's therefore decided to accept the load (one Iroquois word that's translated into English simply as "warrior" evokes in the mind of those in the know an image of "a man who's chosen to carry the burden of peace on his back"). With such an inheritance, I feel obliged to, now and then, give His Name the nod.

And if I'm right in my cogitating and, ergo, am such a playwright, it would have been more daring had I not invoked the Man and had attempted instead to break, like a conventional adolescent of our Western culture, with tradition, such "breaking with tradition" itself traditional. But I'm too old for that, old enough to have experienced, more often than not, an enduring admiration for The Playwright's works. No, I'm not one who needs or wants, like my friend Louise H. wanted in the fall of 2007, to declare "Shakespeare's dead!" (But consider also that, unlike monolingual me, she has the twinned burdens of English and Cree . . .)

I do agree with her impulse, though, and admit that we do need to get on with our own writerly work in this sixth century after Columbus in the country of Canada in the land on Turtle Island without any further colonizing encumbrance as The Playwright often

seemed when we first were—and probably still are—taught about
him and his works in our educations. I even once found myself the
"Who let him in here?" guest at a conference of secondary school
educators, close on the occasion of the first edition of Terry Goldie's
and my *An Anthology of Canadian Native Literature in English*, 1992.
I was the one on the panel who mused that perhaps we, in our
democracy, might be better off *not* teaching impressionable and
inexperienced teenagers those plays of The Man that focused on
the English tradition of Monarchy. My suggestion was not, after
some fluster, welcomed or taken with any seriousness—I guess it
was amusing. But I've not been invited to such a conference since.

I'd add to my suggestion, now that I've had a few years of
learning about teaching at a university, that young folk seem to see
in those works mostly a weird nostalgia for the increasingly foreign
other's (their parents') Old and/or Mother Country and are mostly too young to perceive in, say, the Princes Hal or Hamlet, their
selves' surrogates. (Romeo and Juliet, understandably, do speak
to their hormonal experience.) Perhaps that's another face of the
disconnect, the irrelevance, so many of them feel for such works.

II

Let me glance at the latter question first.

Humor is surely not out of line as one of many ways of
approach to The Playwright. He was a bloke who didn't hesitate
to wright a pun, that lowest humor form, The Playwright was. Hey,
He dared name a character Bottom, didn't He, a gesture at once
simple, poetic, and scatological? Surely He or His Reputation can
take whatever some lowercase playwright might throw at or around
Him or It when dealing with plays and the playful?

Let's gaze in the first question's direction next.

This question I realize is the one dear storyteller Alice Munro
named a book with, a Canadian title changed for the American edition to *The Beggar Maid*, which transformation suggests it's a typically Canadian question or, to be more exact, a typically English
Canadian, lower- to middle-class, Protestant one. One might narrow
the focus down to even southern Ontario, upper Canadian stock,
early twentieth century, but this one hasn't usually, because it might
not be in good taste to be that regional and historical when we've
only just got through (it still seems to the sixty-one-year-old I am in

the summer of 2012) a late twentieth-century era when the Canadian urge was most national. One's probably treading on the *outré* by even mentioning "class" . . . But all of that gazing could be a good beginning of telling who I think I am, except that the "who I am" grew up also knowing I was "an Indian."

I didn't know, in any clear way, what "Indian" might mean until I got out and about a bit in the world, my folks, bless them, so provided me with shelter. Though the Six Nations Reserve was a creation of some of the political and societal myths promulgated around the word "Indian," it's also the place I simply call home and with its mix of underdeveloped woodlots and farmland, with my family's struggling farm along its northern border caressed by the leisurely flow of the Grand River, the place seemed and seems more, to the earnest little Anglican who still dwells somewhere off inside me, a bit of Eden.

What I didn't know then and there, for instance, is that that word "Indian," a perpetrated misnomer when the country India weighs on the world's other side, had been declared legally, under the Dominion of Canada—we still called it a "dominion" when I was a kid—a blanket identity for all of us descendants of the original folk of the place. A legalized, rich, and strange confusing blanket.

My growing Canadian Indian experience out in the world, and the knowledge of its mythologies shared by my fellow Indians, around, for instance, small pox, made me and us suspicious of such blanket efficiencies. The warning out of the English vernacular is "Don't look a gift horse in the mouth!" But I looked, especially since I didn't see then why we couldn't have just been called by the names we were first given by our families or familiars, Haudenosaunee, Lenape, Anishinaabe, for three of countless instances. Haven't governments managed to find uses for words like Toronto, Canada, canoe . . . ?

But this is late in the game for us Indians to begin understanding the shiftingness of the rules and the progress of the competition when we all, not just us Indians, are constantly being given the news of the end of the game and the world, certainly as we know it. This is likely why so many of us Indians, instead, pay renewed attention to Trickster stories. But it seems that we do still have the human impulse to try, which may be why, in part, we came up with our own contribution to the naming game, adding to the roseate varieties growing up between language and culture, history and intention, the local Canadian blooming moniker "First Nations."

How do you like them apples?

III

In the fall of 2007, I now see, I was hesitating on the path. Near, probably past, the midpoint of my journey through the shadowed and bright wilds of my life and art, I stood, swayed, and looked back. I now see I must have arrived, unawares, at a point where the long familiar gaps in my education, experience, and understanding suddenly loomed too wide, strangely, to continue leaping in unexamined faith or passion. I looked back, trying to imagine or remember the path I knew or thought I knew before I discovered or was told the world it cut through was considered "New" and that I was an Indian. "O brave new world" . . .

Or is that fiction, sophistry, camouflage?

Because, as I am putting these words to paper, I'm hesitating over something I've only tried to talk about until now in a single isolated venue at an event where I was sure of compassionate if not comprehending attention. (Yes, yes, the same time and place dear Louise declared Shakespeare mortal.)

And some part of me fears a larger repetition of the confusions around that early "You aren't Indian enough!" incident, even though the two of us involved now know more about who put such measurement rulings into play. I may be misremembering this, but didn't we agree to remember that an Iroquois, say, doesn't need to be the same as a Cree or Ojibwa?

I admit now those gaps in my knowledge generated that autumn one apparently Un-Indian set of activities. I admit now I spent all the spare time I had in an already too busy teaching season—I had no time for my own writing projects—rereading three of Shakespeare's plays (*King Lear* for the first time since high school!) as well as reading a couple of books on the Bard and his works, one called *The Sacred Art of Shakespeare: To Take Upon Us the Mystery of Things*, by Martin Lings (with a foreword by Charles, H. R. H. The Prince of Wales), and the other simply called *On Shakespeare*, by Northrop Frye.

The Department of Drama at Queen's University in Kingston, Ontario, Canada, where I find myself a professor of playwrighting, was then producing a revision of *Lear*, one that had several of the male characters, including the King himself, turned into women (this is what you do when you have a preponderance of young women enrolled and still want to nod to The Man), so perhaps I could blame my attention's perverse and persistent non–First Nations focus on that atmosphere.

And of course the late Professor Frye's work as a thinker here in Canada—he was one repeatedly proclaimed "our own" during those years of worry about the Canadian identity—is deemed so essential that my not having read any but a few scattered and, I admit, unremembered essays until now can likely be blamed on my prejudiced perception (someone will please correct me if I'm wrong since I doubt I'll get around to further research) that the drama of Canada that Professor Frye's work contributed to only (more of the same old official story) contained Indian folk like and unlike myself as, say, the embodiment of the landscape or the Other, and not as human persons.

It wouldn't surprise me. It is hard to escape the zeitgeist of your age and dominions and we Indians have only had the vote since 1960. The ideas come at you from all directions. Despite my apparent status as a playwright and a citizen, a contributing member of society, I was still cut when, for instance, an American border officer as I crossed through New York, heading home, doubted, when I couldn't answer a question about the hockey play-offs, that I was Canadian. I had been away for a couple weeks. Did Professor Frye have to answer such questions?

All of which I now realize may be more fiction, sophistry, camouflage, because the simple memory appears to me of these Bardish books presenting themselves side by each on a table in a bookstore in my Toronto neighborhood on a sunny afternoon at the end of August 2007, long before I'd even returned to Kingston and the university.

IV

All of which puts me at last up onto a stage at Brandon University, Brandon, Manitoba, Canada, one afternoon late in October, 2007, where and when I'm chairing a panel on Writing and Life (Men) as part of the Brandon Aboriginal Literary Festival.

We guys are following a panel from the morning session where the Writing and Life (Women) had their turn and proclaimed, it seemed to me, once again, in their various ways, the tradition of, even in the twenty-first century, the women being the keepers of our various wounded but healing cultures. I'm thinking we men need to try to explain our writing and lives as somehow in contrast or complement to that role.

So I start out by talking, with more energy than clarity (I've since listened to the tapes of the session), about the writing of my

second play and the writer's crisis I came to and through because
of it, because it was a crisis with an idea of women's identity at
its center.

I had been asked by the artistic director of a small theatre
company that produced dance-influenced storytelling plays for
young audiences to create a play from my cultural background,
one that was "universal," and she had given me the example of the
story of the Sleeping Beauty as one such story she had staged in
the past. Coming from my Iroquoian community, with its so-called
matriarchal traditions, I had immediate doubts that a story like that,
where the heroine literally goes to sleep in the middle of the action
and has to be rescued, was universal, mostly because I couldn't
picture any woman in my family behaving that way.

(I also had doubts about such a story as a play because the
action of waiting for rescue isn't at all dramatically or theatrically
interesting, pace *Waiting for Godot*.)

I decided to test out *The Sleeping Beauty* example to see if
there might be something in it that really had some broader meaning. I dropped images from our Iroquoian traditional culture into it,
replacing, for instance, the king and castle with extended matrilineal
family and village; the fairy godmothers with the spirits of corn,
beans, and squash; and the hundred years of Beauty's sleep with
a five-hundred-year-long dream of winter.

I also decided the Beauty in my version of the story had to be
an active participant if she was to be a credible Iroquoian human
person (and dramatic character) and not, say, just the prince's prize
at the happily-ever-after end. She had to be the heroine of her own
story. The action of the play was the action of a dream, a nightmare
Beauty had to find a way to awaken from.

I gradually realized that this second play I'd ever written pro-
fessionally, this play the artistic director had now promised to get
me a grant to wright, had become, in the Iroquoian context, a story
that was about a young woman's coming of age as well as an oblique
meditation on the colonization of North America. I was pleased to
have accomplished the latter narrative but suddenly unsure about
the former.

It was the late 1980s and I think I had only recently paid attention to ideas from white, capital "F" Feminists about the problems
of men telling women's stories. Or maybe it was the news media's
Harpy personifications that made the impression on me? However,
having seen how white writers could and did persistently misunder-
stand, misinterpret, or simply bowdlerize Indian stories, I suddenly

felt unsure and my writing stopped. "This is a woman's story and I'm, for most intents and purposes, a man. Should I be doing this?" But when I mentioned my iffy feelings to one of my women friends from home (Hi, Cat, long time, no see!), she just shrugged her shoulders and said, "You grew up there. You know what's going on."

I felt like I'd been given permission to explore, and the project came clear in my mind once more and became the play *The Dreaming Beauty*.

I look back on it now, I want to say, as an example of the idea that if our women are going to be the ones who are the guardians of our cultures—tending the longhouse and the fields, in Iroquoian imagery—then I, as a man, have to be doing the hunter-gatherer thing, going out into the cultural wilds and finding stuff that is valuable for us that I can bring back to the village. (The "warrior" is probably also part of that male image complex historically, but a lot of our women have taken that on too as part of being "guardians.")

So I next find myself, on that stage in Brandon, as an example of such hunting and picking behavior and despite Louise's remark about The Playwright, perhaps even inspired in part by that remark made during the women's panel, confessing all the time I've spent reading *The Sacred Art of Shakespeare*.

What's an Indian doing, doing that? What's a more or less secular person doing, doing that?

Well, I did find myself first entertained by the way Professor Lings insists on calling contemporary folk, by which he seems to mean every Western human since the Renaissance, by the name of "progressivist"—it does sound vaguely like something dirty.

But then I'm also intrigued by the idea he insists on, a contradiction to the image of Shakespeare I imbibed early on, of The Man as one of the first Renaissance Men, a guy at the beginning of the great awakening of the humanist modern world who created new ways of thinking about theatre, all of it proclaiming him as very much "our own."

Professor Lings says that Shakespeare is actually a Medieval Man: ". . . Shakespeare seems in a sense to go back as time goes forward and by the turn of the century he had become, unlike many of his fellow dramatists, the continuer and the summer-up of the past, the last outpost of a quickly vanishing age" (Lings 1998, 9). A kind of guardian of the culture, perhaps?

So what's so good about that vanishing medieval outlook that we're still reading Shakespeare and still see other works it produced, cathedrals, and paintings as more than worth our whiles?

(I'm remembering my surprise at being moved, not bored, by a nunnery full of such paintings, Crucifixions, Nativities, Madonnas, in Prague.)

When Professor Lings quotes Professor Schuon, I recognize something. "When standing in front of a Romanesque Gothic cathedral, we feel like we are at the center of the world; when standing in front of a Renaissance, Baroque, or Rococo church we are merely conscious of being in Europe" (qtd. in Lings 1998, 3).

I remember also feeling like I was at the center of the world when I was witnessing a Sun Dance out in the country near Saskatoon in 1992.

The trouble with humanism, according to Professor Lings, is that it "considers man and other earthly objects entirely for their own sakes as if nothing lay behind them" (1998, 3).

And though I have to hesitate when he characterizes (hey, what can you do, it's his zeitgeist) what's there behind the earthly as the Christian's God, I don't question the impulse he describes toward transcendence.

Our cultures have their own dream quests and shamanic journeys. So maybe the Man, Shakes Spear, living and creating prodigiously in the midst of the Elizabethan police state, has something to teach us Indians too?

So that is why, I realized, back in the fall of 2007, that I had to try to take his example home.

7

Theatre

Younger Brother of Tradition

Floyd Favel

J'ensevelis les morts dans mon venture.
Cris, tambour, danse, danse, danse,
Danse! Je ne vois même pas l'heure
Ou, le blancs debarquant, je tomberai
Au neant

[I bury the dead in my belly.
Shouts, drums, dance, dance, dance,
Dance! I cannot even see the time
When, white men landing, I shall fall into
Nothingness]

—Arthur Rimbaud, "Mauvais sang," section 5

I

The presentation of Native performance has a long history in North America. Mainly these presentations, primarily traditional song and dance, are the result of the subjugation of the Native peoples by the settler society and these performances remained one of the few places that Native people could openly practice their culture to an appreciative audience. For decades government policies outlawed the practice of spiritual dances and songs of the Native peoples, in part due to misunderstanding and also deliberately, as government people observed that these dances were the expression of a unique worldview. The government rightly deduced that without their worldview, Natives ceased to be Natives. Native peoples had fought hard for their independence and their lands, many tribal leaders like Geronimo of the Apaches and Chief Joseph of the Nez Perce remained prisoners of war far from their homelands until the day they passed on into the spirit world. Government policy and intent was for the total assimilation of the Native people into the values of modern society and in order for this to succeed, their culture and independence had to be eradicated.

In the former Soviet Union, Native peoples' dances were outlawed and their spiritual and cultural leaders were jailed or killed. One of the few places that Native peoples in the former Soviet Union could express their culture was through folkloristic performances. That is, dances and songs performed out of their ritual and social context on the contemporary performance stage. The tradition of folkloristic performance became the vehicle where Native peoples could practice their culture, so much so, that according to Marina Idham, Tuuvan actress from Buryatia, Russia,

> [t]he tendency of the theatre is to keep and extol traditions as much as possible, so that not to let people to be separate from the roots. Nowadays we can see our generation having this tendency of separation from the roots. The theatre is attracting everything back to the roots; and not only the theatre; the whole culture does that. All our activities further the preservation of our culture and traditions. (Interview with the author in Moscow, 2003)

Shortly after the destruction of the Plains Indian cultures in the late 1800s, impresario Buffalo Bill Cody hired former warriors to perform in his Wild West Shows. These shows toured the world and brought romantic notions of Native peoples, notions that still exist today in Europe and beyond. Most importantly, these shows allowed Native peoples to express their dances in freedom, as back at home, their people were being killed and massacred simply for dancing, as in the Ghost Dance, which led directly to the Wounded Knee Massacre of 1890 in South Dakota.

The contemporary stage was one of the few places that Native peoples could once again live in freedom and this led to a tradition of performing among many Native peoples, and the stage became the vehicle and the refuge where ancient songs and dances could be kept alive and shared with the world. It enabled the performers to send monies home to their starving relatives. In the Battleford region of Saskatchewan, the Plains Cree and Assiniboine peoples, in the 1880s, a time of starvation, began to dance for the public in exchange for food, "Begging Dances," they were called, but nowadays we could also call it "busking." Famed medicine man Black Elk, a Lakota, performed for many years, sharing staged rituals and dances for appreciative tourists in the Black Hills. Black Elk in his youth had been a warrior and a visionary medicine man, made famous by the book *Black Elk Speaks*, written by John Neihardt. Black Elk also performed in the Wild West Shows and spent one year in France, where it is rumored he had dinner and shared insights and knowledge of Native worldview with scientist Albert Einstein.

In modern times, one of the dancers who brought native dances to a professional level was Boye Ladd, a Ho-Chunk/Winnebago Indian from Wisconsin. Boye has been an entertainer, war veteran, cultural leader, and champion pow wow dancer. Over the years Boye has staged shows at Foxwoods Casino and other major American Indian casinos, and on the PBS network where he staged a concert by composer Robert Mirabel. Although innovative with regard to presenting traditional Native dance, his work remains in the domain of traditional dance taken out of its tribal ritual and social context, and placed directly on the performance stage with the addition of modern music, lights, and smoke machines. To be truly innovative, this style of performing needs to take one more step to break it out of its traditional form and also to extend the dance to a new frontier. There needs to be a strong measure of theatrical process applied to the dance.

II

One of the dancers who has taken traditional Native dance to another level is Anishinaabe dancer Buffy Handel. She is also a protégé of Boye Ladd and, like a true student, she has taken the teachings of her teacher to another level. Based in Winnipeg, Manitoba, she has succeeded in extending native dance beyond its perimeters, the Hoop Dance in particular. The Hoop Dance is an ancient medicine dance where the dancer dances with a series of hoops and makes intricate designs all the while dancing. In this regard her process is similar to the process used by Cirque du Soleil, who took the traditional circus to another level by applying in great measure a theatrical process (story, music, and lights). Buffy has extended Hoop dancing by integrating acrobatics, showmanship, and the Brazilian martial art capoeira. Despite the innovations in her dance, the dance retains its spiritual roots as Buffy states that "there is a spiritual dimension to all of my performances" (interview with the author, June 2009). The spiritual dimension is always present in Native performances. What is most interesting is that Buffy has elaborated her unique artistic vision and practice in isolation from Native artistic dance trends in Canada, and Buffy does not apply for arts grants. This independence has led her be one of the most interesting and unique Native dance artists in Canada today.

The game of lacrosse, invented by aboriginal people, was called "the younger brother of war." This game taught the players all of the skills the players would need as warriors on the field of battle. Similarly, I believe that for many aboriginal artists theatre can be called the younger brother of our tradition.

Gaetan Gingrass, an aboriginal contemporary dancer, once asked me whether aboriginal performance was a technique, a style, an ethnic category, or was it a separate art form? In order to answer this question we have to look at structural foundations that support the voice and the written drama of aboriginal performances. It is similar to peering through a murky glass as we are naturally faced with the confusion of different continents, histories, and world-views. Our only reference point is the reality and the context of this land to which we are indigenous.

What is theatre then? There are so many ways of practicing theatre, and many ways of defining it. Theatre within the context of aboriginal people simply cannot avoid contact with tradition. In this essay I will work with narrow definitions of theatre and tradition in order to avoid lengthy interpretations of their meanings.

Theatre can be defined as a set of performative skills of the body, voice, and narrative structures presented in an idealized space for the public at large. Meanwhile, ceremony within tradition can be understood as ways of "doing" through song, dance, and narrative structures taking place within a sacred ritual space, as presented within the context of an aboriginal nation's social and ritual activity. If we accept both definitions, it is quite clear upon observation of theatrical and traditional activities that they share a heightened use of the body, voice, and narrative structures to achieve their apotheosis within a special sacred "space," that is, an idealized space separate from daily life.

When I visited Japan, I stayed once at a house where I would often sit outside in the afternoon. Soon I figured that in the next house, separated by a high fence from the one where I stayed, lived a Noh master. Noh theatre is a stylized indigenous theatre form of Japan. This unseen master would practice every afternoon and therefore I could hear from behind the fence his otherworldly voice, an eerie sound that made me think of the voice of our ancestors reaching across time and space in order to call us, deafened by the daily routine of traffic and urban congestion. The voice of the master reminded me that theatre must be separate from daily life.

Both theatre and tradition inexplicably connect us to our "higher self" in the very moment of action. It is this connection with this "higher self" that makes them brothers. Theatre comes from across the big water. It is new to our turtle island. Yet it does retain some traces of its origin in ancient Elysian mysteries. We welcomed this art form to our land as a younger brother of tradition. In the same manner our people taught the newcomers how to live on this land when they first came here. It is this connection that takes place at a metaphysical level that binds them to each other, as soul brothers.

What differentiates these two brothers is that their context and purpose are at the opposite ends, and most importantly, that they serve two very different audiences. We can simplify their differences, for the sake of framing this discussion. Generally speaking, theatre has social and cultural functions and it serves the society while tradition is at the service of spirit and spiritual forces. Between these two brothers is a shadow zone where a dialogue happens. This is the place where we as aboriginal people find ourselves when we practice the craft of theatre foreign to us. To successfully navigate this zone, an aboriginal artist needs to have the instincts of a hunter and a stalker that help him/her to successfully navigate in the fields of the unknown.

I borrowed the term "stalker," as well as the concept of "zone," from the film *Stalker* made by Russian director Andrei Tarkovsky. Stalker is a man who takes people into "the zone," a curious area around a Russian town, where some years ago a cosmic meteorite fell and since then all kinds of strange things have happened. The main character takes people through the enigmatic and dangerous area of "the zone" to realize their innermost dreams. He is a stalker;

it is his gift and his vocation. He guides people through a ravaged landscape that is subject to laws not made by humans, remembering his sick daughter whom he left behind in a poverty-stricken home. Dramatically, his family is a part of his motivation to be a stalker.

There is an inner chamber in the zone called "the room" where people, if they manage to get through all of the mazes and the dangers of the zone, can ask for the fulfillment of their innermost desire. The two journeyers, Writer and Scientist, who hired Stalker to accompany them through the zone, manage to overcome all the journeys obstacles but in the end do not have the courage to enter the room. And then Stalker relates to them an anecdote of his predecessor who trained him, a man named Porcupine, who reached the room and entered it. Shortly afterward his dream was granted. He became rich but soon after committed suicide. No doubt Porcupine entered the zone with good intentions to benefit his people. But in the end the truth came out, and his wish, tragic in its banality of personal greed, was granted. If we interpret his suicide metaphorically, it came after an ethical, spiritual, and creative suicide. It was a suicide in that Porcupine sacrificed the noblest instincts for baser instincts, that is, financial gain. We can interpret this as something similar when an artist sacrifices the higher goals of art for money and ego.

Both this film and aboriginal performance have a strong spiritual element. Both are nonlinear and work from that hidden world beneath the mundane surface of current existence. The zone is a maze, a spiritual journey where space and time are not linear and where it is the journey that is most important: a journey that confronts us with our inner truths and reveals to us the false idols we hold dear. Many people are not capable of looking so deeply into themselves as they are afraid of their innermost dreams. Aboriginal performance is a spiritual art that lives in contradiction with its public face but it has a dimension that is hidden from the public. Aboriginal performance is an investigation, a maze that brings us back to the sources of our soul. The room we can interpret as the moment when the journey becomes defined and set, when the journey becomes motivated by success or greed.

A sacred aboriginal dance, a traditional story, an invocation or any ritual act taken out of its context and placed on the stage, does this make it aboriginal theatre? Is the ritual act of a traditional society alien to the contemporary stage? There is an artist named Christo, who wraps public buildings with various materials. In 1995, he wrapped the Reichstag in Berlin. The changing light of the day, the deliberately placed lights at night upon the material, endowed this building with chameleon-like powers. Through an artistic process, the building became something else. But is it enough for the audience to believe in genuine transformation? Underneath the wrapping materials, there exists the same building. We have not changed the architectural foundations of the building.

It is important to have clarity when we enter the zone and to let our motivations guide us. If we say that life is a drama, then the main objective that guides the protagonist in us needs to be transcended in order to make sure that the drama does not become tragically banal, like that of Porcupine in the story of the Stalker. And if our motivation is too weak, then we must create a strong enough motivation that does not let us succumb to mediocre desires, because all our wishes in the end can be granted.

Also, we must remember our people and our families.

It is important that we constantly reevaluate our profession, and that we search for different new ways for framing our discussions and our quest. This novelty will allow us to avoid traps made by our own mental systems that may block creative growth. Our words can take on a life of their own and begin to dance circles around us. In aboriginal theatre the function of novelty is performed by the character of the Trickster who constantly makes his new appearance. One of the modi operandi of this figure is his constant shedding of worn-out paradigms while keeping commitment to contradictory modes of behavior and thought. Similarly, in Tarkovsky's movie, the Stalker asks the men he is taking through the zone not to take the same path twice. We can take this condition of behavioral disequilibrium and apply it to ourselves. In this manner, we are paying homage to this culture hero who is the prototype of aboriginal behavior.

There are moments of joy in working on a non-aboriginal show, or in doing an aboriginal show in a non-aboriginal professional venue or circumstance. There is also joy in being involved in the traditional practices of my people. But these are not enough in themselves; every once in a while you get a call or an e-mail from your colleagues or a proposal to participate in a project that entails entering "the zone": the zone between theatre and tradition, the meeting points between tradition/process/performance.

Like The Stalker who arises from bed, you pack your bag, kiss your family goodbye, and you set out to the designated meeting point where you are joined by your fellow stalkers. We meet in a studio, an idealized imagined space where we confront the creative questions that trouble and intrigue us. Perhaps it is a personal tragedy that compels us to go beyond the conventional boundaries of performance, or maybe it is the love we feel for our people. For a number of days or weeks we disappear into The Zone, following our impulses and subjected to the laws that are not made by humans. There is neither glory nor money in the work. Our creative exploration takes place in a realm that does not exist, since there is no formal or written knowledge that speaks of these investigations. Each person has different reasons for being a part of the work, otherwise the futility is exacerbated. There is no system or ideology that binds us or that we impose upon each other. The only imposition is that of rigor, and it is precisely this rigor that allows us to be free.

An interesting problem presents itself when we look at the two-row wampum belt of the Haudenosaunee nation. This belt was created during a treaty with the Dutch, and it outlines the nature of their relationship. The belt is bordered by two rows of purple beads separated by an expanse of white beads. The two purple rows are the two nations of the Haudenosaunee and the Dutch. In a way, the belt symbolically tells that the aboriginals and the whites should stay in their own boat and paddle their own canoe. To mix the two is like standing with your feet in both canoes.

Inevitably, you will fall into the water.

Then you may ask whether in our artistic investigation we are standing with our feet in separate canoes? Indeed, are we taking all of the white man's belongings and getting into our own boat? Are we sometimes just entering the white man's boat, that of theatre? Shouldn't we just stay in our own boat of tradition?

I don't know if we will ever reach the room where our wishes will be granted, or if we do reach The Room, if we will have the courage to enter. But I think the journey in itself is enough, and we have elaborated a large body of work that can keep us occupied for a number of months and years, work that guides us through a landscape made up of the ruins and fragments of our cultures, training, and of our nostalgia. Take a fragment of this movement, extend it with some music, alter the position of the spine, and something mysterious appears. I think we realize the hopelessness of our task, yet we continue. I think that is what art is all about; a romantic striving for the ineffable, the indescribable, and the magic "something" that can fill our solitude, the passion to save our culture and to express our worldview. Isn't that why we became artists?

8

Chocolate Woman Dreams the Milky Way

Monique Mojica

I

I have been thinking for quite a while about knowing and not knowing.[1] What we know and *how* we know it. There is a saying in Spanish—*saber sabiendo*—literally "to know knowingly." But it also carries the connotation of knowing the unknown, the intuitively known or what we do not know that we know.

Most of the work that I have done over the past two decades reflects tapping this kind of knowing. I have not always done it consciously and I have not done it alone. Since 1991, I have collaborated with Floyd Favel and Muriel Miguel, among others, in performance research and laboratories searching out how to do consciously what we do *un*consciously. This work has resulted in studio investigations and produced performances that aim to identify and hone a methodology that Floyd has called "Native Performance Culture." These two visionary directors have had an enormous influence on me and I will talk more about them later.

So, I have been doing this performance thing for a long time. It has been fifty-two years since I first started training (yikes!); twenty-nine years since I first worked with an all-Native theatre company, Indian Time Theater, directed by Bruce King out of the now defunct Native American Center for the Living Arts in Niagara Falls, New York; and nearly twenty-four years since I moved to Toronto to be one of the early artistic directors of Native Earth Performing Arts. Those were the times just preceding the infamous "Native theatre explosion" in Toronto when our small circle included the Highway brothers Tomson and René, Billy Merasty, Makka Kleist, Maariu Olsen, Gary Farmer, Shirley Cheechoo, Graham Greene, and Doris Linklater. Over the years, I have accumulated quite a bit of material. Some there is no record of; some are lost on floppy discs that my computer can no longer read. Some are drafts that hide in my not so organized filing cabinet, and still others are scraps of paper folded into notebooks: fragments of stories and notations of improvisations. In preparation for this essay and as someone whose writing process includes doing laundry, making lists, and sifting through papers, I excavated some two-decades-old writings, dusted them off, and had a look. What I found is that not only could I recognize recurring themes and imagery, but I could also trace a trajectory, a personal transformation as an artist and as an Aboriginal woman. A trajectory that transforms amnesia through stories drawn from conscious memory, muscle memory, blood memory, then births organic texts allowing me to emerge trusting the Indigenous knowledge encoded in my dreams, in my waking visions, and in my DNA.

The theme of being lost in my motherland finding no trail to follow because my grandmothers and great-grandmothers left no written records of themselves or their experiences weaves through my early work.

This is how the theme appeared in *Princess Pocahontas and the Blue Spots*:

> CONTEMPORARY WOMAN #1:
> No map, no trail, no footprint, no way home
> only darkness, a cold wind whistling by my ears.
> The only light comes from the stars.
> Nowhere to set my feet.
> no place to stand. *(rising)*
> No map, no trail, no footprint, no way home.

"No map, no trail, no footprint, no way home" is a refrain echoed by the character Lady Rebecca, as Pocahontas was renamed when she was converted to Christianity and then taken to England's Elizabethan court as an advertising gimmick.

Narratives of wandering, without a map, having forgotten my way, evolved to another recurring theme: memory/remembering/memorializing.

II

Another one of the recurring images in my work is the bag of bones carrying girl/woman. A character I'll refer to as Bag of Bones / Rebecca first appeared in an early Native Earth production, *Double Take / A Second Look* (1983) written by Billy Merasty, Gloria Miguel, Maariu Olsen, and myself, and directed by Muriel Miguel. Rebelda is another aspect of the same character. In retrospect, they are both early versions of Esperanza, my massacre-collecting atrocity tour guide from Turtle Gals' *The Scrubbing Project* (2002 & 2005). My original inspiration for this character came from Gabriel García Márquez's *One Hundred Years of Solitude*, which I read for the first time at age sixteen. This is a passage from García Márquez's magical novel:

> That Sunday, in fact, Rebecca arrived. She was only eleven years old. . . . Her entire baggage consisted of a small trunk, a little rocking chair with small hand-painted flowers, and a canvas sack which kept making a *cloc-cloc-cloc* sound, where she carried her parent's bones. (García Márquez 1971, 47)

I carried this bag of bones around for a long time—these "bones of my ancestors," and with the bones, the history of Native women on this continent. The history of being the sexual commodities for the conquest, the stories from the female side of the colonization experience were not being told in the course of the "Native theatre explosion." I wanted to work with other Native women who felt the void and who had the courage to tell their own stories.

Jani Lauzon, Michelle St. John, and I first worked together in 1990 on the set of a CBC mini-series, *Conspiracy of Silence*. At that time, during predawn conversations on the way to set in subzero temperatures, we discovered a common interest in a theme that had left its mark on us all. Each of us had, or knew someone who had, tried to scrub off or bleach out their color. These conversations and recognitions were the first seeds of *The Scrubbing Project*. It was not until nearly ten years later in 1999 that we gathered to create the work and Turtle Gals Performance Ensemble was formed.

In *The Scrubbing Project*, the Bag of Bones / Rebecca character was fully developed and her story expanded to include the massacre imagery that I'd been working with since The Centre for Indigenous

Theatre's residency at the Banff Centre in the winter of 1995. This was a program Floyd Favel and I co-directed that included Muriel Miguel, Pura Fé, Michelle St. John, Archer Pechawis, Maariu Olsen, Jennifer Podemski, Alex Thompson, and others. There were several questions from this residency that carried over into the creation process of *The Scrubbing Project*. They were:

1. What are the consequences of creating art out of atrocity?

2. Is there such a thing as internalized genocide? (If so, what does it look like?)

A question from a subsequent research project I did with Floyd Favel was:

3. How do we create memorials to the holocaust in the Americas?

To which Turtle Gals added:

4. Once Native women have put down the bundles of grief and multigenerational trauma that we collectively carry—then what?

and

5. How do we get from victim to victory?

The Scrubbing Project is a study of the manifestations of internalized racism and genocide. Esperanza, my Earthplane character, is a persona formed from my deepest victimization. She carries with her at all times a bag of bones she recovered from a clandestine mass grave; bones which she scrubs, feeds, and cares for. She also carries a bag filled with shoes she collected from massacre sites, which she treats as prayers and offerings, which the play's three characters transform into tobacco ties.

In contrast, my Starworld character, Winged Victory, was created from my strongest vision of victory: the huge copper- and bronze-winged beings, round breasted and full in the thigh, who crown the tops of the triumphant neo-Greco/Roman statuary our colonizers have erected in order to commemorate *their* victories.

She is also rooted to the knowledge that the Kuna Rebellion of 1925 led by Nele Kantule and the Mayan uprising of 1994 led by the Zapatistas are evidence that sometimes we get to win.

This is an excerpt from *The Scrubbing Project* where Esperanza crosses into a "Massacre Portal" and tells the story of the recovery of the bones. By the end of the story she cradles the bones in her arms and addresses them.

MASSACRE PORTAL
ESPERANZA: Crack! / Thud! Crack! / Thud!

BRANDA tries to hang on to tradition. DOVE spirals down to Earthplane, back to OPHELIA

It's that once you see you can't ever pretend you don't see.
And I see,
I see the men lined up on one side, the women trembling on the other. I've never witnessed a massacre / I see them all the time.
    I see the soldiers raise their rifles—
    I see
    Skulls shatter
    I see
    Bodies fall:
    Friends
    Companions
    Husband
Crack! Thud! Crack! Thud!
I've never seen a body fall under the crack of
 bullet splintering bone / I see them all the time
And once you've seen, you can't ever pretend you don't see
 And I see . . .

ESP & OPH: Little rivulets of blood . . .
ESPERANZA: . . . soaked up by the thirsty earth.
ESP & OPH: All the colors of the rainbow . . .
ESPERANZA: . . . dried to a rusty brown crust.
 I've never seen my relatives' bodies piled on the
 blood soaked earth / I see them all the time.
Spit on blood fades the stain.

But once you've seen, you can't ever pretend you don't see
and I see.
(as she gathers up bones)
I will carry you, I will care for you, I will feed you, and I
will sing you songs of comfort.
I will wash away the dirt, and the ragged flecks of flesh and
skin
And you will be warm
And you will be loved
And I will build memory.

I am very grateful to the process that Turtle Gals went through
diving headlong into the dark places of our victimization. The
willingness to go there has allowed me to use those depths as a
springboard—a trampoline that offers me the possibility of ground-
ing myself in another place. A place where I cease to identify with
my own victimization and no longer recognize my reflection as "the
victim."

Which brings me to mirrors as a recurring theme; mirrors as
reflections, illusions, distortions, and shattered identities—mirrors
as magical tools that multiply images, deflect negativity, refract
and concentrate light. This next piece was developed for *The Only
Good Indian . . .* , a Turtle Gals production. The text was generated
in several workshops directed by Arturo Freselone and Guillermo
Gomez-Peña.

I come from a family of show Indians. My Grandpa con-
cocted snake oil in the bathtub and sold it to tourists.
The future Spiderwoman Theater ballyhooed to attract
customers to see the latest John Wayne western. They'll
openly admit that's where they got their start. Show biz
Indians!

III

I'd like to talk now about two veteran theatre directors who I consider to be light-bearers in our movement. They have consistently
held up a beacon, shed light on the path, and given me a direction through their incredible vision. They are: Floyd Favel from the
Poundmaker Reserve in Saskatchewan[2] and my aunt, Muriel Miguel
of Spiderwoman Theater in New York City.

I'll start with this equation that Floyd came up with, and though it's somewhat "tongue in cheek" and pseudo-scientific—I think it works.

TrAd (social / ritual) x M = NpC
Or Tradition, social or ritual x Methodology = Native Performance Culture.

Instead of trying to interpret what Floyd means, I'll read a quote from an essay he wrote called "The Shadowed Path":

> One of the ideas of Native Performance Culture is to search for accessible ritual and social structures that can act as a catalyst for creative action. I believe that there needs to be a bridge from a ritual and social action to the professional stage. Tradition needs to be filtered and transformed for the objective needs of the theatre. Without this bridge, theatre risks presenting "Artificial Trees" on stage. "Artificial Trees" is the superficial or clichéd presentation of ritual and social structures on the professional stage. (Unpublished manuscript, n.p.)

In another article entitled "Waskawewin" published in 2004 for *Topoi*, an international philosophy journal published in the Netherlands, Floyd defines the concept of "Artificial Trees" this way:

> to take the traditional sacred dance as it is and transplant this to the modern stage. This process I feel turns the dance into folklore, or an "artificial tree." A tree cut off from its roots, a facsimile of culture and sacredness. (Favel 2005, 114)

He describes the methodology for Native Performance Culture he has been searching for in these words:

> One would have to isolate the technical principles of the dance and use these as starting points for contemporary performance. What is meant by technical principles is: the position of the body to the earth, the relationship of the feet to the ground, the head to the sky, the different oppositions in the body, balance. It is the enigmatic relationship between these technical principles that

create the dance. These enigmatic relationships are the
shadow zone where ancestors and the unknown dwell,
and this is where creativity is born, where the impulse is
born. In Japan, they call this the Ma, the pause between
beats and notes. In my tradition, they say the ancestors
dwell in the space between the dancers. (Favel 2005, 114)

One of the things that I love about Floyd is that he does not get
stuck in his own dogma. Since the beginning of our collaboration
on the interdisciplinary performance project "Chocolate Woman
Dreams the Milky Way" in 2007, there has been a shift in the articulation of NpC. We have grown away from the term "methodology"
and are now calling the transformative journey to the stage (and
back to our origins) simply—process.

Tradition ↔ Process ↔ Performance—a fluid multi-direc-
tional continuum where the three elements all relate to
each other in an equal manner.

However, Floyd warns against his equation being applied as
a formula saying that each artist must work from his or her own
equation. In a recent phone conversation he also said, " 'artificial
trees' is its own valid form." And that's true. It's what my grandpa
did performing Indian medicine shows—it's the "Lakota" commercial. Which is the perfect segue to . . . Spiderwoman Theater.

I have known Muriel Miguel all my life; she is my mother's
youngest sister. I grew up watching her, my mother (Gloria Miguel),
and their older sister Lisa Mayo perform long before Spiderwoman
Theater was founded. They are my lineage and I am proud of the
precious gifts that I have inherited from them.

As the director that I have worked with most consistently over
the past two decades, Muriel has truly been the one to mold the raw
material of my writing into performances. This is how she describes
what she does. It's from the director's notes from *The Scrubbing
Project* program in 2002.

As indigenous people, we see all disciplines as intercon-
nected, with roots in traditional forms of storytelling. As
the artistic director of Spiderwoman Theater, I have, over
the past 30 years been using a methodology called *storyweaving* to entwine stories and fragments of stories with
words, music, song, film, dance and movement, thereby

creating a production that is multi-layered and complex;
an emotional, cultural and political tapestry.

I was thinking, over the past year, about the way Muriel works—
how she does what she does when she directs. She helps generate
materials, she dramaturges that material and weaves it together in
a way that is very intuitive—not at all an intellectual process. As
a matter of fact, do not even try to justify something to her intel-
lectually! She'll wave it away with her wrist and say, "That sounds
very intellectual." As if to also say, "I can't do anything with *that*,
Dearie—you're going to have to go deeper." Muriel does not allow
an actor/creator to stay in her head. Muriel works from that place
of what is unconsciously known, intuitively known—*saber sabiendo*:
to know knowingly. Nor is she satisfied for a piece of theatre to be
one- or two-dimensional when it could be three-, six-, nine-, or even
twelve-dimensional. And dynamics!—Don't play her the same note!
    So I had this brain flash! Now maybe it was just menopause
but I could see, I thought, what Muriel does. She makes *mola*s out
of theatre! *Mola*s are her palette and her dramaturgical tool. *Mola*s—
the art of Kuna women.
    *Mola*s are the traditional textiles of the Kuna nation from the
autonomous territory of Kuna Yala in what is known as Panama.
Kuna women wear two *mola* panels—front and back—sewn together
to form our blouses. Kuna women are renowned for their skills in
creating their designs and combining color. Originally, the designs
were painted and tattooed on our bodies; designs born from dreams
and visions from the *chicha* ceremony—the most important in Kuna
ceremonial life because it honors a girl's first moon cycle. Kuna
perception, Kuna cosmology, Kuna identity is encoded in the layers
of our *mola*s.
    *Mola*s are made by the combined techniques of reverse appli-
qué, appliqué, and embroidery. They require several layers of fabric
and the designs are cut out freehand to allow the colors from the layers underneath to show through. Stitching the edges of the designs
with the tiniest of stitches is the most fastidious part because it
is what connects the layers. The *mola* gets thicker and thicker.
Sometimes a corner will be torn apart and another color or pattern
of cloth will be inserted. Some areas will be built up with appliqué
and details embroidered on. There are no even edges and they are
never truly symmetrical. Even two panels of the same blouse will
not be exactly the same but will sometimes show two different perspectives of the same design motif. Ironically, sewing machines were

introduced to make Kuna women's work faster, a more economically sound enterprise. They did make the work faster, but these *mola*s are thin with square edges to their designs and inferior overall. It is possible to trace the design of a *mola* and reproduce its outline, but it would lack the multidimensional layers of meaning that make it Kuna. I have never made a *mola*, neither has my mother or my aunts, but we all grew up living with them, touching them, tracing their texture and designs, smelling them, sleeping on them, and wearing them. It is this thickness, this multidimensional knowing applied from the principles of Kuna women's art that I believe is my inheritance from Spiderwoman's theatrical methodology. And I want that thickness in my work.

When I was very small I had a *mola* that belonged to my mother since before I was born. I used to put in on to dance around our apartment. It was too long and fell almost to my knees; it would slip off my shoulders. I always wore it accompanied by a little red ballet tutu, and I would dance and create performances all by myself. I would spend hours dancing in my *mola* and red tutu to Tchaikovsky, Mendelssohn, Rimsky-Korsakov. I have not thought about that outfit in fifty years but I can feel myself going back to where I began, only now with more experience and more information. *Saber sabiendo.*

There are four artistic principles ever present in the traditional and contemporary Kuna cultural aesthetic:

- *Duality and repetition*—Kuna aesthetic and all of Kuna culture are based on duality and repetition; everything reflects and honors the duality of Baba/Nana, the Mother/Father.

- *Abstraction*—Kunas use abstract geometric designs; by further abstracting these we protect the integrity of traditional designs and pictographs.

- *Metaphor*—presenting image and story metaphorically, as if through the smoke screen of Chocolate Woman's smudge, protects its true meaning by encoding it.

- *Multidimensionality*—the eight levels of Kuna reality are reflected in Kuna art.

Key collaborator in the Chocolate Woman Collective, Kuna visual artist Oswaldo (Achu) DeLeón Kantule has been working with these principles in his paintings and art installations for decades with stunning results. By seeking a creative process that translates his work to the performing body, we wish to explore relationships between Kuna pictographs, *mola* textile designs, Achu's contemporary paintings, story narrative structure and content, memory, the dramaturgical process, and body movement. The simultaneous development of the system of visual notation for the body moving through space is an intrinsic component of our interdisciplinary process.

IV

Tracing the themes in my work over the past two decades has allowed me to see up close my trajectory from victim to victory. Returning to the first fragment in this essay, I can affirm that I am no longer calling to the spirits of heartbreak and sadness, blood and rebellion, or back-breaking endurance because transformation is a continuum and I must conjure myself into another place on my map.

It feels like shedding a skin that, although familiar, has become too constraining. I spent a long time digging around in massacre imagery and now I must call out to other spirits. My writings and the theatre I create from them are my offerings, my prayers, my healing chants, my history, my identity—my *molas*.

Cacao beans are what chocolate is made from. In the central part of the Americas (from Mexico south) they are very important. They are used as currency; they are burned as smudge to purify, pray, and heal; and they are an important part of the traditional diet. *Siagua*. Without it many Kuna have developed diabetes and high blood pressure. I have started eating these beans. In Kuna culture almost all the medicines are women, so *siagua* is referred to as Cacao Woman—*Puna Siagua*. Intrigued by the yummy image of a chocolate woman, I began to invoke Chocolate Woman. This excerpt from the current work-in-progress piece is in part a dream I had over a decade ago.

Chocolate Woman Dreams the Milky Way: An Invocation

PUNA SIAGUA and TULE GIRL:
Now . . .

TULE GIRL
In this time when my blood is held inside,
the cries of my dolphin children are carried farther out
    to sea into the arms of *Muu Bili*, Grandmother Ocean.
Now that my blood is held inside,
Purified by the smoke of Red Cacao Woman's beads—
    siagua—here on *Abya Yala*, "Land of Blood."

PUNA SIAGUA and TULE GIRL
Puna Siagua, Siagua kinnit!
Be an anwe be sagua waale waaletgine

TULE GIRL
Wrap me in the arms of your purifying smoke.

PUNA SIAGUA
Burning like coals my eyes of fire turn my necklace of
    cacao, my *sabured* to sacred smoke
On my smoking body I carry helpers—

TULE GIRL
—*uchugana*—

PUNA SIAGUA
—and seers—

TULE GIRL
—*nelegana*—

PUNA SIAGUA
Through the eight layers
searching
hunting pestilence, malevolence
unbalance, illness
boni
In my golden net I capture
entangle and leave them powerless
I am Puna Siagua daughter of the morning star

TULE GIRL
Olowaili / *nisgua dummad*

PUNA SIAGUA
Olowaili, the morning star, is the sister of the sun.

TULE GIRL
My grandfather, whose broad chest was tattooed with an
    eagle's wingspan open full,
saw *Olowaili* fall to earth over New York harbor and
    named me for her.

(chants) *ani we / we ani*
ani we / we ani
ani we / we, ani

PUNA SIAGUA and TULE GIRL
Olowaili guile birya birya!
Be nak odoe an nakine!
Be an saban enoge nizgana guallu gine

TULE GIRL
Olowaili, swirl and dance!
Spiral and place your feet in mine!
Fill my belly with starlight!

PUNA SIAGUA
eyes like coals
my smoking body
carries helpers through the layers
captures *boni*

I am Chocolate Woman
it is only my chocolate essence that you need
if you only ask
I can rescue your *burba*

TULE GIRL
In heavy chocolate dreams I swim to shore
I am naked as the warm turquoise water breaks over
    my face.
I can see the shoreline. There are houses made from cane
    stalks lashed together their palm-thatched roofs hang
    low.
Swaying in the sea breeze—

Puna Siagua
—burwa—

TULE GIRL
—palm fronds.
The beach burns brilliant.
Sand blinding white.

PUNA SIAGUA
Kuna Yala!

TULE GIRL
I stand and walk out of the sea. Salt water slides off
    my naked skin.
Against the starkness of the sand there are *mola*s
    neatly laid out.
Layers of code—a blanket of red—*kinnit* against white
    sand, *kinnit* against white sand.

PUNA SIAGUA
Sue mola, cansu mola, yar burba mola, kwage mola

TULE GIRL
To my left, a few steps away from the *mola*s, stands a
    beautiful young woman.

PUNA SIAGUA
Kikadiryai

TULE GIRL
She wears the clothes of *Kuna* women: a red blouse . . .

PUNA SIAGUA
Mola

TULE GIRL
printed skirt

PUNA SIAGUA
sabured,

TULE GIRL
a red and gold head-scarf

PUNA SIAGUA
muswe,

TULE GIRL
beads wrapped tightly around her wrists almost to the
    elbow, adorning her ankles almost to the knee

PUNA SIAGUA
winis

TULE GIRL
a gold nose-ring and a gold necklace that falls over
    her entire chest like a breast-plate. A delicate line of
    blue-black paint traces the centerline of her nose.

PUNA SIAGUA
sabdur

TULE GIRL
Her round cheeks are shiny with moisture and stained
    achiote red.

PUNA SIAGUA
nisar

TULE GIRL
Her black hair cropped short frames her face. There is
    something on her head like . . . a . . .

PUNA SIAGUA
. . . *gurgin* . . .

TULE GIRL
. . . a golden bowl whose sides undulate in constant
    motion.

She is smiling. Smiling at me. Her arms outstretched,
fingers spread wide. She shows me her *molas*, neatly
arranged in rows on the sand. *Kinnit* against white sand.
Kinnit against white sand. She is proud of her work. She
begins to spin and spin and spin. Faster faster.

PUNA SIAGUA and TULE GIRL
Olowaili, guile birya birya!

Be nak odoe an nakine!
Be an saban enoge nizgana guallu gine

TULE GIRL
nizgana guallu gine

PUNA SIAGUA and TULE GIRL
Puna Siagua! Siagua kinnit!
Be an anwe be sagua waale waaletgine

TULE GIRL
Let my smile mirror *Kikadiriyai* spinning, stitching *mola*s
   on the sand!
. . .
Full moon hangs low over the Ocean.
Shards of moonlight like fragments of broken disco ball
   bob in the black water—laying a path of stars to the
   Milky Way—

PUNA SIAGUA and TULE GIRL
—negaduu.

TULE GIRL
If I could place my feet upon those stars like stepping
stones, I would follow them to visit my ancestors.

PUNA SIAGUA
—sergan—(throws her net)

TULE GIRL
And we would drink chocolate—

PUNA SIAGUA	TULE GIRL
—siagua nisa—	*(whispers) ochi . . . ochi . . . ochi*

TULE GIRL
—mixed with ground, roasted corn from gourds. We
would smack our lips; wipe our mouths on the backs of
our hands and talk. Wouldn't we talk! *Tegi!*

PUNA SIAGUA
(chant) nabiree . . . nabiree . . . nabiree (continues under
the next speech)

TULE GIRL
I, too, am a granddaughter fallen from the stars
I call to Sky Woman: send me your courage!
The courage of the valiant Morning Star,

PUNA SIAGUA and TULE GIRL
—Olowaili—

TULE GIRL
—when she rises each morning to greet her brother—

PUNA SIAGUA and TULE GIRL
—Ibeler—

TULE GIRL
—the sun, at daybreak
And there, for some moments, we hang in the liquid
    pigment of a watercolor sky.

PUNA SIAGUA and TULE GIRL
Puna siagua negaduu gi gabdake
Gabdakmai gi negaduu
Negaduu gi gabdake

TULE GIRL	PUNA SIAGUA (*underneath*)
Puna siagua negaduu gi gabdake	*nabiree*
Gabdakmai gi negaduu	
Negaduu gi gabdake	
nabiree	

Notes

1. A previous version of this essay was published in 2009 in *Performing Worlds Into Being: Native American Women's Theater*, ed. Ann Elizabeth Armstrong, Kelli Lyon Johnson, and William A. Wortman (Oxford, OH: Miami University Press).

2. See also Floyd Favel's essay, chapter 7 in this volume.

9

"I don't write Native stories, I write universal stories"

An Interview with Tomson Highway

Birgit Däwes

Tomson Highway is the most influential Native playwright in Canada today, and one of Canada's most prominent aboriginal voices. He was born as the eleventh of twelve children in a tent pitched in a snow bank just south of the Manitoba/Nunavut border (near Saskatchewan). His father, Joe Highway, was a legendary caribou hunter and world championship dogsled racer.

Of the many works Tomson Highway has written to date, the best known are his plays, *The Rez Sisters*, *Dry Lips Oughta Move to Kapuskasing*, *Rose*, *Ernestine Shuswap Gets Her Trout*, and the best-selling novel, *Kiss of the Fur Queen*. Between 1986 and 1992, when Highway served as artistic director for Canada's most renowned professional aboriginal theatre company, Native Earth Performing Arts, the production of *The Rez Sisters* brought international fame to indigenous theatre and initiated a wave of success for this intriguing genre. Among his many honors are the Floyd S. Chalmers Award, five Dora Mavor Moore Awards, the Toronto Arts Award, the Wang Harbourfront International Festival of Authors Award, the Silver Ticket Award, the National Aboriginal Achievement Award, the Order of Canada, and six honorary doctorates.

Although most of Tomson Highway's work is in English, he is in fact a native speaker of Cree: "I use the English language filtered through a Cree imagination," he told his audience at a Canadian studies conference in Grainau, Germany, in 2009. Most of all, Highway believes in the universal languages of music and emotion. In

November 2008, he toured Germany—a country where most people enthusiastically think of North America's indigenous people in terms of Karl May's *Winnetou*, Kevin Costner's *Dances with Wolves*, or Walt Disney's *Pocahontas*. In light of this stereotypical "Indian" imaginary (which has also fueled the most successful German movie of all times, Bully Herbig's *Der Schuh des Manitu* [*Manitou's Shoe*]), Highway's humorous approach to cultural specifics was an enlightening experience for audiences at the sold-out venues in Würzburg, Munich, Marburg, and Mainz. For his Cree cabaret, "The History of the World in 60 Minutes, from an Indigenous Perspective," he was joined by Peruvian-Canadian singer Patricia Cano and by Berlin-based saxophone player Ulrich Kempendorff.

The following conversation took place on November 10, 2008, in the (reconstructed) medieval city center of Würzburg. Tomson Highway talks about his involvement in the history of contemporary Native theatre, his emphasis on music, and his understanding of art as a universal form of communication; and he also addresses specific questions regarding his plays *Rose* and *Ernestine Shuswap Gets Her Trout*.

BD: First of all, let me thank you for agreeing to do this interview, despite your busy tour schedule. As I mentioned previously, this interview is going to be published in a volume on the history of indigenous theatre in North America.

TH: You know what we do in my culture when we react to an introduction like that? We moo with pleasure. Like this: Mmmmh.

[*laughter*]

BD: So, to begin at the beginnings: where would you see the origins of Native theatre, drama, and performance?

TH: The beginnings, of course, are dance, and pow wow. And chants. And storytelling.

BD: Drew Hayden Taylor once said that theatre is just the "logical extension of storytelling," from the campfire to the stage (1997, 140). But in the twentieth century, this has developed into fascinating new formats, and you play a major role in the development of Native theatre in Canada. Some people say that the genre started in 1986, with the opening of *The Rez Sisters* in Toronto—that that was the beginning of modern First Nations theatre in Canada.

TH: People say that? Oh, I think it started way before that. There were certainly plays produced before that that people do not really know about. There was, for instance, *Son of Ayash* by Jim Morris [Ojibway], a wonderful production. That was in 1982, in Sioux Lookout, Ontario. It was produced by Northern Delights theatre company, and it was fantastic. It was the first time a Native myth was adapted for the stage. *Son of Ayash*, an ancient Cree/Ojibway myth. It is about the journey of a young man, but ultimately, it is like the *Odyssey*—a Native version of the *Odyssey*.

BD: Was it a small production?

TH: Yes, six actors, two acts, about two hours long. A full-scale production. And then it went on tour, to many, many places—about sixteen or twenty reserves in Northern Ontario. It was fantastic.

BD: So the productions were mostly on reserves?

TH: Yes. You know, it was originally produced in Sioux Lookout, which is a town, and then the company, Northern Delights, took it to about twenty reserves. It was beautifully produced. Beautiful directing, beautiful acting. And there were lots of other people. So I was far from the first.

BD: And before you came into theatre, were you familiar with other Native productions at that time? Was it already visible?

TH: Oh yeah. And that really inspired me.

BD: You also worked with James Reaney for a while.

TH: At the University of Western Ontario, yes. I was a student, and I attended a couple of his workshops. He always workshopped plays before he produced them. I participated in *Wacousta!*, and I participated in the sequel to it, which was called *The Canadian Brothers*. Those were two early Canadian novels by John Richardson. The first one has to do with the Pontiac wars, as they are called [which took place in 1763]. So this one is about Chief Pontiac, the leader of the Confederacy of the Three Fires: the Odawa, the Pottawatomi, and the Ojibway. And the second one has to do with Chief Tecumseh and the war that he fought in 1812.

BD: So would you consider James Reaney one of the influences on your work?

TH: Yes, totally. You know he just died.

BD: Oh, I'm sorry to hear that. When?

TH: On June 11. I remember the precise date. It was a big day in Native culture, because of the apology for the residential school system.[1]

BD: Who else would you consider influential on your work?

TH: On my writing: James Joyce and Homer. I did a major paper once, which was way too big for my britches. It was an essay comparing the structure of Homer's *Odyssey* and Joyce's *Ulysses*. It almost killed me, but I did it. And it was at the same time that I was perfecting my English, so it was a double challenge for me.

BD: So did you start out writing in English, or did you start in Cree?

TH: In English. I really started writing mostly because I wanted to master the language. And it was never my intention to be a writer. I still don't want to be a writer.

BD: Well, you're not being very successful with that wish. [*laughter*]

TH: My first dream was to be a piano player. A concert pianist. But coming from the kind of land that I come from, it was a totally impractical dream. Because where I was born, the nearest piano was three hundred miles away. So I was comparing myself to the likes of Glenn Gould and Martha Argerich, and other major concert artists, but to be a concert artist of any kind, and in classical music especially, you want to be born and raised in a major city, where the best musical education is available from an early age, so you can start at three or four.

Glenn Gould is an excellent example: His mother was a piano teacher and on top of this, it so happens that the best music-education facility in Canada, namely the Royal Conservatory of Music in Toronto, was a mere half-hour streetcar ride from his home. So he was lucky. I've always been very jealous of Glenn Gould. And Martha Argerich, who has a great story, from what I know. She was born in 1941 in the very major city of Buenos Aires, Argentina. Her father was a diplomat who, when she was still a girl, was appointed Argentina's ambassador to Austria by Argentina's then-president himself. So that by age thirteen, she was living in Vienna where the best training in the world for a classical musician is available. So that by the time she was eighteen—and not, of course, without her awesome natural talent—she was a world-class concert artist. And I was born three hundred miles away from the nearest piano. She was a genius, and so was Glenn Gould.

BD: I think you even mentioned somewhere that Glenn Gould has been a more direct influence on you.

TH: Yes—my teacher had the same teacher as Glenn Gould.

BD: Would you consider music a bigger influence on your work than literature?

TH: Oh, yeah. And my biggest teachers are Germans! Their names are Bach, Beethoven, Brahms, Schubert, Schumann, and then Mozart, of course, was Austrian.

BD: So was Schubert, but we like to count him in. [*laughter*]

TH: In any case, I still think in those terms: language is music, and we're all musical instruments. Whether I write a play, a novel, or a piece of music, a song, I think in those terms. Sonata form, sonata structure; fugal form, fugal structure. I am convinced that the best songs ever written in the history of songwriting were written by Franz Schubert and Robert Schumann.

BD: And isn't that one of the wonderful things about theatre—that you can merge all those different forms of art?

In *Rose*, for instance, the music is an integral part of the performance—the play wouldn't work without it.

TH: Yes, and *Rose* is, of course, a musical. But to me, this works for my other plays, too: *The Rez Sisters* and *Dry Lips* are gigantic fugues for eight voices. And I create like that. I am thinking of Bach's fugues, or Beethoven's fugues and sonatas, like Opus 109. A fugue is like a Rubik's cube made of sound waves, you know. And as a music student you have to study all these kinds of works. The last quartets of Beethoven, string quartets, especially the Razumovsky quartets, Opus 59, there's three of them; and then the last ones. His very last composition before he died was called the *Grosse Fuge*, the Grand Fugue; the biggest fugue ever written in the history of fugues. Incredible. And when you study that it becomes a part of your subconscious. It affects your whole life.

BD: I can imagine. The subtitle of *Ernestine Shuswap Gets Her Trout* reflects that too: You call it "A 'string quartet' for four female actors."

TH: I think fugally. I think sonata. And I think symphonically. I always do.

BD: That's an intriguing insight into your creative process. I would be interested in hearing more about how you got from the point of being a musician to that of the director and playwright, how you first started translating that musical training into the medium of drama. Did you conceive of your own work as "First Nations" theatre? Or did you just consider it theatre?

TH: I just wanted to have fun. [*laughter*]. Well, my brother [René] was a dancer. But unfortunately by the time a dancer turns thirty, or approaches thirty, he has to start thinking about something else. It's the most cruel of all the art forms, dance. Aside from the fact that the pay is terrible, and the lifestyle brutal, the lifespan of a dancer is very short, you know, his career span. So by the time you are turning thirty, you already have to start thinking of a second career. A lot of dancers turn to teaching. And a lot of dancers turn to something completely different, a totally different career. And then, of course, there's choreography. So he was moving into choreography, and he would have made an excellent choreographer if he'd had the time to live.[2] He was working on some choreography, and one of the first things that choreography needs is music, of course. So he asked me to write some music for him. But I had never expected for one second that I was gifted for writing music or anything. Even though I had all this extraordinary musical education behind me. Of course, we learned orchestration, we learned how to write for a symphony orchestra, and I had an extraordinary teacher. So quite legally speaking, I have the skills to write a symphony. But I wouldn't do it, because it's just prohibitively expensive and a tremendous amount of work. And at the end of it, who would play it? Just to have one rehearsal, and to pay one hundred musicians for two hours, we're talking $10,000.

BD: Right, that's even worse than the financial challenges you have to face with a play.

TH: Yeah. So anyway, I wrote music. I wrote a ten-minute piece for him. And then the pieces became longer and longer. I also started adding words into the score, into the musical tapestry. Words in Cree and English. And that's how it started. So over the years, those things, those performance pieces, morphed into plays; experimental plays, but plays nevertheless. So writing plays was never my intention. It was more like an accident.

BD: What a happy accident. And in the process of that metamorphosis, wonderful things followed. *The Rez Sisters* is always said to be the play that opened the floodgates for the success of First Nations theatre today. How did you perceive that moment, the opening of this play's first production at the Native Canadian Centre of Toronto in November 1986?

TH: I just remember being surrounded by a number of extraordinary people in Toronto: the performers and an extraordinary director [Larry Lewis]. And also in Europe. They were extraordinary and insane—insanely fun. It was the big decade from [19]84 or [19]85 to [19]95. During those ten years, we lost many many of the best artists in theatre and dance and literature to AIDS. A lot of people died in their thirties and forties. And my brother was one of them. So I just remember being surrounded by extraordinary people. And I remember being extraordinarily excited, extraordinarily busy, and tying all my talents to the promotion of Native writing. And it was also a very poor experience of my life, because I had to go through all this stuff myself and I was very poor financially. But I don't remember that. I remember being extremely happy. It was a very happy time, a very creative time in my life. What made it so much fun was being with all these people. That's what mattered to me. And to a very large extent I still think "Good Grief"—that that particular piece, and others that followed it, have affected people. But the point is, it surprises me. And I cannot believe that I've written something that—and those two plays in particular—that they have a worldwide effect. I can't believe that. I just can't believe that I've written something like that. Because I think I was just basically following orders, you know, doing what I was told to.

BD: And it's highly fascinating, I mean, your work has been produced all over the world. As you're saying, it has an effect all over the world. Yet at the same time it is also remarkably culturally specific. We have this Cree reserve with the women in *The Rez Sisters* and the men in *Dry Lips*, and the issues they discuss are highly specific from their own regional and cultural context. But at the same time they are also universal, so that these plays work on stages around the world. *Dry Lips* was produced in Tokyo in 2001, for instance. How did the reception work there? How did people react in Asia?

TH: Wonderfully. They loved it. They always love it. *The Rez Sisters* was also produced in Tokyo, in 2002 and 2003, at the KAZE theatre, near the Sumo Museum.

BD: Did you get different reactions in different countries?

TH: No. And I'll tell you what: the most amazing thing about art is that after the first five minutes during a work, it doesn't matter what race people are. They're just human beings, human hearts, human desires, and human frailties. So when I write and when I produce, I don't think in Native terms. I think in universal terms.

BD: That works very well with your plays. And the Trickster may be a figure from Native mythology, but we also have equivalents all over the world, such as Sun Wukong in China, Eshu in Yoruban culture, or Till Eulenspiegel in German culture.

TH: Well, precisely. *Romeo and Juliet* has an Italian setting, but it's universal. Chinese actors play *Romeo and Juliet*. These are just roles, and they can be performed by Nigerian actors in Nigeria, Mongolian actors in Mongolia, or Russian actors in Moscow.

BD: That's also what you write in your essay "Should Only Native Actors Have the Right to Play Native Roles?"—that it's always better to be color-blind when it comes to casting than not have your play performed at all. That was an issue with the production of *Rose* especially, wasn't it?

TH: Yes, that was one of the reasons. It took a long time to get *Rose* produced because of its complexity, and then in brackets, it was also considered "unwieldy." I have an answer to that. I mean, I have no business comparing myself with these people, but why not . . . well, Wagner is unwieldy, too.

BD: You could certainly say that.

TH: You know, giants singing, dragons singing . . . it's a whole cycle of that. Oh my god, Wagner. In *The Ring* [*of the Nibelung*] you have the Rhine Maidens singing underwater, enormous scene changes, and gigantic opera singers in harnesses being lifted up and down.

BD: That is pretty unwieldy, I agree.

TH: So nobody thought those things could be done, and the country was bankrupt, too. It served as one of the reasons why King Ludwig II's political opponents labeled him mad, so they could get rid of him. And they labeled him mad for a number of reasons, but one of which was because he went bankrupt over funding Wagner's operas, until Wagner was literally chased out of Bavaria by angry creditors. But look what he did: he changed the world. And for me, it's only a matter of time before Native artists get the same treatment as well. You see operas at the Metropolitan Opera, or in Vienna, Toronto, or Montreal, with eighty singers on stage, and sixty people in the orchestra. One hundred and forty artists being paid. And [in *Rose*] I'm only asking for twenty-seven. Twenty-two actors and five musicians, that's all. That's nothing. And it's only a matter of time until we break through that next ceiling, and it becomes ordinary human theatre as opposed to us as circus acts.

BD: It would be high time indeed. And I think the success of Native theatre so far confirms that development, if you consider what's been done over the past twenty years.

TH: Yes, and it's still very young.

BD: Your first international experience was the production of *The Rez Sisters* at the Edinburgh Festival in 1988. What were your feelings about that? Were you wondering about the reception overseas?

TH: I didn't worry about it at all. It was just exciting to go to the Edinburgh Festival, and being in Edinburgh, which I'd never seen before. So it was exciting. It was fun. I thought: "we're going to put on a show in Edinburgh!" And we all had a wonderful time.

BD: In terms of the inter- or transnational reception of theatre, the language plays a big role, of course. Obviously, that was no problem in Edinburgh; but I can imagine it posed a different challenge in Japan. So, on the practical side, you'd need translators, and Japanese actors . . .

TH: Yes, all of that. But it worked. The performance was incredible. One of the best productions I've ever seen of my plays was in Tokyo. Wonderful.

BD: So if you had to choose your favorite place, internationally, where your work was performed, that would be Japan?

TH: Yes, probably Tokyo.

BD: In terms of the productions of your plays in Canada, is there a difference between the reception of your plays on reserves and in other places?

TH: It's hard to describe. I guess my work is better received in Native communities because it's a reflection of them. It's a reflection of their reality, and most people are very proud of it. But obviously, the majority of my plays are performed in cities, because most theatre is performed in the cities. Theatre is a city thing.

BD: That's similar in the United States, of course. A lot of Native plays are performed in New York, obviously, Chicago, St. Paul, Seattle, and Los Angeles, but there are also successful theatre companies in other areas, such as the Thunderbird Theatre in Lawrence, Kansas, or the Tulsa Indian Actors Workshop in Oklahoma. Has your work been performed on your home reserve, in Brochet, Manitoba?

TH: No, it's too far away. Too small, and too remote, you know.

BD: What's the population?

TH: Oh, just one hundred.

BD: Do you still go back home sometimes?

TH: Oh yeah, every summer to see my family. I should say that was when my parents were still alive, but they are dead now. Which reminds me—I noticed the dedication in your book [*Native North American Theater in a Global Age*, which is dedicated to Mathilde Däwes]—who is that?

BD: That was my grandmother, the most amazing woman I ever knew. She passed away three years ago [in 2005].

TH: I noticed she was fairly old when she died.

BD: That's true—she was ninety-nine years old. She lived through almost the entire twentieth century.

TH: We just went to Lima for Patty's [Patricia Cano's] grandmother's twenty-second birthday.

BD: The . . . twenty-second?

TH: Yes, she was born on February 29th. [*laughter*].

BD: Do tell me more about your cooperation with Patty. You've been working together for quite a long time. How did you meet?

TH: I met her as a child. The house where her family lives is still there, and up until eight years ago, my partner's

sister lived just down the street from them. And they
have three daughters about her age, and a son. And my
sister-in-law's family has children the same age, so they
were playmates, because they lived on the same street.
I met Patty there, when she was six. And then we lost
touch. And fifteen years later, I was teaching at the University of Toronto, and she was a student. She happened
to be in one of my classes. And then, at the University
College Drama Program [UCDP], where I was teaching,
she played in an audition.

BD: So how long have you been doing tours together?

TH: For seven years.

BD: That's a long time!

TH: Yes, but we've only done about forty shows in total.
We do about six or seven per year. So in New York terms,
in Broadway terms, we'd still be in preview.

BD: Well, I look forward to the show tomorrow night! It
will be amazing to see Patty [who also played Emily Dic-
tionary in the UCDP production of *Rose* in 2000] perform
the songs from *Rose*. Would you also like to see another
full production of the play sometime?

TH: That is out of my power. Producers do that. And good
ones are hard to find. Just like directors: good directors
are hard to find. But I don't worry about it. In fact, I'm
happy with a lot of the success that I had, but a little bit
of me is scared of more. I don't really want any more.
I'm happy maintaining this level. I don't like being recognized, and I'm tired of seeing my name in print. I think
it's time for others to get the spotlight. That's quite the
way how I feel. I just love my life way too much now,
and I don't want to jeopardize it. Famous people have
to hide all the time.

BD: True—you couldn't even go to the bakery anymore.
So do you still get recognized in the streets?

TH: I do. Not when I'm in Europe, but I mean I don't live
in Canada for a number of reasons, and that's one of
them. One of the scenes that made us decide to move
to Southern France was when I was standing at a urinal

in Toronto, at a bar downtown, and the door behind me
went open at one point, and I heard a couple of guys
passing by in the hallway, and one very loud voice said:
"Look, there's Tomson Highway taking a piss." And I don't
want any more of that. Just to be watched peeing, you
know. I had to move away.

BD: That's awful indeed. But don't be too confident: after
your shows here, you'll have a huge crowd of fans in Germany, too. They might follow you around . . . [*laughter*].

Let me ask you about *Ernestine Shuswap Gets Her Trout*
(2004), which is very different from the other plays you
wrote, and it addresses history much more openly.

TH: That was a commission by people from Kamloops
[a joint commission by Western Canada Theatre and the
Secwepemc Cultural Education Society], and they had a
very specific project in mind, so they gave me this document [the Laurier Memorial, a document dictated by the
political leaders of the Shuswap, Okanagan, and Thompson Nations to a Scottish secretary, James A. Teit] and
asked me to dramatize it, and I couldn't. So I turned it
on its head and talked about the women who were not in
the document. The document very much has to do with
Native chiefs presenting a set of grievances to Wilfrid
Laurier, who was prime minister of Canada, and it's a very
important document. But I couldn't find a way of doing
that. They sent me a newsletter from that reserve, the
Kamloops Indian Reserve, which is just across the river
from Kamloops, British Columbia. And in that newsletter
were these pictures of old Shuswap women, and I just
loved them. I wanted to do their life stories, so that's
how I started writing about the wives of the chiefs. And
the Laurier Memorial is very dry; it's like a manifesto, a
political document where the chiefs moan and groan to
the prime minister about what has happened to them
and their land being taken away from them. But I don't
like to complain. So finally I put the body of the text into
the play in the best way that I knew how to.[3] But that's
not the text I care about. Without wanting to insult the
people who commissioned me to do it, what I've always
cared about in my life is not the specifics of this situation.

The specifics of this situation should be embraced and well told, but what's important to me is the universal element in that story. That's what I really care about. And the universal question that I ask in that play is: Why are there no women in the picture? Who prepared that meal [for the political visitors], and who set the table, and worked in the background? Whoever that is, they are never recognized, their contribution to human history is never given recognition. They have never been thanked. And that's the story I wanted to tell, that's what the play is about.

BD: As a final question on the genre of drama: what is your perspective on the more recent developments of Native theatre in Canada? What are its challenges and its possibilities for the coming years?

TH: Well, I wish it the best. I've made my contribution. Let me look at it as a relay race. You know, it's the responsibility of not just one person but of an entire community. And we all take our turns carrying the baton in the relay race, and you take the baton and you run as fast as you can, and as well as you can, and then you pass the baton on. We certainly have a much larger number of Native playwrights now than ever existed before, and that is one thing I hope I have contributed to: the development of a whole generation of Native playwrights.

BD: So there is reason for optimism.

TH: Absolutely.

BD: You also said that you were currently writing a new novel. What will it be about, and what other projects are you working on in the near future?

TH: That's about it, in terms of creative projects. Maybe some new songs this winter, one song at a time, but that doesn't take much time at all. It's more like a hobby. One song every two weeks, so it doesn't take much work. And the novel is, like all of my work, about women and the unjust distribution of power in this society, and the need to readdress that question, to rebalance that gender imbalance. As all my work, it's about the return of God as a woman. It's about what I see happening out there, in society as a whole: the slow death of a male god.

BD: In conclusion, I should apologize for this interview, since you said you were so tired of being interviewed all the time, so thank you all the more. I appreciate this very much. And I'm awfully sorry.

TH: [*laughs*] Well, honestly—and I can't lie to you. But I appreciate your work, too, very much.

Notes

1. On June 11, 2008, Canadian prime minister Stephen Harper apologized to former students of Indian residential schools, saying that "The burden of this experience has been on your shoulders for far too long. The burden is properly ours as a government, and as a country. There is no place in Canada for the attitudes that inspired the Indian residential schools system to ever again prevail." Tomson Highway and his brother René attended the Guy Hill Indian Residential School in the 1950s; an experience which he wove into his novel, *Kiss of the Fur Queen*.

2. René Highway died of AIDS in 1990, just two and a half weeks short of his thirty-sixth birthday. Tomson Highway explains that René "used to count the days to his birthday by tapping his chest with one forefinger, the only thing that he could move on his entire body during the fourth and third last weeks of his life, the only thing that moved, at the end, being his heart until that, too, finally stopped."

3. At the end of *Ernestine Shuswap Gets Her Trout*, audience members are handed a copy of the Laurier Memorial as they leave the theatre.

Part III

Representations of History

Critical Perspectives

10

Voices of Cultural Memory

Enacting History in
Recent Native Canadian Drama

Marc Maufort

The dramatization of the painful history of colonization, oppression, genocide and its aftermath, constitutes a salient feature of recent Native dramaturgies on the Canadian stage.[1] Rewriting history/ies from the perspective of previously marginalized constituencies is a staple characteristic of postmodern and postcolonial[2] literature, a phenomenon that has been abundantly documented in fiction.[3] However, the fraught issue of historiography is equally important in Canadian drama, as evident for instance in the historical plays of Sharon Pollock, most notably *Blood Relations*.[4] Further, over the past three decades or so, prominent Native Canadian playwrights such as Tomson Highway, Daniel David Moses, and Drew Hayden Taylor, to cite but a few examples, have consistently examined the legacy of history in their varied indigenous voices. As much as defining what it means to be "Native," or indeed determining what "Native drama" exactly consists of, would prove an impossible task, it seems futile to try to homogenize Native historiography, a tendency too often perceptible in Western criticism. In the same way as Drew Hayden Taylor has voiced his opposition to the widespread concept that Native plays should necessarily stage a Trickster, the multiple formulations of Native historiography should be acknowledged (Taylor 2003, 28). The danger of ghettoizing Native historiography recalls the issue of Native authenticity, which, as Alan Filewod has rightly pointed out, exists primarily as a nostalgia for a lost innocence in the gaze of Western critics; it is a construct

159

that betrays a reinscription of hegemonic patterns of thought (File-wod 1994, 364–65). In an attempt to evade this pitfall, then, these pages will seek to illustrate the complexity of Native reenactments of history on the stage, indeed the tricksterish evanescence of this process, in focusing on three significant case studies (plays by Shirley Cheechoo, Tomson Highway, and Marie Clements), especially selected for their contrasting aesthetics. These plays shed considerable light on the ways in which Native playwrights reinscribe cultural memory in their works in an age of transition.

Further, as I shall demonstrate, the works examined in this essay articulate a dramatic aesthetic akin to magic realism. The history of magic realism dates back to the beginning of the twentieth century. In the course of the century it was used to designate various aesthetic forms, including German post-expressionist realism in the twenties, Spanish American marvelous realism, and Dutch fictional realism in the fifties (Zamora and Faris 1995, 1–11). In its later postcolonial phase, it can be regarded as a literary movement intent on rejecting binary forms of Western rationalist perception, that is, the clear distinction between ordinary reality and the surreal or indeed the supernatural. As Stephen Slemon has argued, magic realism can be decoded as a (post)colonial manifestation of the "Other" through a subversion of dominant aesthetic patterns (Slemon 1995, 407–26). As a number of postcolonial critics have pointed out, the term "magic realism" remains highly problematic for various reasons, not least of which are its Eurocentric underpinnings. Indeed, its oxymoronic nature could seem to foreground the supremacy of mimetic representation in a Western sense. How could it, therefore, justifiably be applied to the literary production of Native cultures, in which the "magic," being contiguous with reality, can hardly be distinguished at all from ordinary life? I would argue that the ontological difference of the status of "magic" in European and Native cultures does not entirely invalidate the use of this concept. First, one should bear in mind the high level of hybridity of Native postcolonial literatures, which freely blend Western and indigenous aesthetic elements.[5] In addition, the Native texts under scrutiny in this essay do not entirely conflate the ordinary and the supernatural realms of existence, despite their indisputable contiguity. In the plays I shall be looking at, the world of Native legends clearly intrudes upon secular reality in unexpected moments of epiphanic revelation.

Second, the concept of "magic realism" still meets with resistance among scholars who exclusively link it with South American literatures. However, the recent work of Zamora and Faris, among others, has shown that the magic realist aesthetic pervades post-colonial literatures in English (Zamora and Faris 1995, 163–263). In addition, some theatre practitioners still only reluctantly accept the validity of the concept, as they fail to perceive the distinction between expressionism and magic realism. I would argue that "expressionism," a term favored in theatre circles, could be fruitfully substituted by "magic realism" in postcolonial contexts. Indeed, magic realism designates an aesthetic whose very fluidity reflects the hybrid postcolonial condition to a larger extent than expressionism did, at least in its classic manifestations. The violent expressionistic projection, indeed concretizations of the *Ich* of the protagonist in the stage set or design, through a Christ-like *Stationen*-drama,[6] does not entirely apply, in its messianic and psychological overtones, to the more collective, societal or mythical, concerns expressed by the magic realism of Native literatures. Further, the German expressionism of the beginning of the twentieth century usually presupposes a high level of abstraction differing from the sporadic hybrid blend of realism and antirealism so typical of magic realism.[7]

These problematic aspects might tempt one to replace the Western concept of "magic realism" with terms coined by Native artists themselves. One case in point is Australian novelist Mudrooroo's definition of "Aboriginal realism" as a literary mode apparently predicated on the same codes of referentiality as Euro-American dramatic realism, but which subverts them through reminders of the oppressed culture such as the use of myth, distortion, abstraction, transformations, storytelling, and special sound effects. Thus Mudrooroo writes: "Aboriginal realism expands European realism by taking in certain supernatural aspects, characters and situations found in Aboriginal storytelling" (qtd. in Balme 1999, 153). If one turns to North America, Diane Glancy's own articulation of Native dramatic realism as "Imaginative realism" or "Realized improbabilities" in *American Gypsy* (Glancy 2002, 201) might prove useful alternatives. However, these terms remain somewhat problematic, mostly through their vagueness, a flaw that in my view can only add to the theoretical confusion. Despite its shortcomings and contentious nature, then, I have chosen to retain the use of the concept of "magic realism" in this essay, mostly for want of a clearly better term. The challenge for a Western critic such as myself is therefore to remain strongly aware of the provisional and arbitrary nature of one's terminology, while refusing to adhere to the assumption that "magic realism" merely constitutes a downgraded version of the superior form of unadulterated Western realism.

Numerous variants of magic realism exist in different contexts, about which countless theoretical models have been developed over the years. As I have mentioned elsewhere, I personally favor Jeanne Delbaere's definition of the concept, particularly for its nuanced fluidity (Delbaere 1995, 249–63; Maufort 2003, 22–25). Like Delbaere, I regard magic realism as an aesthetic translating in fiction or, in this particular context, on the stage, the ephemeral and uncanny fusion of apparently irreconcilable objects, ideas, or situations, which thus rejects the basic Western rational dichotomy between reality and the supernatural. Magic realism, often found only sporadically in plays or in novels, seeks to express the sudden and fleeting transgression of the otherwise water-tight boundaries between the real and the supernatural. Delbaere articulates three variants of magic realism, all found to some extent in the plays discussed in this essay. In what Delbaere terms "psychic realism," a variant on magic realism, the "magic" constitutes "almost always a reification of the hero's inner conflict" (1995, 251). This form of magic realism records the character's fissured vision of the real. Delbaere's second subcategory defines a form of "grotesque realism," which tends to further distort and amplify reality. Delbaere suggests that "grotesque realism" be used "for any sort of hyperbolic distortion that creates a sense of strangeness through the confusion or interpenetration of different realms like animate/inanimate or human/animal" (1995, 256). A third subcategory, which Delbaere terms "mythic realism," emanates from the supernatural features of the environment itself rather than from the character's psyche (252–53). Magic realism, whose role consists in showing the "interface between realms," constitutes a prominent feature of the historiographic project of the works considered in this essay.

I. *Path with No Moccasins*

My first example, Shirley Cheechoo's monologue play, *Path with No Moccasins*, addresses a specific historical problem, that is, that of the residential school and its concomitant oppression of Native children by white teachers. This monologue-like play was premiered at Lakeview Public School, West Bay First Nation, Manitoulin Island, in 1991. Conceived as a semi-autobiographical account of Cheechoo's early life, it conflates the historical with the personal. Marked by a confessional and lyrical style, this play foregrounds the protagonist's painful journey toward self-discovery. As a result, the monologue-like structure of this work focuses our attention onto the Native body of the main protagonist, highlighting the woes of a specific historical experience: the adoption of Aboriginal children into white families.[8]

Path with No Moccasins opens with a searing image of entrapment as "Shirley [is] locked in a room at the residential school" (1991, 9). At the outset, as a little girl, Shirley suffers deeply from the fracture of her family unit, her brother having been sent to another residential school. The memory of her grandmother, symbolized by the moon, offers some consolation: "When the moon comes into my room, it's a ball of smoke surrounding me. . . . Inside it's cold, but I don't care. I can find my feather blanket that my grandmother gave me. It comes with the moon" (9). The special light of the moon, associated with the grandmother, creates a form of psychic magic realism emanating from the character's thoughts. Cheechoo's aesthetic thus departs from conventional stage realism. The process of assimilation into white society forces Shirley to learn how to write and speak English, although she misses the Cree language, associated with the lost mother figure. The Cree language nevertheless resurfaces from time to time, notably when Shirley sings a lullaby to herself. Memories of her mother also crop up: "The smell of smoke tanning the moosehides, my mother's rough chapped hands work day and night. Her face never changes. She's not an angry woman. I wonder if she knows what I go through at school" (19). This first part then powerfully articulates a crisis of identity.

Part 2 further explores this sense of alienation, expressed through Shirley's poignant interrogation: "Who am I?" (31). The chorus eventually reinforces the motif of the quest for a home: "No one knows how to get home too" (32). This section of the play equates the crisis of identity with the evils of drinking, which further destabilize Native families. Shirley now speaks to an imaginary bottle, to which she turns for comfort in her loneliness: "My true friend. You who takes away the sins of the world. . . . My bottle is my friend, you protect me like I'm your baby" (23–24). Images of suicide abound in this part of the play, as a result of heavy drinking. As Shirley is aware, the bottle "play(s) tricks on us, I know [it does]" (26). Shirley remembers her uncle and her father abusing their wives after drinking excessively. Further, one of Shirley's friends died from alcohol abuse. Images of rape also resurface in Shirley's memory: "They pulled me off the bike, dragged me into the ditch. They took my clothes off. They didn't rip at them. I didn't fight back. I recognized all their fuckin faces. It seems like

no matter how old I am, someone always wants to do this to me"
(30). By metaphorical extension, this rape equates the oppression
of Native culture by white society.

Part 3, which marks a transition toward the epiphanic conclusion, amplifies the magic realist mood of the earlier sections. Shirley,
who is now twenty-eight and has ceased to drink in the hope of finding who she is, talks to the water spirits: "Water spirits of the black
rocks" (34). She invokes the Native spirits in order to retrieve her
cultural roots: "Why won't you show me a sign?" (35). After reporting
she had a dreadful vision of herself being shot, she delivers a song
in Cree, a translation for which is provided in a footnote. In the song,
she implores the help of her grandparents in her quest. She does not
want to become "a wandering spirit walking with holes in my moccasins with no place to go and mend them" (37). The moccasins thus
symbolize Native identity. She recounts a dream of mutilation, whose
grotesque overtones conjure up a magic realist atmosphere: "In a
dream I was having an operation, and I wasn't quite asleep . . . the
doctor said 'first the clitoris'. . . . I screamed from pain, but they
can't seem to hear me. Then 'the tubes' he said. . . . I felt a sharp
pain and out came this glass ball from my womb" (37). This image
suggests the erasure of her female identity by white society. Further,
she blames the spirits of the water for taking her father away, leaving
her alone on a road that seems "to have no end" (39). The dream she
evokes at the very end of part 3 suggests a glimmer of hope, especially in view of her love for her husband Blake and her son Nano:

> I dreamt that small layers of steel were growing all over
> my body. There were two steel blades growing out of
> my mouth, pushing my mouth apart. I was able to pull
> them out and when I did this the rest of the blades disap-
> peared. . . . Nano . . . put his hand into his pocket and
> showed me a steel blade, just like the ones that were
> growing in my body. (40)

The uncanny overtones of this dream evoke Delbaere's notion of
grotesque magic realism. They suggest that Shirley and her offspring
can free themselves from the wounding impact of white society, by
removing its "steel blades."

Part 4 further amplifies the magic realist aesthetic of the work,
while moving toward a positive outcome. It takes place at Dreamer's
Rock, a place known in Native mythology to inspire visions. The
scene occurs on August 17, 1987. Shirley invokes the soul of her
father, in an effort to accept his death. She initiates a journey of

healing, which she associates with the color red. Incidentally, these positive connotations can be interpreted as a rewriting of traditional Western color codes, which typically liken the color red with negative images, such as blood, murder, and death. Shirley is trying to reconnect with her past and with her future life, in a process of successful mourning for her father: "Today's supposed to be a powerful day for making connections. Today the planets align" (43). This speech qualifies as an instance of mythic magic realism, which conflates the natural with the world of Native mythology: Shirley asserts the power of Nanabush, the Native Trickster, over her life. She describes Nanabush as a universal element/force: "Nanabush, to me, is the trickster in everybody. He's half-spirit and half-human . . . and we are half-human and half-spirit" (44). This acknowledgment of her hybrid instincts, of her Native culture, brings Shirley to some form of reawakening: "Those sleeping Indian children taking their path with no moccasins slowly awake. I am one of them" (45). In her road toward reconnection, Cheechoo thus reasserts her link with the spirits of her ancestors. The Native environment itself reflects this sense of rebirth: "*The sun rises. The wind whistles and the trees whisper and a hole appears in the sky. A perfect circle forms around the rock. The sky looks like waves of water*" (45). While celebrating in a dance of life, she "see[s] the spirits" (46). She suggests that we should all weave a "starblanket full of healing colors made by us with no judgement of the past" (47). Upon which, she manages to free herself from the painful memory of her father. During her final gesture of reconnection with the spiritual world, the sound of falling rain suggests renaissance and fertility (48). In a traditional Native ritual, she "covers herself with the starblanket and she turns to the four directions. I'm going to be able to move towards my healing . . . with no future, no past, just a beginning. . . . it's all up to me" (48). This epiphanic conclusion affirms the possibility, on a personal level, of escaping the woes of history. On a purely formal level, one could argue that the entire play evades rigid Western codes of stage naturalism, especially through its monologue-like structure and its reliance on magic realism. Through its weaving together of fragmented stories, the play could also be equated to a Native starblanket, a further sign of its aesthetic emancipation.

II. *Ernestine Shuswap Gets Her Trout*

Tomson Highway literally revolutionized Native Canadian drama in the 1980s with two highly successful plays, *The Rez Sisters* and *Dry*

Lips Oughta Move to Kapuskasing, in which Nanabush, the Trickster, figures prominently.[9] In his recent *Ernestine Shuswap Gets Her Trout*, Tomson Highway develops a slightly different kind of dramaturgy, one that helps him to reconsider how we should look at Native history. The play was premiered at the Sagebrush Theatre, Western Canada Theatre, Kamloops, British Columbia, in 2004.[10] It hinges on a single historical moment: on the occasion of his visit to Kamloops in 1910, Prime Minister Wilfrid Laurier heard the complaints of fourteen chiefs of the Thompson River basin about the confiscation of their fishing rights. Like Cheechoo, Highway reinvents historical reality in a highly idiosyncratic aesthetic, which calls to mind magic realism. The whole play can be decoded as taking place within the consciousness of the four female protagonists, Ernestine Shuswap, Isabel Thompson, Annabelle Okanagan, and Delilah Rose Johnson. The musical structure of the play is manifest from its very subtitle, which describes the work as "a 'string quartet' for four female actors" and undoubtedly constitutes a reminiscence of Highway's own educational background in Western classical music. In other words, this play echoes the notions of cultural hybridity, as related to historiography, articulated by Homi K. Bhabha in *The Location of Culture*.

Indeed, Bhabha envisions hybridity or "in-betweenness" as a flexible pattern of reciprocal cultural exchange between colonized and colonizer: "Hybridity . . . unsettles the mimetic or narcissistic demands of colonial power but re-implicates its identifications in strategies of subversion that turn the gaze of the discriminated back upon the eye of power" (Bhabha 1994, 112). Further, the colonized subject resorts to mimicry, an affect of hybridity (Bhabha 1994, 120), to unsettle the artistic domination of Western dramatic realism. This use of mimicry is clearly subversive and creates an ambivalent, hybrid "Third Space" (Bhabha 1994, 36). It projects a desire for a "reformed, recognizable Other, as a subject of difference that is almost the same, but not quite. . . . the discourse of mimicry is constructed around an ambivalence; . . . mimicry emerges as the representation of a difference that is itself a process of disavowal. Mimicry . . . poses an immanent threat to both 'normalized' knowledges and disciplinary powers" (Bhabha 1994, 86). Bhabha's celebration of hybridity and mimicry characterizes Tomson Highway's historiographic project in this work.

The Trickster spirit is manifest only in an indirect way in this play, not in the very form of the Nanabush, but through the "tricksterish" aspect of Highway's use of language itself. In fact, none of the female characters speak English. Conceived as a mere translation tool, the play's English reproduces typically Native images and metaphors, thus revealing the subtle spirit of resistance of an oppressed culture:

> . . . the Native people of the Thompson River valley . . . spoke Shuswap, Okanagan, Thompson . . . and other Native languages. In this play, they speak Shuswap, a tongue that works according to principles, and impulses, different entirely from those that underlie, that "motor," the English language. For instance, because the principle that "motors" the Shuswap language is, in essence, a "laughing deity" (i.e. the trickster), it is hysterical, comic to the point where its "spill-over" into horrifying tragedy is a thing quite normal, utterly organic. That is to say, as in most languages of Native North America . . . , the "laughing god" becomes a "crying god" becomes a "laughing god," all in one swift impulse. (2005a, 11)

The tricksterish character of this work lies in the extreme flexibility of its language and in the rejection of clear-cut binaries between comedy and tragedy. In a spirit calling to mind Bhabha's theories, this tricksterish use of language bespeaks the hybrid nature of the entire play.

The work's prologue reinforces this hybrid pattern. It consists of three monologues addressed to the moon, a feature reminiscent of Cheechoo's play, over which we hear *"the gurgle of a river,"* a sign of the power of Nature. In this case, the river evokes the special link uniting Natives to Nature. In contrast the soundtrack "bleeds," in Highway's very words, the low notes of Bach's cello music. Further, the prologue is meant to establish *"an atmosphere of ominous foreboding and . . . the counterpoint of comedy and tragedy"* (13). Highway further comments:

> . . . these faces look like masks in a Greek tragedy. In fact, that is what their voices should sound like as well, like those in a play by Euripides, that is, a mesmerizing weave of chant and prayer. The point here being: though, at first glance, this may appear to be a very funny play, right from the start, there are undercurrents of darkness, of horrifying tragedy. (13)

This hybrid blend of Western and non-Western elements, of comedy and tragedy, characterizes the play's elusive structure, which demonstrates affinities with Bhabha's theories. While Ernestine announces her desire to secure a gigantic rainbow trout, Isabel and Annabelle lament the loss of Native fishing rights, a metaphor for the wider colonial enterprise.

Act 1 further displays musical overtones, the characters' *"promenade increasingly resembling a syncopated dance, a fractured tango"* (18). The initial dialogue between Isabel and Annabelle provides background information about the reasons for the prime minister's visit, alluding again to the deprivation of fishing rights. It also indicates that a big meal will have to be prepared in his honor. Ernestine, who joins them later on, announces that she wants to cook a big trout for the occasion. The women appreciate the Quebecois prime minister because, being a Catholic like them, they think he might help them in their conflict with the local Protestant authorities. In the background of this conversation, Delilah Rose Johnson is constantly seen sewing away feverishly to the music of Bach's cello suite. She utters a monologue, revealing that she is on the edge of madness, perhaps even schizophrenia. She recounts the central tragic story of the play, that is, her marriage with the son of the Protestant leader who enforced the restriction of Native fishing rights. Her uncomfortable position of in-betweenness, interracial and cross-religious, results from her falling in love with a cowboy named Boy Johnson:

> Why? Because he was different, because he was special, because he liked . . . classical music, yes, that's what he called this curious music I still don't understand . . . Somehow, says Billy Boy to me, that music—that's the only thing that could assuage the pain, the unbearable pain of feeling . . . out of place, of not belonging. (47)

This passage underlines the throes of the colonial experience for both whites and Natives. While Boy Johnson suffers from his exile, Delilah falls in love with the beauty of European culture. She then experiences what W.E.B. Du Bois termed "double-consciousness" in *The Souls of Black Folk*, while referring to the predicament of African Americans in a white society: "It is a peculiar sensation, this double-consciousness, this sense of always looking at one's self through the eyes of others . . ." (Du Bois 1964, 45). Delilah's desire to assimilate is never fulfilled, the more so as the boy is Protestant: "An Indian girl does *not* fall in love with, much less marry, a white boy. . . . A Roman Catholic does *not* marry, or love, a Protestant" (48, emphasis in original). Her problematic pregnancy offers concrete evidence of her hybridity. The concluding moments of act 1 again focus on Delilah who resembles a *"goddess emerging from a river"*—the river being actually symbolized by her sewed tablecloth (56). This touch of mythic magic realism, blending the real and the mythological, finds echoes in the mournful cello sound. It also recurs in the shadows of the other women, who look *"like spirits—the land is talking, through them"* (56). Thus, the conclusion of act 1 asserts the validity of a Shuswap worldview.

The tragicomic act 2, in its grotesque magic realism, prolongs the women's complaints about various sorts of rights being confiscated, including the right to speak Native languages. In a spirit of farce, the women then start neighing. A background recitation of the memorial presented by the Natives to the prime minister, which we hear in English, is supposed to be delivered in horse language. Ernestine subsequently evokes an argument between Natives and whites including the murder of two men, Franklin Coyote and Don Jenkins Sr. Her speech definitely contains magic realist overtones, as in the night mist, one can often detect the eyes of the dead men. This blend of the real and the supernatural is reenacted in front of us, as *"we see the 'eyes' just described, two pairs of them, like lamps, hovering in the air, on the backdrop, as in a mist"* (68). Ernestine counterpoints this gloomy image with her horse language recitation of the memorial addressed to the prime minister and *"the speech itself ends up sounding like a funky piece of music . . ."* (74). Annabelle and Isabel perform movements that transform into a tango dance accompanying the speech. Once again, this contrast testifies to the hybridity of the play's structure.

The next focus, endowed with tragic overtones, lies on Delilah, who now *"looks like a cross between a bride and a statue of the Blessed Virgin Mary"* (77). This image suggests the uncomfortable cultural in-betweenness of the protagonist. Again in a movement of oscillation, Ernestine appears on the bottom of the river, in search of the trout her inefficient husband seems to be unable to catch for her. This conjures up a magic realist atmosphere, which pervades the play until the very end: *"Ernestine is not only on the banks of the Thompson River, she's in it, walking on its bottom as in a dream . . . this dream-like 'aquarium/underwater' visual will hold true for the next two scenes as well . . ."* (78). In contrast, Delilah seems to collapse from a nervous breakdown, during which she starts neighing. Delilah feels self-hatred for bearing a white child in

her womb: "There was a white man in her stomach, a white man
who communed with the devil . . ." (85, emphasis in original). She
then kills her baby with a pair of scissors. In a mythic magic realist
moment, a third pair of eyes, Delilah's, joins the supernatural eyes
of the murdered men we had earlier perceived in the mist.

The next scene provides a striking opposition, in its hybrid
fusion of Native mythology and Christianity. It records the actual
meeting with the prime minister, which looks both like "*a funeral
and a banquet*" (87). Like a "priestess in a ritual" (88), Ernestine
triumphantly serves the prime minister her trout. Nonetheless, the
ghost of dead Delilah appears as the scene starts looking like the
Last Supper, the prime minister being likened to Christ and the
chiefs to the apostles. Ernestine concludes the play in reasserting
female emancipation, and, by metaphorical extension, the spirit of
Native endurance: she confesses she caught the trout with her own
sharp teeth (90). The stage directions indicate a hybrid blend of a
river sound, "*the voice of a land*" (90), and Beethoven's cello sonata,
Opus 69. Metaphorically, it is as if Ernestine had managed to accept
the hybridity Delilah could not assume, a positive message for the
future of Native communities. Reverting to the historical framework
of the play, Highway stipulates that audience members receive a
copy of "The Laurier Memorial" as they leave the theatre (91).

All in all, in this chamber music-like play, Highway offers a
highly personal treatment of a forgotten incident of Canadian history, while foregrounding the wealth of Native identity. His tricksterish aesthetic resorts to magic realism and to the hysterically
farcical in order to assert the strength of Native identities, in their
hybrid configurations.

III. *Burning Vision*

Burning Vision, by British Columbia Métis playwright Marie Clements, certainly constitutes the most experimental play dealt with
in this essay. It was premiered at the Firehall Arts Centre in Vancouver in 2002. Focusing on historical events that took place in the
Northwest Territories in the late nineteenth century and throughout
the twentieth century, the play offers us a glimpse of yet another
historical reality of Canada. It recounts the economic exploitation of
radium ore at the expense of the health of Dene Indians. While this
substance was primarily meant to cure cancer, it ironically served

to destroy Hiroshima and Nagasaki. This play links together events that took place in nineteenth-century Dene communities, in contemporary North America, as well as in Japan. The first pages of the published version of the play provide a map of the Great North, on which various events are chronologically listed in small inserts. This distortion and expansion of conventional time-space coordinates indicates Clements's wish to redefine the very boundaries of what constitutes drama. Even the characters are only metaphorically related. The play could be decoded as a vast oratorio for voices, an idiosyncratic technique that admirably serves Clements's questioning of official and imperialistic discourses of history.

The musical structure of the play is reinforced by its division into four "movements," which resonate with the increasingly intensifying clicks of radioactivity. The entire play seems to take place in a wasted landscape, more often than not in a hole, from which uranium can presumably be extracted. Metaphorically, one could argue that Clements engages in a process of historical excavation. Likewise, one could suggest that the entire play follows the pattern of "radio waves" (Clements 2003, 19). Movement 1, "The Frequency of Discovery," offers a kaleidoscopic presentation of the characters. It first focuses on a little Indian boy, "scared and huddled in the darkness of the centre of the earth" (20), symbolizing uranium itself. He voices how uranium is misappropriated by materialistic people: "It is only a matter of time . . . before someone discovers you and claims you for themselves. Claims that you are you because they found you" (20). Without any transition, Clements focuses on the LaBine brothers, who explored the North in search of uranium, of black rock, in the 1930s. We then discover a Native Widow, whose Dene husband worked as an ore carrier. A young Métis girl, Rose, is subsequently introduced. She regrets the disappearance of her Native mother and embarks on a quest for roots. She is contrasted to Koji, the Japanese fisherman, killed during the Nagasaki bombing. The latter is counterpointed by the Fat Man, a dummy used by Americans to test nuclear bombs on the continent, who embodies materialistic American values.

In a first psychic magic realist moment, taking place either in a dream or in memory, Koji sees his grandmother walking in front of him. He feels transported onto her shoulders as if through a tunnel of light (31). Their dialogue introduces the theme of the fractured family, which like the very structure of the play, was literally exploded:

KOJI: I am riding on my Grandmother's back. This is what
I see. I am riding on her back yet I am a man. All man
legs and tall arms. I am a man and yet she is carrying
me like I weigh nothing.

THE JAPANESE GRANDMOTHER: If we ever get separated
wait for me here. Wait for me here and I will come for
you. Remember this tree, remember my words. . . . I say,
you will be safe as long as you talk to the cherry tree's
back. (32–33)

She then repeats this sentence in Japanese, a sign of the linguistic
hybridity of the play. Her lines bespeak the necessity of honoring
one's cultural roots, in spite of outside attacks from imperialistic
powers.

Movement 2, "Rare Earth Elements," emphasizes the transcultural dimensions of the play. It first focuses on a miner before
switching to the Widow's complaint about the death of her husband.
A following scene takes place in the Fat Man's dummy house, a
bomb shelter, as he encounters the little boy, who wants "to go
home" (46). Koji then resumes the motif of the wasted landscape,
alluding to the Japanese nuclear bombing: "this charred landscape
of hell" (51). He expresses doubts about his identity, as does Rose
when lamenting the fact that she is a "Métis" (54). Rose recounts
how her father met with her Indian mother: "She saved my father,
the Irishman . . . he was a stowaway at fourteen on a clipper that
traveled the Orient and by accident discovered my mother" (58).
Her concern is echoed by a repetition of the quest of Koji's grandmother: "Koji, it is your grandmother. I have left this note here on
the cherry tree like I used to do when we were separated. I have
left this note to let you know that I am still looking for you" (59).

Movement 3, "Waterways," amplifies the wave-like structure
of the play: "The movement of scenes through, under, and over
dangerous waters. Worlds swirling in brief currents that throw them
together and then separate" (75). This section focuses on the waterways transportation of ore sacks. In the midst of this realistic passage, the Widow again laments her lost love. She underlines her
fractured identity in a psychic magic realist mode: "This love of
mine remembers the first day I met him like it was yesterday but
not quite yesterday, like it was almost a different life this yesterday. . . . I am in parts this life now hollow so his spirit can pass in

front of me, whispering and drifting like smoke and staying like a shadow" (87). Her confession emphasizes the sense of fragmentation that permeates the entire play. In a subsequent mythic magic realist scene, reminiscent of the world of fairy tales, Koji is transformed into a trout and fished by the sailors transporting the ore on the Canadian waterways: "There was this light in the sky when I was talking to this trout and then I was flying and I landed on a branch and then I tried to grab a loaf of bread then and I was swimming and . . ." (89). He subsequently meets Rose, as if their respective hybrid and diasporic identities united them. Koji rearticulates the theme of the quest for self: "I want to be" (94), before kissing Rose.

Movement 4, "Radar Echoes," constitutes the most obviously magic realist of all sections, to which all the threads of the plot converge: *The waves of radar getting closer to the heart of everything. The visions, the bombing, the burning. . . . The sound of worlds, and hearts beating, truths colliding and the tunnels of internal time digging deeper"* (102). The Sahtu Dene See-er, a kind of shaman, plays a major role in this fourth movement when he reveals his vision of doom, which occurred in the late 1880s: "I told them I sang many things and in the singing I saw the future, and I was disturbed. . . . In the singing I felt they would hurt my people. . . . I sang this strange vision of people going into a big hole in the ground—strange people, not Dene. Their skin was white. Strange" (104–06). The See-er felt apparently at a loss on how to interpret his vision. In it, matter extracted from the earth rose in the sky and then burned, an explicit allusion to the Japanese bombing. His account of his vision is interrupted by a scene in which Rose, now pregnant, sees some hope for the future in the hybridity of her child, a motif calling to mind Bhabha's celebration of hybridity: ". . . he can give the world my hope" (114). This statement announces the affirmative stance of the very last moments of the play. This joyful moment is counterpointed by an encounter between a miner and a radium painter, in which they express concerns about cancer. As *"THE MINER pulls her hand tenderly and turns her around in her wedding dress," "THE RADIUM PAINTER turns around. Half her face is missing and her beautiful hair is entirely gone"* (116–17). This horrific vision bespeaks the radioactive danger of uranium and suggests that Northern Canadians involved in this industry suffered from a kind of internal explosion, whereas the Japanese were literally bombed. A few moments later, Clements stages a reenactment of the first nuclear explosion, which penetrates the bodies of all the characters: *"The sound of the bomb falls downward and into their own bodies that glow bright . . . A huge white light whites out their world into blackness"* (118–19). The See-er asserts the link between Dene Indians and Japanese people: "The people they dropped this burning on . . . looked like us, like Dene. . . . This burning vision is not for us now . . . it will come a long time in the future. It will come burning inside" (119–20). The fact that the Japanese grandmother becomes the Dene Widow underlines a sense of transcultural suffering. The Widow releases the soul of her husband into the netherworld: *"Released, her husband begins to walk towards the fire shadows of DENE ore carriers waiting. He disappears into the spirit world"* (121). The Japanese grandmother/Widow is met by Koji, who decides to bring her home, in a gesture of reconciliation and healing. The last moments of the play reinforce this epiphanic sense of healing, as Slavey,[11] Japanese, and Canadian radio announcers use their respective languages to call for a family reunion of all loved ones, a positive coda which reaffirms the transcultural aspect of the play. When Koji concludes: "They hear us, and they are talking back in hope over time," *"cherry blossoms fall"* on the stage, as tokens of reconnection (122).

Clearly, then, in *Burning Vision*, Marie Clements forces us to redefine what a Native play really consists of. Her revisionist project, giving a voice to oppressed people across cultures, broadens the ways in which we conceive of Native historiography and expands the exclusively Native viewpoint of Cheechoo's and Highway's plays. This innovative approach is sustained by her idiosyncratic stage aesthetic, which relies on a blend of magic realism, exhibits an exploded structure evocative of the detonation of the atomic bomb, and further displays the musical shape of a symphony of voices in four movements. Clements's take on history thus amplifies the tricksterish dramaturgies of her predecessors into visionary modes of playwriting.

The historiographic agendas of Cheechoo, Highway, and Clements reveal the complexity of a Native stage aesthetic that resists the colonial gaze of homogenization. That the conclusions of these plays should converge toward an epiphanic reaffirmation of identity and cultural memory in spite of the woes of history contributes to a subtler definition of postcolonial dramaturgies at the dawn of a new millennium. Clearly, these plays are poised in a delicate balance between the search for reconstruction typical of modernism and the rejection of totalizing systems and simplistic binarisms so central in postmodernism's praise of the "ex-centric." This in-betweenness, questioning Western epistemologies and literary categories, testifies to the vitality of Native Canadian dramaturgies and historiographies in the twenty-first century.

Notes

1. For further information about the dramatization of Native history in Canada, the reader may profitably turn to Ric Knowles's *The Theatre of Form and the Production of Meaning: Contemporary Canadian Dramaturgies* (especially the chapter entitled "Replaying History," 1999, 121–58); and to Robert Appleford's edited critical anthology *Aboriginal Drama and Theatre* (2006). Further, Birgit Däwes's *Native North American Theater in a Global Age: Sites of Identity Construction and Transdifference* (2007a) will help the reader linking the related concepts of Native identity and historiography.

2. I have chosen to use the word "postcolonial" without any hyphen, thus following in the wake of Helen Gilbert who favors this spelling in order to emphasize the discourse of opposition against colonization inherent in this term. Thus, this concept is endowed with more than chronological connotations (see Gilbert 1998, 6–7).

3. For general background information on historiographic metafiction, one may wish to consult Linda Hutcheon's *A Poetics of Postmodern: History, Theory, Fiction* (1988, especially chapter 7), and Bill Ashcroft, Gareth Griffiths, and Helen Tiffin's *The Empire Writes Back: Theory and Practice in Post-Colonial Literatures* (1989).

4. Anne F. Nothof's *Sharon Pollock: Essays on Her Works* (2000) offers valuable insights into the work of this noted Canadian playwright.

5. For a more detailed discussion of the related concepts of syncretism and hybridity in postcolonial theatre and drama, the reader should turn to Chris Balme's *Decolonizing the Stage* (1999, 1–24) and Marc Maufort's *Transgressive Itineraries* (2003, 11–25).

6. This phrase designates a type of dramatic structure reproducing, through a series of short scenes, the various stages of Christ's road to the Cross.

7. For a more thorough examination of the aesthetic of expressionism, the reader should consult Mardi Valgemae's *Accelerated Grimace: Expressionism in the American Drama of the 1920s* (1972) and Sherrill E. Grace's *Regression and Apocalypse: Studies in North American Literary Expressionism* (1989, 11–42).

8. For historical information about the adoption of Aboriginal children and the residential school system, the reader is advised to turn to Armand Garnet Ruffo's "A Windigo Tale: Contemporizing and Mythologizing the Residential School Experience" (2005) and Ric Knowles's "The Hearts of Its Women: Rape, Residential Schools, and Re-membering" (2003).

9. I have analyzed these plays in detail in my book *Transgressive Itineraries* (2003, 148–57).

10. For more details about the writing and production of *Ernestine Shuswap Gets Her Trout*, see also the interview with Tomson Highway, chapter 9 in this volume.

11. This term designates one of the Aboriginal groups of which the Dene First Nations are comprised. Slavey communities are located in the northern parts of Canada. They live in the Mackenzie River region, more precisely in the area of the Great Slave Lake.

11

"If you remember me . . ."

Memory and Remembrance in Monique
Mojica's *Birdwoman and the Suffragettes*

Günter Beck

Being one of North America's leading Native actresses, (theatre-) activists, and playwrights, Monique Mojica was guest editor of the *Canadian Theatre Review*'s 1991 special edition on Native American theatre. Her editorial programmatically describes as the most prominent features of Native theatre the possibility to offer "an alternative world-view (one in which many worlds coexist); the possibility of another interpretation of 'historical facts'; the validation of our experiences and our images reflected on stage" (Mojica 1991b, 3).

In her half-hour radio play *Birdwoman and the Suffragettes: A Story of Sacajawea* (1991) Mojica therefore reconstructs the story of Sacajawea from different perspectives, a classic stereotype and a virtually mythical figure of the American collective imagination from the early frontier era.[1] Mojica reclaims the legendary guide of the Lewis and Clark expedition from her incorporation into American popular mythology, either as an "Indian princess" who subscribed to the expansionist goals of America, or as an early crusader for the Suffragette movement.[2] To achieve this, Sacajawea is provided with a voice of her own, and in several differing but intersecting circles the story/stories of her life get/s told by two antithetical groups. One group is comprised of the Grannies and Grandpas of a reservation, and the other confronts us with a turn-of-the-century assemblage of Suffragettes who plan to erect a bronze statue in Portland (Oregon) in honor of the "trusty little Indian guide" (Mojica 1991a, 67) and embodiment of the "Eternal Womanly." Both groups represent two different conceptions of memory and remembrance, and therefore two different conceptions of history. While the Suffragettes' Western "memorializing-as-monumentalizing, which buries the past rather than keeping it alive" (Knowles 2003a, 252) relies on writing and documentation as materialistic approaches to conserve the past, the Native approach keeps memory, and therefore history, alive via storytelling and personal memory. I will show how memory and remembrance work in this play by contrasting the Western and the Native views on history.

Already in *Princess Pocahontas* Mojica presents and simultaneously deconstructs the continuing stereotypes of a construed female "Indianness" that positions Native women between the poles of "noble" and "ignoble savagesse." Here, excessive parodies of the stereotypical images of female indigeneity have an exorcizing effect and meet with several counter-images. The play's different stories "bring to the surface," as Knowles describes

> the brutal materiality of the sexual violence and coercion that underlies the stories of all the women in the play and that underwrites the colonial project. Each of Mojica's principal historical characters is made the object of sexualized exchange between men, each mother's a mixed-blood line, and each is both blamed by her own people and celebrated by the colonizer as the agent (translator, traitor, mistress, and whore) of the destruction of the people. (2003a, 253)

The play's single sequences intertwine, cross, and construct hybrid discourses and thus avoid renewed attempts of heteronomic definitions, that is, by Western feminism: "So many years of trying to fit into feminist shoes. O.K. I'm trying on the shoes; but they're not the same as the shoes in the display case. The shoes I'm trying on must be crafted to fit these wide, square, brown feet" (Mojica 1991a, 58). In *Birdwoman* these "feminist shoes" do not fit, as they, too, present a recent political and economic instrumentalization of Native women, and they, too, tell a falsified version of history. Both plays fall back on historical and documentary material and incorporate it. The dramatis personae list counts the three Suffragettes merely by number and therefore without any real individuality. They are the representatives of a certain mentality that is not limited to the time of the early women's movement, but is expanded until the present day. However, already in the second scene one of them identifies

herself as Eva Emery Dye, Suffragette from Oregon and author of
the historical novel *The Conquest: The True Story of Lewis and Clark*
(1902), that substantially contributed to Sacajawea's transfiguration:

> . . . Dye . . . went looking for a heroine to embody her
> vision of feminism. She wanted a historical figure whose
> life would symbolize the strengthened power of wom-
> en. She found Sacagawea (or Sacajawea) buried in the
> journals of Lewis and Clark . . . and through Dye's work
> Sacagawea became enshrined in American memory as a
> moving force and friend of the whites, leading them in the
> settlement of western North America. (Allen 1998, 215)

The three Suffragettes open and close *Birdwoman* with a mélange of
song and spoken text. Their opening song sounds like the music of a
children's TV program with echoes of marching feet. This "childish"
music contributes to the caricaturing depiction of the Suffragettes,
but the incorporation of the marching feet alludes to their uncondi-
tional, almost military attitudes. In all three scenes the choir's litany
of enumerations of places and objects bearing Sacajawea's name
also "frames" her. First, these are basically geographical locations
in the American Northwest, while the choir enumerates commemo-
rative plaques and statues later before ending on purely artificial
and kitschy expressions of adoration like "a silver service set now
/ on the battleship Wyoming / [or] a Sacajawea mural in Montana"
(Mojica 1991a, 84).

It is a cyclical meshing of beginning, middle, and end points
of a never-ending chain of misinterpretations, and the continual
instrumentalization of Sacajawea, who is enclosed within that circle and therefore remains invisible as a historical person. Cyclical
repetitions are also found in the lyrical passages of Sacajawea's
speech parts, and stand in marked contrast to the prose of the
other characters. In three of her six scenes she refers to her name
"Tsakakawea," given to her by others, and comments upon events
from her personal viewpoint without anyone else paying attention.

Knowles's statement that Mojica's play "[is] eschewing chronological order" (2004, 132) is only partially correct. Though the
plot jumps between the Suffragettes in 1905, the Grannies in 1926,
and the expedition in 1804 without any discernible connections,
the basic structure of *Birdwoman* (as opposed to *Princess Pocahontas*) follows a linear pattern. The Suffragettes are planning a
memorial, chat about Sacajawea's life story, and then inaugurate

the statue. The Grannies seek a name for a newborn baby, come up with "Sacajawea," remember her personally, reminisce about stories, and finally recall an interview with the Suffragettes and the erection of the statue. In their conversations they try to grant Sacajawea her rightful place and role in the community, and finally arrive at the conclusion: "I think I'll find another name for my new great-great-granddaughter. Let Sacajawea rest" (Mojica 1991a, 81). Their commemoration of Sacajawea is inscribed into the landscape but cannot be captured in an artificial rendering like a statue.

Sacajawea's story itself starts with her captivity with the Mandan, the arrival of Lewis and Clark and the hiring of Charbonneau, followed by the dangerous river raft, the adoption of Pomp, and finally ends with the unveiling of the statue in 1905, at which Sacajawea's "presence" is clearly an anachronism.

The characters in the play are well-defined, historical persons like Clark, Lewis, Charbonneau, and Sacajawea whose antagonists are the Suffragettes, who, nevertheless, also partially portray historical role models like Susan B. Anthony, who speaks at the unveiling of the statue. Only the Grannies and Grandpas have a certain timelessness of character but they are also reduced by the exact date of their conversations at tea hour in 1926.

While *Princess Pocahontas*, despite its reference to historical personalities like Pocahontas and Malinche, is generally situated on a more abstract level of historical reckoning, *Birdwoman* is more in line with a conventional "history play" in its concentration on a single person, her epoch, and the aftermath of her life until today. Yet the continuous appropriation of indigenous women by white feminism is criticized and Sacajawea is elevated to be the prototype of all those with a similar fate: "*Dedicated to Sacajawea, 1786–1884 whoever she may have been; and to all the unnamed women who share her story*" (1991a, 65). Mojica's dedication is twofold: First, the figure of Sacajawea cannot be traced accurately due to a want of factual knowledge, thus actually inviting for a larger-than-life mythology; and second, tragic fates like hers still happen today, although more often than not they go unrecognized. Finally, all that Mojica does (and can do) just adds a further variant to the Sacajawea legend by letting her make her own statements and by resorting to the popular mythology already surrounding Sacajawea, albeit missing historical accuracy. Mojica lets her heroine recount how Charbonneau won her in a bet, yet this is historically unproven. The relationship between the two must remain in a historical twilight since "[h]is relationship with Sacajawea is also sufficiently unclear to leave a wide margin for speculation in the historical accounts and in the novels" (Knowlton-Le Roux 2006, n.p.).

Evoking the different places named after Sacajawea by the Suffragette Choir remains an artificial, inauthentic relation that is intensified by the play's fairy tale-like beginning. It confers upon the places an unreal distance: "Far away o'er the mountains / lived a brave Indian maid— / so that her name ne'er be forgotten, / and her mem'ry never fade: Now remember: there's Sacajawea Creek in Montana / Sacajawea Lake in Washington . . ." (Mojica 1991a, 67). Meaning cannot be made by any connection to places that received their names solely through a colonial process of naming and are recited ad nauseam. Sacajawea already has a completely different relationship to place, as expressed in the lyrical translation of her name Pohenaif:

> Pohenaif, from where the tall grass dances / laughs and ripples / where the sky meets the earth / the grass dances to the east of me / whispers mysteries to the north of me / sighs its sorrows to the west of me / and sings again in the south. (Mojica 1991a, 69)

Sacajawea's relationship to her environment is not only marked by a strong connection with an animate, anthropomorphic nature. She is also an integral part of it through the meaning of her name— "Grass Woman." Additionally, the numerical symbolism of the four directions, with her placed in the middle, charges the environment with spirituality as mythological thinking forms her worldview. Though she misses the exuberant, subversive Trickster humor, she nevertheless possesses the traits of a Trickster figure, as her different names simultaneously point to a crisis of identity and contain the possibilities of shape shifting.[3] This becomes obvious when the expedition is almost doomed to failure during a stormy river raft, but is heroically saved by Sacajawea. This is rendered in an interior monologue of Sacajawea's. A hawk scream heralds the transformation:

> SACAJAWEA (INT.): They call me Tsakakawea—Birdwoman!
> I fly high above the river
> hover and glide—watch the boat
> no sound but leaves as wind
> ruffles their light underside—rain coming . . . [. . .]
> Rain coming! a shout, my beak frozen

as the sky turns black, purple, yellow, grey.
No sound—then the river roars angry
spitting white foam, rising, rising.
The storm opens wide its mouth to
suck us under!
Tsakakawea—Birdwoman, wings spread
diving for the boat!
Hawk's screech, heavy winds, rapids. (Mojica 1991a, 73–74)

While Sacajawea's scenes are distinguished by continuous earnest-ness, humor and esprit lie in the Suffragettes' self-deconstructing commentaries and their proclivity for all imaginable prejudices and stereotypes. Also the contact between Lewis and Clark and the Natives is a cliché-ridden depiction in an overtly ironic tone:

CLARK: (clears his throat) Hail Redskins! I bring greet-ings from the Great White Father in Washington—No, no . . . Washington . . . Redskins . . . um . . . no. Hello Savages! You may now discard the flags of France and Spain and accept these medals bearing the likeness of the Great White Father in Washington. See how they shine! [. . .] We have already several boxes of Indian gifts which include: fancy coats, Jefferson Medals, flags, knives, toma-hawks, looking glasses, handkerchiefs, paints, beads and other assorted ornaments. (Mojica 1991a, 71)

The punning is based on the naïve, hit-or-miss addressing of the Natives as well as on the anachronistic allusion to the Wash-ington Redskins, that, like other American sports teams, has an "Indian" name or mascot. Clark's list of donations sounds like the assortment of a junk dealer but also clearly evokes the stereotypical image of the Indian who does not know about the "true value of things" and falls for the glimmer of bric-a-brac. The trading goods serve the purpose of dispersing "civilization," and at the same time they symbolically manifest and reinforce the American sovereign rights. The colonial center's imperial claim to power becomes even more evident when Clark, in a letter, informs the illiterate Charbon-neau about the adoption of Sacajawea's son. This letter is exclu-sively addressed to Charbonneau, not to Sacajawea.[4]

The historical memory and remembrance of the Grannies and Grandpas is based on orality and finds its expression in lively story-telling. This is confronted with the Suffragettes' emphasis on literacy to document the past and their "memorializing-as-monumentalizing."

Memory and remembrance are thus central issues of Mojica's play, especially in the form of a female experience of history.

Both the Grannies and the Suffragettes situate events from the past in the context of the present, but despite this formal similarity—both groups are depicted drinking tea—there are essential differences. Initiated by their search for a suitable name for a newborn, the Grannies' memory is a spontaneous, biographical and personal recollection. Their memorizing is non-utilitarian in its discursive centering on the personal relationship as a memorizing of casual everyday communication; it remains related to the group and does not exceed common experiences, that is, it is the biographical memory of the group. The Grannies' reminiscences open with a formulaic "I remember." The succession of their memories provides a different and more differentiated picture of Sacajawea than that of the Suffragettes, and finally demonstrates their understanding of Sacajawea's role for them:

> Well, we Shoshones never thought too much of her taking those white men over the mountains to the big waters. It never was important to us. It made her important to the white people, though. So they gave her a medal and some papers to prove that she was worth something. (Mojica 1991a, 77)

The Grannies and Grandpas elaborate on this: from the more general level of the tribe and the impersonal white world they continue to a personal, individual perspective and finally they position Sacajawea again in the collective of the tribe:

> "Personally, I would like to ask, what is all this fuss about?" We remember our grandmother for who she was to us . . . not with medals, papers and monuments. "She is here on the hill in the cemetery. She can only be buried in one place." (Mojica 1991a, 81)

The objective of this oral memory serves neither the purpose of heroizing nor rejecting. Nevertheless, due to her hybrid status between the cultures, Sacajawea's position is also difficult for the Grannies:

> We never knew that my grandmother had married a white man by the name of Charbonneau. . . . She was perfectly familiar with the white people at the fort. I mean that she

was not afraid to mingle with them. The white people
respected her. (Mojica 1991a, 76–77)

Despite these doubts, no above-average individual achievement that
finds expression in a materialized symbolism is important for memory, save the connection to the natural environment, the community, and its collective memory. The Grannies and Grandpas do not
produce historical factual knowledge. Part of their memory culture
is the concrete relation to the person who is alive in memory and
is thus creating identity, even if there must remain some doubts in
the demands to absolute truth as expressed by Granny #2: "What I
have said is absolutely the truth. I am not trying to pretend at all.
I am telling the truth" (Mojica 1991a, 77). They do not sympathize
with the Suffragettes' search for Sacajawea in which they have also
questioned the Grannies as contemporary witnesses; this "memory
work" that centers on a single person and finds expression in sym-
bolical objects seems ridiculous to them: "See, look here, these—
women for suffering came and gave us these little spoons, eh? That
woman on the spoon here, it's supposed to be Sacajawea" (Mojica
1991a, 77). The fact that the Suffragettes in their reconstruction of
the past fade out disagreeable aspects from their idealized picture
does not go unnoticed by the Grannies: " 'I remember her once
telling that she had fed the white with dog meat.' Why don't they
put that in their statues and big picture of her?" (Mojica 1991a,
70). Instead of delineating a selective and opportunistic image of
a heroine, the Grannies' anecdotal memory work places the *whole*
person at the center of interest, who remains alive as long as orally
transmitted memory goes back.

The Suffragettes do not dispose of this personal connection;
they must refer to a different spatial and temporal frame in which
the personal memory of historical remembrance crosses over into
the collective memory of historical consciousness and must assure
itself of the phenomena and dimensions of historical culture. "To
remember" for them means primarily a symbolic consolidation of
memory in representative objects, in the naming of places, and
in formal-ritual actions like the inauguration of the statue, so that
the remembered person finally takes on larger-than-life dimensions.
Remembrance replaces memory, which, as Aleida Assmann points
out, is different in that the first is spontaneous while the latter is
more formal and often embedded in ritual reenactments and reifica-
tions like symbols and memorials (see Assmann 1997, 36).

Cast in bronzes or plaques, remembrance is removed from
active cultural memory to a place where it can safely be visited

for specific celebrations. Although the Suffragettes have tried to collect all imaginable and available information about Sacajawea, the result remains a mere construct—Sacajawea is deposed from her biography and identity and is created anew by the Suffragettes in a God-like act of creation:

> I then hunted up every fact I could find about Sacajawea. Out of a few dry bones I created Sacajawea and made her a living entity. For months I dug and scraped for accurate information about this wonderful Indian maid. (Mojica 1991a, 76)

In a book Sacajawea's story is filed, musealized, and safely stored. The facticity of scholarly research becomes an instrumentalized fictionalization that only pretends to be authentic. Dye undermines the claim to validity of her statement right at the beginning of the play: "In order to ensure that the identity of Sacajawea is known to you and above all, that *veracity* itself is upheld, I will now read from my historical *novel . . .*" (Mojica 1991a, 68, emphasis added).

The truth claim—later also made by Granny #2—is expanded, in an ironic turn, to fictional genres. Dye's novel approaches Sacajawea through a translation in familiar terminology that should evoke certain culturally secure recollections, and at the same time incorporate her into an ideal of attractive femininity. Mojica interlaces a passage from Dye's fictional epopee into her play:

> Sacajawea's hair was neatly braided, her nose was fine and straight, and her skin pure copper like a statue in some Florentine gallery. Madonna of her race, she had led the way to a new time. To the hands of this girl, not yet eighteen, had been entrusted the key that unlocked the road to Asia. (Mojica 1991a, 68)

Dye adjusts Sacajawea to a Western cultural understanding, endows her with a quasi-religious aura, and deprives her of any liveliness. However, she is commissioned to the imperialistic project of expanding the frontier across the continental borders toward the Pacific Rim.

The Suffragettes themselves, in their affectionate and nostalgic approach, deconstruct any subversive potential the story of Sacajawea might have because they transfer their own desires onto her. The expedition's hardships are turned into a romance that not only promulgates the image of the "noble savage," captured in a

natural state of grace, but eventually also reveals the repressive
sexual morals of their own society by unsheathing their hidden
fantasies:

> Imagine! Oh how I've always wanted to be like a wild
> Indian—an Indian maiden dancing naked in the wilder-
> ness to the light of the bonfire! . . . Imagine the excite-
> ment, the romance of trekking across the untamed,
> untouched, VIRGIN territory with those two handsome
> captains!! She must have been terribly in love with one
> of them . . . (Mojica 1991a, 75–76)

For the Suffragettes, wishful thinking substitutes for facts, and
a strangely inappropriate romantic longing for male dominance
replaces the need for individual self-realization. Remembered is
what cannot be remembered because it never took place—and it
is exactly this which encroaches on cultural memory and thus (de-)
forms historical consciousness. "Who are these strange sisters?"
(Mojica 1991a, 82 and 83), Sacajawea skeptically asks, oscillating
between some form of kinship and bare lack of understanding. In
her statue she cannot recognize herself, as it bears in its arbitrari-
ness no likeness to her, just as the speeches or the novels quite
obviously portray someone else. Sacajawea feels entrapped again,
and is alienated by "her" monument. She wishes for a completely
different kind of remembrance, contrapuntal to that of the Suffragettes. While they monotonously repeat their incantation three
times to remember the places and objects named after Sacajawea,
she simply appeals to audiences to let her descend from the high
pedestal of veneration and to escape the clutches of monopolizing
appropriation:

> If you remember me, / remember a child fighting to stay
> alive / remember a slave girl gambled away / remember
> a mother protecting her child / remember a wife defying
> the whip / remember an old one who loved her people /
> remember I died at home on my land. (Mojica 1991a, 84)

History, as construed by the Suffragettes, has no relationship to any
real-life experience and thus can offer no guidance. History con-
served in inscriptions and materialized in monuments involves the
risk of a musealization and the dissolution of active memory cultures.
This is confronted with a form of oral storytelling that can keep
memories alive and subversively counteract instrumentalizations.

The Suffragettes' history of Sacajawea is the history of a heroine, a "modest princess," a "Madonna of her race," a "wonderful Indian maid," a "woman who accomplished patriotic deeds," a "modest, unselfish, enduring little Shoshone squaw" who embodies "the eternal womanly" (Mojica 1991a). Sacajawea as a person vanishes behind the pompous verbiage, and her fate of a continuous exploitation through enslavement, women trafficking, and the forced adoption of her child eviscerates. With the erection of the statue, Sacajawea is being commercialized—instead of participation follows expropriation: "We need to raise $7,000.00! [. . .] We will sell Sacajawea buttons and Sacajawea spoons . . . !" (Mojica 1991a, 68).

The discourse of the Suffragettes denies Sacajawea the rights to her own voice and to a franchise in the actual sense of the Latin *suffragium*. The excerpt from Anna Shaw's speech is already characteristic in its diction for the denial of voice. Except when dealing with her own people, Sacajawea is depicted as the voiceless sufferer, "the little Shoshone squaw, who uncomplainingly trailed . . . silently strapping her papoose upon her back she led the way, interpreting and making friendly overtures to powerful Indian tribes . . ."; and as a "patient and motherly woman" (Mojica 1991a, 83) she becomes a role model.

It is significant for their relationship that Sacajawea refers to the Suffragettes as (albeit "strange") "sisters," while in turn, the latter refer to her as the stereotypical "Indian" and therefore the outsider within the dominant society. Hence, the Suffragettes' civilizing mission can only aim for an assimilation analogous to America's colonial project of Manifest Destiny: "Well, the wheels of progress do turn. How fortunate for her people that the wilderness has been tamed and civilized—they're all Americans, now, and maybe we can teach them something about true equality" (76).

Mojica's critique in its parodistic intentions is not so much directed against the early women's movement in particular; she rather sees it in its contemporaneousness as a continuing appropriation of indigenous women into the Western feminist discourse (which attempts to level cultural differences in favor of a universalistic "eternal womanly"). Generally, many indigenous women approach this form of feminism with skepticism, especially as they prioritize a different problematic:

> Indeed, women activists shied away from being defined
> as feminists or as having any particularly female agendas.
> They saw feminism as a white, middle-class movement
> with little relevance in their lives. . . . Indian women

must address their concerns within the context of those
of the total group. (Hoikkala 1998, 270–71)

Sacajawea is not only subject to selfish interests, but during her life-
time she also becomes the passive object of economic and sexual
exploitation. Here, Mojica's play is nonpartisan in its approach as
she also critically reviews the roles of the indigenous cultures to
revise ideologically charged notions of the past. The indigenous
society Sacajawea is forced to enter is definitely not based on mutual respect between the genders. She is captured by a Mandan war
party, enslaved, and sold to the well-known rapist Charbonneau.

When Lewis and Clark decide to take Sacajawea along as an
interpreter they note only her "native" naïveté and humbleness—
and since "the squaw is a wife of Charbonneau, she won't be expect-
ing to be paid" (Mojica 1991a, 72). As the only reward for her efforts
she receives a medal, which she continues to wear even when Clark
adopts her son in a deal among men with Charbonneau, without
her consent. Together they assess Sacajawea's "value"—Clark out
of well-meaning paternalism, Charbonneau out of pure disgust
(see Mojica 1991a, 79). Thus silenced and bereft of her identity,
Sacajawea is a dehumanized and exploited worker, a commodity
and victim of sexual abuse, exposed to constant discrimination and
appropriation from all sides in one form or another because of her
gender and her ethnicity.

Despite their experimental plots Mojica's plays gain a certain
documentary quality, and refer formally to their hybrid textual character with autobiographic elements, historical narratives, and lyrical passages that challenge conventional forms of discourse. While
the one-sided, privileged Western "memorializing-as-monumentalizing" approach tends to distort history and appropriates it for
political-ideological purposes, it is foremost necessary to refer back
to the idiosyncratic modes of historical narration. "Remembrance"
and "memory" for Mojica are not static acts best left to "history,"
but are rather dynamic processes rooted in the community: "For
Mojica . . . memory, unlike history in its European operation, is
embodied and therefore potentially active. . . . Memory serves, not
to keep the dead dead, but to keep the ancestors alive" (Knowles
2003a, 252). In *Birdwoman*, Mojica resorts to historical material and
examines and deconstructs stereotypical images of Native women
by confronting two different conceptions of history—the play's
hybrid form find its counterpart on the thematic-historiographic
side since both ways of narrating history are necessary to finally

restore Sacajawea's voice and to demonstrate her hybrid status between cultures.

Notes

1. *Birdwoman* was first aired in 1991 by CBC Radio Drama in its series *Vanishing Point: Adventure Stories for Big Girls*; it was published together with Mojica's first feature-length play *Princess Pocahontas and the Blue Spots* (1988/1989) in 1991. While the meta-theatrical mélange *Princess Pocahontas* is regarded as "a significant American history play" (D'Aponte 1999, 102) and as "[s]tructurally . . . both challengingly disjunctive and ultimately visionary" (Knowles 2004, 133), its complementary counterpart *Birdwoman* remained somewhat unnoticed by scholars.

2. The Shoshone Sacajawea (ca. 1787–1812 or 1884) was the guide of the Meriwether Lewis and William Clark expedition, who in 1804–1806 were the first white men to cross the continent from east to west. As a young girl Sacajawea was captured by the Mandan (Hidatsa), ransomed by the Franco-Canadian trapper Toussaint Charbonneau, and then became one of his wives. Lewis and Clark hired Charbonneau as a scout and took Sacajawea along as an interpreter. Sacajawea's son, Jean Baptiste, nicknamed "Pomp" (or "Pompy") later grew up under Clark's custody. Sacajawea repeatedly managed to save the expedition from failure (e.g., when she recovered the expedition's recordings from a capsized canoe). This expedition gathered essential scientific knowledge about the flora, fauna, and topography of the West, which later yielded political profit. Sacajawea died either about 1812 or in 1884: Mojica's play mentions the latter date. The reports of the expedition made her famous, numerous landmarks were named after her, monuments were erected in her honor, and works of literature transfigured her into a folkloristic legend. *Collier's Encyclopedia* states that "there are more monuments to her than to any other American woman."

3. She is called Pohenaif, Porivo, Tsakakawea, Sacajawea, but also "Grass Woman" and "Birdwoman," and for the sake of simplicity, she is anglicized by Clark as "Janey."

4. Here, Charbonneau's triple "Oui" as a rather speechless answer to Clark's intentions supports Knowlton-Le Roux's thesis of the purposefully negative representation of the Frenchman. Without rehabilitating Charbonneau, Knowlton-Le Roux traces his demonized depiction in works on the expedition that was intimately connected to widespread anti-French resentments, so that the American protagonists could appear even more glorious. This negative picture can finally be found in *Birdwoman*, too. Sacajawea can be set apart positively, because Charbonneau's demeanor reveals callousness, indifference and his lack of refinement while she responds emotionally to Clark's paternalistic boarding school policy (see Mojica 1991a, 79).

12

Translating Ab-Originality

Canadian Aboriginal Dramatic Texts in the Context of Central European Theatre

Klára Kolinská

The images of the North American continent's aboriginal inhabitants have haunted the minds of Central Europeans for centuries and inspired many of their, largely unrealistic, aspirations. The emblems created thereby habitually distorted the picture of reality, serving a complex whole of projections, desires, and issues concerning the Europeans' relation to the New World. In the twentieth century, the time has come to recognize and represent North American aboriginal cultures in their original forms and means of expression, and, accordingly, to introduce their achievements to the rest of the world.

For European researchers and cultural workers, the task involves a set of serious conceptual, methodological, as well as ethical implications. With the historical experience of exposure to the cultural commodities of the Euro-American civilization, there gradually arose a realization of need with the aboriginal people to accommodate these and assign them for their own political, cultural, and also individual concerns. Among such commodities, as Tzvetan Todorov reminds us in *The Conquest of America*, the most conclusive one was the acquisition (initially imposed) of the English language. The situation of the aboriginal culture is one of complicated in-betweenness, of which code-switching is a constitutive element. Its distinctiveness needs to be preserved, if the culture as such is to survive, but at the same time must not amount to the extent which would make it totally impenetrable from outside influence. And it is precisely this distinctiveness that constitutes not only its inescapable essence, but also its persistent appeal for the outside world. The interpretation of aboriginal literature involves reconciling its innate ethnic character with the Western theoretical and exegetic apparatus. Kimberly Blaeser, a writer and scholar of partly Anishinaabe background, protests candidly about "[t]he insistence of reading Native literature by way of Western literary theory [that] clearly violates its integrity and performs a new act of colonization and conquest" (Blaeser 1993, 55). Blaeser concedes, though, that her own work as a Native scholar working within the fabric of Western academy is implicated by "this distinction between applying already established theory to Native writing versus working from within Native literature or tradition to discover appropriate tools or to form an appropriate language of critical discourse" (Blaeser 1993, 56).

Not only Native but likewise some non-Native scholars have become acutely aware of the current position of aboriginal literature, as well as of their own predicaments stemming from the realization of their academic responsibilities in the task of reconciling their culturally specific exegetic equipment with the aboriginal material and its subject matter. In her study *Travelling Knowledges: Positioning the Im/Migrant Reader of Aboriginal Literature in Canada*, Renate Eigenbrod, a German scholar living and working in Canada, employs Said's, and also Deleuze and Guattari's, notions of the intellectual as a migrant, nomadic figure, from which she develops her potent and culturally sensitive methodology of interpretation and instruction. Eigenbrod's approach to critical practice stems from her agreement with Anishinaabe scholar Armand Garnet Ruffo's caution that

> For the outsider . . . attempting to come to terms with
> Native people and their literature . . . is more a question
> of cultural initiation, of involvement and commitment, so
> that the culture and literature itself becomes more than
> a mere museum piece, dusty pages, something lifeless.
> (Ruffo 1993, 174)

For such a positioning of Eigenbrod's notion of "im/migrant reader" the figure of the translator is a particularly apt metaphor. Besides being a skill, and a complex qualification, translation is, by its very nature, a service industry, reentering the vicarious role of establishing, maintaining, and also problematizing communication between different perspectives. Translation is thus laden with constantly reemergent potentialities for modeling new meanings, either at the demand by the master (narrative), or inadvertently, by the process of trans-locating the old, "original" ones. A whole new meaning has been attributed to the act of translation from the onset of the colonization by Europe of all possible spheres of interest in the world. Europe saw itself as a fixed, absolute point of reference, and strove to reproduce copies of its own patterns in the newly conquered territories. In many senses, while demarcating areas of influence, Europe was thus recognizably and systematically translating itself:

> Europe was regarded as the great original, the starting point, and the colonies were therefore copies, or "trans-lations" of Europe, which they were supposed to dupli-cate. Moreover, being copies, translations were evaluated as less than originals, and the myth of the translation as something that diminished the greater original estab-lished itself. (Bassnett and Trevedi 1999, 4)

Not only on the metaphorical level, but even on the purely literal plain of actual language practice, translation became a crucial instru-ment of power. Theorists of postcolonial translation have declared that "colonization and translation went hand in hand" (Bassnett and Trevedi 1999, 3), and some, such as Eric Cheyfitz, even argue that translation was "the central act of European colonization and imperialism in America" (Cheyfitz 1991, 104).

In the context of North American aboriginal literature, meth-odologies of translation stem not only from the linguistic character-istics of the languages involved, but also from the extra-linguistic and extra-literary realities surrounding them. Brian Swann, a leading theorist of Native American literatures, explains:

> If translation itself is problematic, the translation of Native American literatures is twice so. To questions of para-phrasis and metaphrasis, parataxis and syntactis, to epis-temological, aesthetic, and theoretical considerations, are added problems of transcription and recording, as well as moral and political dimensions. In a subversively creative way the question of whether or how we should resist unifying theories and practices is added. Even at its most "definitive," any translation of a Native American text will always partake of the unknowable. (Swann 1992, xvi–xvii)

The situation is further complicated by the fact that today most of the literary production by aboriginal authors comes out in English—English becomes, therefore, their "original" language, while the connection with their ethnic language source is weakened, if not altogether severed. The English language in Native North America has served not only as a matter of pure linguistic appropriation, but also as an instrument of the domination of space—including the space of the aboriginal people's mind. Floyd Favel, a Cree playwright and theatre practitioner, assumes that "[w]hen a native language is not spoken, an understanding of the worldview of that nation is purely theoretical" (Favel 1993, 8) and explains the reasons for that predicament by a fitting observation about the very nature of language as such, in that "[l]anguage is related to place; it is our umbilical cord to our place of origin, literally and symbolically" (Favel 1993, 9).

Favel's former formulation points out two related issues pertinent to the practice of intercultural translation. First, the notion of a native language "not spoken" echoes, again, the idea of "betrayal" by translation, to the extent of silencing the source language altogether by the target one, and second, it highlights the continuing centrality of the oral aspect of language in the paradigm of North American aboriginal cultures, which renders the translation a very broad mission. It is thus perhaps inevitable that in Canada the favored genre of choice among many aboriginal authors is theatre. Even though we may not necessarily be quite convinced by Drew Hayden Taylor's claim that "[t]oday Native theatre is strong, popular and practically everywhere in terms of the Canadian theatrical community" (Taylor 1996, 29), the optimism and cultural self-confidence expressed in his statement form a solid basis for the conceivable growing quantity, as well as quality of both the present and future theatrical production by aboriginal authors.

A number of aboriginal writers perceive theatre as "a logical extension of the storytelling technique" (Taylor 1996, 29). Floyd Favel describes that

> [f]or Native people the theatre is where a lot of our dreams, fears and visions live and dance in the living present. Language is just one of the elements of a total production. I feel that we are at a turning point towards something. The theatre is a puzzle and riddle for us; how do we incorporate our concept of time, space, architecture, language, colours, rhythms, sounds and movements into a contemporary performance? (Favel 1993, 9)[1]

The actual character of storytelling discernible in the structure of contemporary aboriginal drama, the effects of translational betrayal, and the multifarious significances of language, as well as aesthetic transfer, have all resulted in the aforementioned enduring attraction that the North American aboriginal theatre has held for European viewers and give justification to—so far infrequent—attempts at translating its texts back into European languages.

Such and related reasoning lay behind the project of an anthology of Canadian aboriginal drama in Czech translation, published in April 2007 under the title *Waiting for Coyote: Contemporary Canadian Aboriginal Drama*. The collection of six dramatic texts by leading Canadian aboriginal playwrights in translation, accompanied by a detailed study of the subject, intends to facilitate a better understanding in a small country in Central Europe of the real nature of contemporary aboriginal dramatic art, seemingly exotic to many viewers, and to explore possible language, cultural, and aesthetic links between the Canadian aboriginal, and European theatrical fields.

The anthology contains translations of six plays: Tomson Highway's *The Rez Sisters* (1988), Daniel David Moses's *Coyote City* (1990), Drew Hayden Taylor's *Someday* (1993), Shirley Cheechoo's *Path with No Moccasins* (1991), Yvette Nolan's *Job's Wife, or the Delivery of Grace* (1992), and Ian Ross's *fareWel* (1997). The choice of texts was influenced by a number of factors, united by the common perspective of translatability, in the linguistic, cultural, and theatrical sense. Since the publication collects the first translations into Czech of any aboriginal drama ever, demand was for texts that would be sufficiently representative of their area, confirming thus the ideal of creating, or, rather, contributing to the creation of a literary canon—a process to some degree inherent in editing any anthology of texts, regardless of the field.[2]

The Czech anthology thus serves a double-edged role of representation, introducing to Czech audiences a whole new field of theatre by selecting and highlighting six texts to the exclusion of many others that are therewith almost inevitably relegated to the position of more parochial ones, seemingly with more local significance and less artistic worth. For this reason, the criterion of mere translatability was complemented with several others, of which cultural transmissibility was an important consideration.

Considerations of the concept of "cultural transmissibility" give notice of the undisputable limitations of any translational attempt in any linguistic and cultural context, and echo, once again, the idea of translation as an act of betrayal. In the area of contemporary aboriginal theatre and its transmissibility, an interesting situation arises when deliberating texts that contain passages, sentences, or any language material in the aboriginal languages. Such material sticks out, intentionally, of the English "original," and its distinction is to be retained in translation. This is the case with two out of the six plays in the anthology: Tomson Highway's *The Rez Sisters* and Ian Ross's *fareWel*. In their texts, as well as in texts by other aboriginal playwrights that employ aboriginal languages for the stage, English, the language of the mainstream culture, meets the languages of the original North American cultures that often express different philosophical, political, psychological, and aesthetic perspectives. Although 90 percent of aboriginal theatre production is written and performed in English, aboriginal languages, regardless of whether the authors themselves speak them or not, seep through its texts and performances with higher or lower currency. The authors characteristically include passages in their languages in order to make their audiences aware of the different poetics of their perception of the world, and to mediate, if only for the time of the performance, the experience of language misunderstanding and the ensuing sensation of ontological, political, and psychological helplessness that the aboriginal cultures involuntarily lived in for such a long time. These texts thus continually and multifariously "translate" themselves, which creates exciting tensions fostering their dramatic potential. This effect, however, is not achieved easily, as Tomson Highway knows well:

> The difficulty Native writers encounter as writers, however, is that we must use English if our voice is to be heard by a large enough audience: English and not Cree. The Cree language is so completely different and the world view that that language engenders and expresses is so completely different—at odds, some would say— that inevitably, the characters we write into our plays must, of necessity, lose some of their original lustre in the translation. (Highway 2005b, 2)

The difficulty Highway experiences as a writer is further complicated by the difficulty for the audience: Highway indulges in confusing his viewers by conflating Cree and Anishinaabe in one text and creating cunning language hybrids with little transparency; even though it would be difficult, and hypothetical only, to deduce a regular system in the author's usage of these two languages, it is hardly a coincidence that he lets them sound, with undisguised pleasure, in the scenes in which the Trickster appears on stage. Multiplied language hybridity thus forwards the Trickster principle and becomes its symbol:

> Highway gives an example of hybrid space by slipping in and out of Cree and Ojibway. By interspersing First Nations languages in a predominantly English text, he unsettles settlers. We are encouraged to acknowledge cultural difference because there is a linguistic signpost in our cultural landscape that we may not comprehend. Highway's use of Cree serves to alienate non-native audiences; they must struggle with language and the problems of translation. Non-native audiences have a small sampling of the alienation and dispossession that many First Nations have experienced when they have not been allowed to speak their languages, but have been required to speak English. (Horne 1996, 86–87)

The complexity of such language hybridity is acutely felt and accounted for by many contemporary Canadian aboriginal playwrights, whether they themselves actually have mastered their aboriginal language or not. Métis playwright Yvette Nolan describes her own story, symptomatic of the postcolonial condition of today's Canada:

> I am the daughter of two people who have lost their language, lost their connection to their traditional land. I was raised by an Irishman who was trying to assimilate into his chosen country, and an Indian whose country was trying to assimilate her. I was raised speaking only English, the language of my parents' colonizer. . . . I am an invisible Aboriginal. This Irish skin of mine disguises my Aboriginal heart. (Nolan 2005, 39–40)

Like Tomson Highway, Yvette Nolan writes in English; unlike him, though, she has lost the connection with her aboriginal language, and only comes back to it gradually, via the medium of English. To her, English is the mother tongue. Therefore, while both Highway and Nolan are aboriginal writers writing in English, Highway made English the language of his somewhat reluctant choice for "writing back," and Nolan moves, much more perceptibly and out of her choice, along the ambiguous fine line dividing the spheres of the colonizing and the colonized.

Highway usually includes passages in Cree—or in a mixture of Cree and Anishinaabe—in such scenes of his plays that carry a spiritual dimension. The purpose is, on the one hand, to prompt the mythological rootedness of his imagery, and to give it a contemporary manifestation for all to see and hear, but also to create a theatrical effect specifically for the aboriginal audience, which Floyd Favel aptly describes:

> The sound of our native languages on stage is a totally different experience of theatrical sound from English. The voice immediately gets more rooted in the body, it is richer and more musical, and a whole different mood is evoked. Present in the immediate words are the ancestors, which go back generation by generation, right back to the day our language bubbled up from the springs and whispers of the trees and grass. It is a doorway, and a window. (Favel 1993, 9)

Passages in Cree and Anishinaabe in Highway's plays, ironically, represent the smallest of the translator's worries: they remain untranslated, precisely to serve, in Dee Horne's phrasing given earlier, as "linguistic signposts . . . that we may not comprehend" (Horne 1996, 86). Since this incomprehension of the actual words is the predicament inflicted by the author upon most of his audiences, Highway thus gets close to the radicalism present in Floyd Favel's suggestion: "Maybe it's better not to speak in words at all, just make a sound, or sing a song in a language which is neither English, and neither a mother tongue. Or invent a language of one's own that touches more truly the feelings trapped in blood, muscle and genes . . ." (Favel 1993, 10).

The decision not to translate the aboriginal language component in Highway's play was confirmed by an interesting example from a very different context: an analysis of the translation of *The Rez Sisters* into Japanese published in *Theatre Journal* in 2007 criticizes the translator for consistently translating all the language parts into Japanese, creating thus out of the text a homogenous linguistic monolith, at the expense of the original's multivocality. The translation, therefore, reportedly "fails to register the multiple meanings possible in the play by striving for an easily understood transparency" (Curran 2007, 460), which is motivated by the fact that the translator "grounds her translation in social and linguistic accessibility; what was distinguished linguistically in Highway's text is lost in assimilation in the translation" (Curran 2007, 456). This comment seems to argue that translation aspiring at too much uni-fication in the target language in view of the audience's comfort is an injustice to the basic role of translation of mediating meaning, even if the meaning is that of realized incomprehension.

Compared to Highway's, Yvette Nolan's story—and the story of her character Grace from *Job's Wife, or the Delivery of Grace*—chimes in with Favel's rendition of the opposite situation:

> To hear English on stage in the mouths of native people, the voice is higher, less in the body, and resonates less with the total life of the performer. A whole spiritual dimension is lost. We have faint traces of the mystery and magic, but mostly the soul is burdened by the mechanic-ity of a foreign language which has colonized the soul's expression. (Favel 1993, 10)

Nolan's play *Job's Wife, or the Delivery of Grace* documents such a "loss of the spiritual dimension" in unfolding "a strange encounter between Grace, a middle-class, Roman Catholic, non-Native woman pregnant with the child of a Native man . . . and God, or 'Josh,' who turns out to be a large Native man in a rag-and-bone cape" (Mojica and Knowles 2003, 239). The encounter between the char-acters becomes an encounter between cultures and worldviews, and accordingly, between languages—a fact symbolically announced by the double entendre of the play's title. Out of the whole text the title represented the greatest translational challenge; and, after much debate, the name of the main character remained untranslated—a decision that, without doubt, restrains the ambiguity of the original to a certain extent, and, again, demonstrates the limitations of trans-lation. At the same time, nonetheless, it (ideally) shows respect for the original and resignation upon its manipulation and forceful linguistic appropriation.

In *fareWel* Ian Ross includes passages in an aboriginal language (Saulteaux-Anishinaabe in his case) from a different background, and for different reasons. For him, like for Nolan, English is a mother tongue; however, through his family lineage he has not quite lost con-tact with his aboriginal linguistic ancestry, and acknowledges it in the "Playwright's Note" to *fareWel*, in which he gives credit to his mother for "an invaluable aid" (Ross 1997, 9) as a language consultant.

Besides occasional words or phrases in *fareWel*, a long passage in Saulteaux (with an English translation in the text) comes, rather surprisingly perhaps, at a political meeting organized by Teddy, "the play's most unsympathetic character" (Lenze 2001, 48). Teddy, "a clever man," is the only character who seems to be able to face the omnipresent apathy and to rise to some action; moreover, Teddy is the only one who displays enough self-confidence to openly profess his aboriginal identity, and promises its renewal for the whole community. However, Teddy is, likewise, a tireless innovator ready to stand up against the anonymous and indifferent administrative authority, and a wily manipulator and crafty racketeer, who openly bullies the weaker (most of whom are, typically, women), and uses the gained power mainly for his own benefit.[3] The fact that language, and knowledge or ignorance thereof, is the prominent sign of corruption in the play, creates out of Ross's play a compelling contribution to the current discourse of redress, which has evolved, to a considerable extent, around the question of language as a medium of culture. Gilbert and Tompkins rightly observe that "[c]hoosing a language (or languages) in which to express one's dramatic art is, in itself, a political act that determines not only the linguistic medium of a play but, in many cases, its (implied) audience as well" (1996, 168). Moreover, choosing a language involves not choosing another, and so the seemingly passive fact of not translating is also a product of an active reasoning and decision—both the author's, and, consequently, the translator's.

Interestingly, a translator who transforms such a multilingual text into yet another linguistic and cultural context runs even a higher risk than the author: among his/her spectators, there would be none to understand the untranslated passages, which easily creates a strong field of opposition, with the result of betrayal of the author by the translator's work—unless the message and intention of the author's decision is mediated clearly: "In using 'foreign' dialogue, one can subvert the authority of the dominant language of the theatre (and of the culture) from within by making the theatre stage one's own, by establishing an unmistakable presence of minority language and culture" (Byczynski 2000, 33).

Another touchstone of the translation philosophy is, in the context of aboriginal drama, prepared by the plays' inclusion of oral storytelling modes and mythological components. As noted previously, oral storytelling is one of the firm foundation stones of aboriginal theatre, and, contrary to Walter Benjamin's belief, on the North American continent at least, the storyteller shows no signs of dying anytime soon. Rather, he naturally conquers the stage, wherefrom he continues his mission, unthinkable without the element of interaction.

An interesting moment ensues when the storyteller, telling a traditional story, becomes one of the characters. Such is the narrative drive in Daniel David Moses's play *Coyote City*, where Boo, a young female character, in a moment of emotional and spiritual desperation, exchanges lines with Johnny, a ghost of her sister's murdered lover, in telling a traditional Nez Perce myth of Coyote and his dead wife. The Coyote myth—which, interestingly, is not "Native" to Moses's culture—echoes the Greek myth of Orpheus and Eurydice, and thus potentially creates for the non-Native audience one of the "signposts of recognition," although, by the author's claim, that was not a primary intention. Rather, Moses is intrigued by the story's performativity as such, by its purpose on stage: "Attempting to tell the story while the play was happening was my first experiment of trying to deal with the different ways of presenting" (Moses 1991, 165). Interpolating the Coyote myth into the text of the play thus serves as a means of othering (aesthetically as well as culturally) certain layers of the play's narrative, while simultaneously forming gentle, restrained pathways to the audience's (self-)identification. In so doing Moses corroborates his ultimate career goal, which he revealed in a conversation with Hartmut Lutz:

> I'm actually gradually moving towards the idea of gathering a repertoire to actually be a real storyteller in the traditional sense. I find that what I value in the use of language comes from that idea of an oral presentation. As much as I can appreciate the beauty of poems on the page, and can appreciate the concepts behind things like concrete poetry, I find that they don't move me as deeply as something I can hear from someone else's mouth. (Moses 1991, 158)

Telling a story or a myth on stage poses a specific task for a translator; a traditional story is by no means a mere personal, subjective expression—its tone on stage changes from the rest of the text, it adds to the aesthetic multivocality of the message, while at the same time forming a component of its organic whole. This quality should, ideally, be preserved in the translation, which usually implies a shift in the stylistic register of the target language, while bearing in mind the need to avoid the danger of improper archaization. The task, luckily, is facilitated by the very nature of myth, regardless of its cultural origin:

> Myth is a mode of communication, which is by its very nature always already a translation. . . . Myth is not

translation in the strictest sense, that is, the rendering
of a text from one language to another. Rather, its function is to bridge one spatiotemporal context to another
and to grant continued and renewed significance to a
time-tested cultural narrative. (Scott 2004, 58)

Myth then bears striking parallels with the profession, and service
of translation, in that both are "haunted by the myth of origin"
(Scott 2004, 59)—or, in the case of translation, "myth of the original." In her analysis of translating myth Jill Scott argues that, consequently, "mythopoesis in turn denies this privileging of origin,"
and "can be seen as an attempt on the part of myth to transcend
its own roots through translation" (Scott 2004, 59). The key to the
successful translation of myth rests then in its careful reading, and
in resisting the temptation to search for the assumed common original, which potentially leads to creating fictional likenesses, and,
hence, to appropriation.

The result of the aforementioned analysis of one translational
experience shows that translating aboriginal drama is a complex
undertaking, demanding, above all, careful and attentive readings
of both the text and context of the original. The test of quality, and
viability of the translation of drama is, ultimately, its specific production, the "coming alive" of words on stage. The Czech anthology
still waits for its theatrical realization—the production in Czech of
Daniel David Moses's *Coyote City* was planned for 2009. Hopefully,
the production, and others to follow, will suggest some answers to
the questions asked in the roundtable on translating for theatre
by George Eliot Clarke, who boldly admitted that translation and
adaptation are

at once acts of love and acts of violence, because you
cannot render the original in any way that's completely
faithful, no matter what you do. There is a certain degree
of violence. So why not just be violent about it? Ador-
ingly violent or violently adoring about the text, in order
to make something that's faithful to your own context,
your own linguistic, cultural, temporal context? (Clarke
in Knowles 2003b, 50)

Clarke's question proves that good translation is not an act of
betrayal, but of faith—in "being faithful to one's own" the translator
creates relations first of understanding, and, consequently, of recog-

nition, in which languages, cultures, and myths meet one another on equal platforms.

Notes

1. Similarly, influential critics of postcolonial theatre have identified the advantages of theatrical storytelling modes for the reasons of their "stage economy." Informed by Hayden White's argument formulated in his *Metahistory*, Helen Gilbert and Joanne Tompkins's seminal study of postcolonial theatre convincingly determines the storyteller as "one of the most significant manipulators of historical narrative in colonized societies" (Gilbert and Tompkins 1996, 126), and explicates the reasons for the storyteller's original product (and process) to be logically transferred-translated to stage: "Telling stories on stage is an economical way in which to initiate theatre since it relies on imagination, recitation, improvisation, and not necessarily on many stage properties. . . . Th[e] story-telling tradition transfers easily to the stage since its codes and conventions as a mode of communication are already highly theatrical" (Gilbert and Tompkins 1996, 126).

2. This claim, nonetheless, runs counter to the understanding of the canon in aboriginal literature and literary theory. Aboriginal writers typically construe the literary canon as a fabrication by the mainstream culture, which imposes upon texts measurements of hierarchy, and is thus alien to their aesthetics. Many of them explicitly oppose the domestication of the notion of the canon on their literary turf, even when performing the task of anthologizing themselves. In an introduction to one of the first comprehensive anthologies of Native literature in Canada, which he coedited with Terry Goldie, playwright and poet Daniel David Moses explains its methodology and credo: "The decisions on what should go in something that you might call the canon can be easily disguised as aesthetic decisions, but if we are making a canon the decisions are definitely political, especially with a literature that is emerging even as we speak. . . . We are in history and this writing is very involved in that history. It seems foolish to try and take it out of life and put it in a separate canon. Why worry about the immortals?" (Moses and Goldie 1991, xx).

3. The character of Teddy, and his selfish manipulation of the Aboriginal language, has been the strongest reason for the mixed reception of the play by both Native and non-Native audiences. Rachel, the female brave of the play, recognizes his aims in saying to him: "You're the only person I know who makes our language sound ugly" (Ross 1997, 59).

Works Cited

Allen, Paula Gunn. 1998. *The Sacred Hoop: Recovering the Feminine in American Indian Traditions*. Boston: Beacon Press.

Appleford, Robert. 1999. The Indian "Act": Postmodern Perspectives on Native Canadian Theatre. PhD diss., University of Toronto.

———. 2005. Daniel David Moses: Ghostwriter with a Vengeance. In *Aboriginal Drama and Theatre: Critical Perspectives on Canadian Theatre in English*, Volume 1, ed. Robert Appleford, 150–65. Toronto: Playwrights Canada Press.

———, ed. 2006. *Aboriginal Drama and Theatre*. Critical Perspectives on Canadian Theatre in English 1. Toronto: Playwrights Canada Press.

Armstrong, Ann Elizabeth, Kelli Lyon Johnson, and William A. Wortman, eds. 2009. *Performing Worlds Into Being: Native American Women's Theater*. Oxford, OH: Miami University Press.

Ashcroft, Bill, Gareth Griffiths, and Helen Tiffin. 1989. *The Empire Writes Back: Theory and Practice in Post-Colonial Literatures*. London: Routledge.

———. 2000. *Post-Colonial Studies: The Key Concepts*. London: Routledge.

Assmann, Aleida. 1997. Gedächtnis, Erinnerung. In *Handbuch der Geschichtsdidaktik*, ed. Klaus Bergmann et al. 5th ed., 33–37. Seelze-Velber: Kallmeyer.

Baker, Marie Annharte. 1991. Angry Enough to Spit But With Dry Lips It Hurts More Than You Know. *Canadian Theatre Review* 68, no. 3 (Fall): 88–89.

Balme, Christopher. 1997. Reading the Signs: A Semiotic Perspective on Aboriginal Theatre. In *Aratjara: Aboriginal Culture and Literature in Australia*, ed. Dieter Riemenschneider and Geoffrey V. Davis, 149–64. Amsterdam: Rodopi.

———. 1999. *Decolonizing the Stage: Theatrical Syncretism and Post-Colonial Drama*. Oxford: Clarendon Press.

Bassnett, Susan. 1999. Introduction. In *Postcolonial Translation: Theory and Practice*, ed. Susan Bassnett and Harish Trivedi. London: Routledge.

Bassnett, Susan, and Harish Trivedi, eds. 1999. *Postcolonial Translation: Theory and Practice*. London: Routledge.

Beagan, Tara. 2006. *Dreary and Izzy.* Toronto: Playwrights Canada Press.

Beck, Günter U. 2007. *Defending Dreamer's Rock: Geschichte, Geschichts-bewusstsein und Geschichtskultur im Native Drama der USA und Kanadas.* CDE Studies 14. Trier: Wissenschaftlicher Verlag Trier.

Becker, Marc. 1994–2002. *Native Web.* http://abyayala.nativeweb.org/about.html.

Benedict, Nona. 1970. *The Dress.* In *The Only Good Indian: Essays by Canadian Indians,* ed. Waubageshig, 62–72. Toronto: New Press.

Bennett, Susan. 1993. Subject to the Tourist Gaze: A Response to "Weesageechak Begins to Dance." *The Drama Review* 37, no. 1 (Spring): 9–13.

Bhabha, Homi. 1994. *The Location of Culture.* London: Routledge.

Bigsby, Christopher W. E. 1985. American Indian Theatre. In A *Critical Introduction to Twentieth-Century American Drama,* ed. Christopher W. E. Bigsby, Volume 2: Beyond Broadway, 365–74. Cambridge: Cambridge University Press.

Bird, S. Elizabeth, ed. 1996. *Dressing in Feathers: The Construction of the Indian in American Popular Culture.* Boulder, CO: Westview.

Blaeser, Kimberly M. 1993. Native Literature: Seeking a Critical Center. In *Looking at the Words of Our People: First Nations Analysis of Literature,* ed. Jeannette Armstrong, 51–62. Penticton, BC: Theytus Books.

Botsford Fraser, Marion. 1991. Contempt for Women Overshadows Powerful Play. In *The Globe and Mail,* April 17: C1.

Boudreau, Diane. 1993. *Histoire de la littérature amérindienne au Québec: oralité et écriture.* Montréal: Hexagone.

Bricker, Victoria Reifler. 1981. *Indian Christ, Indian King.* Austin: University of Texas Press.

Brown, Kent. 2000. The American Indian Theatre Ensemble. In *American Indian Theatre in Performance: A Reader,* ed. Hanay Geiogamah and Jaye T. Darby, 169–74. Los Angeles: UCLA American Indian Studies Center Press.

Bryson, Bill. 2004. *A Short History of Nearly Everything.* New York: Broadway Books.

Byczynski, Julie 2000. A Word in a Foreign Language: On Not Translating in the Theatre. *Canadian Theatre Review* 102 (Spring): 33–37.

Byrne, Louis. 1995. *Boneman.* In *Boneman: An Anthology of Canadian Plays,* ed. Gordon Ralph, 6–35. St. John's: Jasperson.

Campbell, Maria. 1973. *Halfbreed.* New York: Saturday Review Press.

Canning, Charlotte. 1996. *Feminist Theaters in the U.S.A.: Staging Women's Experience.* New York: Routledge.

Cheechoo, Shirley. 1991. *Path with No Moccasins.* West Bay, Ontario: Kasheese Studios.

Cheyfitz, Eric. 1991. *The Poetics of Imperialism: Translation and Colonization from* The Tempest *to* Tarzan. New York: Oxford University Press.

Chinoy, Helen Krich, and Linda Walsh Jenkins, eds. 1981. *Women in American Theatre.* New York: Theatre Communications Group.

Clements, Marie. 2001. *Age of Iron.* In *DraMétis: Three Métis Plays,* by Greg Daniels, Marie Clements, and Margo Kane, 193–273. Penticton, BC: Theytus.

———. 2003. *Burning Vision.* Vancouver: Talonbooks.

———. 2005. *The Unnatural and Accidental Women.* Vancouver: Talonbooks.

———. 2007. *Copper Thunderbird.* Vancouver: Talonbooks.

Collier's Encyclopedia, 1985 edition, s.v. "Sacajawea."

Courtney, Richard. 1985. Indigenous Theatre: Indian and Eskimo Ritual Drama. In *Contemporary Canadian Theatre: New World Visions,* ed. Anton Wagner, 206–15. Toronto: Simon & Pierre.

———. 1989. Amerindian and Inuit Theatre. In *The Oxford Companion to Canadian Theatre,* ed. Eugene Benson and L. W. Conolly, 20–22. Toronto: Oxford University Press.

Curran, Beverley. 2007. Invisible Indigeneity: First Nations and Aboriginal Theatre in Japanese Translation and Performance. *Theatre Journal* 59: 449–65.

Däwes, Birgit. 2003. An Interview with Drew Hayden Taylor. *Contemporary Literature* 44, no. 1 (Spring): 1–18.

———. 2007a. *Native North American Theater in a Global Age: Sites of Identity Construction and Transdifference.* Heidelberg: Winter.

———. 2007b. From Toronto to Berlin: Canadian First Nations Theatre in the EFL Classroom. *Literatur in Wissenschaft und Unterricht* 40, no. 1–2: 67–84.

———. 2007c. James Luna, Gerald Vizenor, and the 'Vanishing Race': Native American Performative Responses to Hege(mne)monic Image Construction. In *Visual Culture Revisited: German and American Perspectives on Visual Culture(s),* ed. Ralf Adelmann et al., 194–214. Köln: Herbert von Halem Verlag.

———. 2008. "How Native Is Native if You're Native?": Deconstructions of Authenticity in Drew Hayden Taylor's Performative Project. In *Drew Hayden Taylor: Essays on His Works,* ed. Robert Nunn, 17–58. Toronto: Guernica.

———. 2009a. Tricksters on Stage: Contemporary First Nations Theater and Drama in Canada. *Canadian Literature: Letters & Reflections.* http://www.canlit.ca/letter.php?page=archives&letter=24 (accessed December 6, 2009).

———. 2009b. "Fox-trot with me, Baby": Diane Glancy's Dramatic Work. In *The Salt Companion to Diane Glancy,* ed. James Mackay, 131–48. Cambridge: Salt Publishing.

———. 2010. "The Unseen World Intrudes as Though It Were Seen": Spiritual Coordinates of Identity in Contemporary Native American Performance. In *Religion in the United States,* ed. Jeanne Cortiel and Michael Wala. Heidelberg: Winter.

Dandurand, Joseph A. 2004. *Please Do Not Touch the Indians.* Candler, NC: Renegade Planets Publishing.

D'Aponte, Mimi Gisolfi. 1999. Native American Women Playwrights: Transmitters, Healers, Transformers. *Journal of Dramatic Theory and Criticism* 14, no. 1 (Fall): 99–108.

Darby, Jaye T., and Stephanie Fitzgerald, eds. 2003. *Keepers of the Morning Star: An Anthology of Native Women's Theater*. Los Angeles: UCLA American Indian Studies Center.

De la Cruz Cruz, Petrona. 2003. *A Desperate Woman*, trans. Shanna Lorenz. In *Holy Terrors: Latin American Women Perform*, ed. Diana Taylor and Rosalyn Costantino, 291–310. Durham: Duke University Press.

Delbaere, Jeanne. 1995. Psychic Realism, Mythic Realism, Grotesque Realism: Variations on Magic Realism in Contemporary Literature in English. In *Magical Realism: Theory, History, Community*, ed. Lois Parkinson Zamora and Wendy B. Faris, 249–63. Durham: Duke University Press.

Deloria, Philip J. 1998. *Playing Indian*. New Haven: Yale University Press.

Dennis, Darrell. 2005. *Two Plays: Tales of an Urban Indian, The Trickster of Third Avenue East*. Toronto: Playwrights Canada Press.

Diamond, David, Hal B. Blackwater, Lois G. Shannon, and Marie Wilson. 2001. *NO' XYA': A Play About Ancestral Land*. In *Playing the Pacific Province: An Anthology of British Columbia Plays, 1967–2000*, ed. Ginny Ratsoy, and James Hoffman, 391–418. Toronto: Playwrights Canada Press.

Du Bois, W.E.B. 1964. *The Souls of Black Folk*. New York: Penguin.

Dudoward, Valerie. 1986. Teach Me the Ways of the Sacred Circle. In *The Land Called Morning*, ed. Caroline Heath, 1–36. Saskatoon: Fifth House.

Durán, Diego. 1994. *The History of the Indies of New Spain*, trans. Doris Heyden. Norman, OK: University of Oklahoma Press.

Durand, Yves Sioui. 1992. *Le Porteur des Peines du Monde*. Montréal: Leméac Éditeur.

———. 2001. *La Conquête de Mexico*. Montréal: Éditions Trait d'Union.

Dzul Ek, Carlos Armando. 2007. Bix úuchik u bo'ot ku'si'ip'il Manilo'ob' tu ja'abil 1562 / The Maní Inquisition or the Colliding of Two Cultures / El auto de fe de Maní o Choque de dos culturas. In *Words of the True Peoples / Palabras de los Seres Verdaderos*, ed. Carlos Montemayor and Donald Frischmann, Volume 3, 98–117. Austin: University of Texas Press.

Eigenbrod, Renate. 2005. *Travelling Knowledges: Positioning the Im/Migrant Reader of Aboriginal Literatures in Canada*. Winnipeg: University of Manitoba Press.

Elter, Sheldon. 2006. *Métis Mutt*. In *Nextfest Anthology II: Plays from the Syncrude Next Generation Arts Festival, 2001–2005*, ed. Steve Pirot, 9–45. Edmonton: NeWest Press.

Escárzaga, Fabiola, and Raquel Gutiérez, eds. 2005. *Movimiento indígena en América Latina: resistencia y proyecto alternativo*. Mexico, D.F.: Gobierno de Distrito Federal, Casa Juan Pablos, Benemérita Universidad Autónoma de Puebla, Universidad Nacional Autónoma de México, Universidad Autónoma de la Ciudad de Mexico.

Fanon, Frantz. 1967. *Black Skin, White Masks*. New York: Grove.

Favel, Floyd. 1993. The Theatre of Orphans / Native Languages on Stage. *Canadian Theatre Review* 75: 8–11.

———. 2002a. All My Relatives. In *The Great Gift of Tears*, ed. Heather Hodgson, 23–95. Regina: Coteau Books.

———. 2002b. The Skinny Ducks. A Critique of Aboriginal Theatre Policy in Canada. http://www.takwakin.com/articles_main.html (accessed October 21, 2002).

———. 2005. Waskawewin. *Topoi* 24, no. 1: 113–15.

Filewod, Alan. 1992. Averting the Colonizing Gaze: Notes on Watching Native Theatre. In *Aboriginal Voices: Amerindian, Inuit, and Sami Theatre*, ed. Per Brask and William Morgan, 17–28. Baltimore: Johns Hopkins University Press.

———. 1994. Receiving Aboriginality: Tomson Highway and the Crisis of Cultural Authority. *Theatre Journal* 46, no. 3 (October): 363–73.

Flather, Patti, and Leonard Linklater. 1993. *Sixty Below*. Toronto: Playwrights Union of Canada.

FOMMA. *The Demon's Nun*. In *Stages of Conflict: A Critical Anthology of Latin American Theater and Performance*, ed. Diane Taylor and Susan J. Townsend, 318–25. Ann Arbor: University of Michigan Press.

Franco, Jean. 2009. Overcoming Colonialism: Writing in Indigenous Languages. *Latin American Studies Association Forum* 40, no. 1 (Winter): 24.

Freeman, Minnie Aodla. 1980. Survival in the South. In *Paper Stays Put: A Collection of Inuit Writing*, ed. Robin Gedaloff, 100–114. Edmonton: Hurtig.

Frye, Northrop. 1986. *On Shakespeare*. New Haven: Yale University Press.

García Márquez, Gabriel. 1971. *One Hundred Years of Solitude*. Trans. Gregory Rabassa. New York: Avon.

Gatti, Maurizio. 2004. *Littérature amérindienne du Québec: Écrits de langue française*. Montréal: Cahiers du Québec.

Geiogamah, Hanay. 2000. The New American Indian Theater: An Introduction. In *American Indian Theatre in Performance: A Reader*, ed. Hanay Geiogamah and Jaye T. Darby, 159–64. Los Angeles: UCLA American Indian Studies Center Press.

Geiogamah, Hanay, and Jaye T. Darby, eds. 2000. *American Indian Theater in Performance: A Reader*. Los Angeles: UCLA American Indian Studies Center.

———, eds. 1999. *Stories of Our Way: An Anthology of American Indian Plays*. Los Angeles: UCLA American Indian Studies Center.

———, eds. 2010. *American Indian Performing Arts: Critical Directions*. Los Angeles: UCLA American Indian Studies Center.

Gilbert, Helen. 1998. *Sightlines: Race, Gender, and Nation in Contemporary Australian Theatre*. Ann Arbor: University of Michigan Press.

Gilbert, Helen, and Joanne Tompkins. 1996. *Post-Colonial Drama: Theory, Practice, Politics*. London: Routledge.

Glancy, Diane. 2002. Further (Farther): Creating Dialogue to Talk About Native American Plays. In *American Gypsy: Six Native American Plays*, by Diane Glancy, 200–204. Norman: University of Oklahoma Press.

——. 2007. Highlight: The Reason for Crows. In *Nations Speaking: Indigenous Performances Across the Americas*. Special issue of *Baylor Journal of Theatre and Performance* 4, no. 1 (Spring): 95–108.

Goffin, Jeffrey. 1990. Four Strong Winds: Native Theatre in Hobbema, Alberta. *Theatrum* 19 (June/July/August): 23–25.

Grace, Sherrill. 1989. *Regression and Apocalypse: Studies in North American Literary Expressionism*. Toronto: University of Toronto Press.

Green, Rayna. 1988. The Tribe Called Wannabee: Playing Indian in American and Europe. *Folklore* 99, no.1: 30–55.

Griffiths, Linda, and Maria Campbell. 1989. *The Book of Jessica: A Theatrical Transformation*. Toronto: Coach House.

Harris, Max. 2000. *Aztecs, Moors and Christians: Festivals of Reconquest in Mexico and Spain*. Austin: University of Texas Press.

Haugo, Ann. 2000a. Contemporary Native Theater: Bibliography and Resource Materials. In *American Indian Theater in Performance: A Reader*, ed. Hanay Geiogamah and Jaye T. Darby, 367–90. Los Angeles: UCLA American Indian Studies Center.

——. 2000b. 'Circles upon Circles upon Circles': Native Women in Theater and Performance. In *American Indian Theatre in Performance: A Reader*, ed. Hanay Geiogamah and Jaye T. Darby, 228–55. Los Angeles: UCLA American Indian Studies Center Press.

——. 2002. Weaving a Legacy: An Interview with Muriel Miguel of the Spiderwoman Theater. In *The Color of Theater: Race, Culture, and Contemporary Performance*, ed. Roberta Uno and Lucy Mae San Pablo Burns, 218–34. New York: Continuum.

——. 2005a. American Indian Theatre. In *The Cambridge Companion to Native American Literature*, ed. Joy Porter and Kenneth M. Roemer, 189–204. Cambridge: Cambridge University Press.

——. 2005b. Native American Drama. In *A Companion to Twentieth-Century American Drama*, ed. David Krasner, 334–51. Malden, MA: Blackwell.

Heath, Sally Ann. 1995. The Development of Native American Theatre Companies in the Continental United States. PhD diss., University of Colorado at Boulder.

Hemispheric Institute of Performance and Politics. Hemispheric Institute / Instituto Hemisférico de Performance & Política. New York University. http://hemisphericinstitute.org/hemi/ (accessed October 1, 2009).

Hengen, Shannon. 2007. *Where Stories Meet: An Oral History of De-Ba-Jeh-Mu-Jig Theatre*. Toronto: Playwrights Canada Press.

Highway, Tomson. 1988. *The Rez Sisters*. Saskatoon, Saskatchewan: Fifth House Publishers.

——. 1989. *Dry Lips Oughta Move to Kapuskasing*. Saskatoon, Saskatchewan: Fifth House Publishers.

——. 2003a. *Rose*. Burnaby, BC: Talonbooks.

——. 2003b. Should Only Native Actors Have the Right to Play Native Roles? In *Rose*, by Tomson Highway, 152–60. Vancouver: Talonbooks.

———. 2005a. *Ernestine Shuswap Gets Her Trout*. Burnaby, BC: Talonbooks.

———. 2005b. On Native Mythology. In *Aboriginal Drama and Theatre: Critical Perspectives on Canadian Theatre in English*, Volume 1, ed. Robert Appleford, 1–3. Toronto: Playwrights Canada Press.

Hodgson, Heather, ed. 2002. *The Great Gift of Tears: Four Aboriginal Plays*. Regina, Saskatchewan: Coteau Books.

Hoikkala, Paivi. 1998. The Hearts of Nations: American Indian Women in the Twentieth Century. In *Indians in American History: An Introduction*, ed. Frederick Hoxie and Peter Iverson, 2nd ed., 253–76. Wheeling: Harlan Davidson.

Horne, Dee. 1996. Settler Culture Under Reconstruction. In *Diverse Landscapes: Re-Reading Place Across Cultures in Contemporary Canadian Writing*, ed. Karin Beeler and Dee Horne, 79–98. Vancouver: University of Northern British Columbia Press.

Houston, Stephen D. 2006. Impersonation, Dance, and the Problem of Spectacle among the Classic Maya. In *The Archaeology of Performance*, ed. Takeshi Inomata and Lawrence S. Coben, 135–58. Lanham, MD: AltaMira.

Houston, Stephen D, Oswaldo Chinchilla Mazariegos, and David Stuart. 2000. *The Decipherment of Ancient Mayan Writing*. Norman: University of Oklahoma Press.

Howard, Rebecca, and Shirley Huston-Findlay, eds. 2008. *Footpaths and Bridges: Voices from the Native American Women Playwrights Archive*. Ann Arbor: University of Michigan Press.

Howe, LeAnne. 2000. My Mothers, My Uncles, Myself. In *Here First: Autobiographical Essays by Native American Writers*, ed. Arnold Krupat and Brian Swann, 212–28. New York: The Modern Library.

Huhndorf, Shari M. 2001. *Going Native: Indians in the American Cultural Imagination*. Ithaca, NY: Cornell University Press.

———. 2006. American Indian Drama and the Politics of Performance. In *The Columbia Guide to American Indian Literatures of the United States Since 1945*, ed. Eric Cheyfitz, 288–318. New York: Columbia University Press.

Huntsman, Jeffrey. 1980. Introduction. *New Native American Drama: Three Plays by Hanay Geiogamah*, ix–xxiv. Norman: University of Oklahoma Press.

———. 1983. Native American Theater. In *Ethnic Theater in the United States*, ed. Maxine Schwartz Seller, 355–85. Westport, CT: Greenwood Press.

Huston-Findley, Shirley A., and Rebecca Howard, eds. 2008. *Footpaths and Bridges: Voices from the Native American Women Playwrights' Archive*. Ann Arbor: University of Michigan Press.

Hutcheon, Linda. 1988. *A Poetics of Postmodernism: History, Theory, Fiction*. London: Routledge.

Innuinuit. 1996. *Braindead*. In *Stars in the Sky Morning: Collective Plays of Newfoundland and Labrador*, ed. Helen Peters, 398–414. St. John's, NL: Killick Press.

Inomata, Takeshi, and Lawrence S. Coben, eds. 2006. *The Archaeology of Performance*. Lanham, MD: AltaMira.

Ivins, Terry. 2003. *Time Stands Still*. Excerpt in *CanPlay* 20, no. 1 (January/ February): 21.

Jenkins, Linda Walsh. 1975. The Performances of the Native Americans as American Theater: Reconaissance and Recommendations. PhD diss., University of Minnesota.

———. 1981. Sex Roles and Shamans. In *Women in American Theater: Careers, Images, Movements—An Illustrated Anthology and Sourcebook*, ed. Helen Krich Chinoy and Linda Walsh Jenkins, 12–18. New York: Crown Publishers.

Jenkins, Linda Walsh, and Ed Wapp, Jr. 1976. Native American Performance. *The Drama Review* 20, no. 2: 5–12.

Johnson, Troy R., Joane Nagel, and Duane Champagne, eds. 1997. *American Indian Activism: Alcatraz to the Longest Walk*. Urbana: University of Illinois Press.

Jones, Eugene F. 1988. *Native Americans as Shown on the Stage: 1753–1916*. Metuchen, NJ: Scarecrow Press.

Kane, Margo. 1991. From the Centre of the Circle the Story Emerges. In *Canadian Theatre Review* 68 (Fall): 26–29.

———. 1994. *Moonlodge*. In *Singular Voices: Plays in Monologue Form*, ed. Tony Hamill, 78–107. Toronto: Playwrights Canada Press.

Kane, Margo, Greg Daniels, and Marie Clements. 2001. *DraMétis: Three Métis Plays*. Penticton: Theytus Books.

Kenny, George. 1977. *Indians Don't Cry*. Toronto: Chimo.

Kenny, George, and Denis Lacroix. 1978. *October Stranger*. Toronto: Chimo.

Killiktee, Jokeypak, and Malachi Arreak. 1990. SURVIVAL and HELP: Two Plays about Taking Action on Spousal Assault. In *"Gossip": A Spoken History of Women in the North*, ed. Mary Crnkovich, 135–49. Ottawa: Canadian Arctic Resources Committee.

King, Bruce. 1999. *Evening at the Warbonnet*. In *Stories of Our Way: An Anthology of American Indian Plays*, ed. Hanay Geiogamah and Jaye T. Darby, 355–440. Los Angeles: UCLA American Indian Studies Center Press.

———. 2000. Emergence and Discovery: Native American Theater Comes of Age. In *American Indian Theater in Performance: A Reader*, ed. Hanay Geiogamah and Jaye T. Darby, 165–68. Los Angeles: UCLA American Indian Studies Center.

King, C. Richard, and Charles Fruehling Springwood, eds. 2001. *Team Spirits: The Native American Mascot Controversy*. Lincoln, NE: Bison Books.

Kolinská, Klára. 2007. *Čekání na Kojota: současné drama kanadských Indiánů*. Vyd. 1. Dramatické texty, sv. 42. Brno: Větrné mlýny.

Knowles, Ric. 1999. *The Theatre of Form and the Production of Meaning: Contemporary Canadian Dramaturgies*. Toronto: ECW Press.

———. 2003a. The Hearts of Its Women: Rape, Residential Schools, and Re-membering. In *Performing National Identities: International Perspectives on Contemporary Canadian Theatre*, ed. Sherrill Grace and Albert-Reiner Glaap, 245–64. Vancouver: Talonbooks.

————, ed. 2003b. Turning an Elephant into a Microphone: A Conversation on Translation and Adaptation. *Canadian Theatre Review* 114 (Spring): 47–53.

————. 2004. Drama. In *The Cambridge Companion to Canadian Literature*, ed. Eva-Maria Kröller, 115–34. Cambridge: Cambridge University Press.

Knowlton-Le Roux, Laura. 2006. Sacajawea vs. Charbonneau. *Transatlantica*, vol. 1, http://transatlantica.revues.org/index300.html (accessed October 6, 2009).

Krieg, Robert Edward. 1978. Forest Theatre: A Study of the Six Nations' Pageant Plays on the Grand River Reserve. PhD thesis, University of Western Ontario.

Krupat, Arnold. 1989. *The Voice in the Margin: Native American Literature and the Canon*. Berkeley: University of California Press.

Lakevold, Dale, and Darrel Racine. 2006. *Misty Lake*. Barrows, MB: Loon Books.

————. 2007. *Stretching Hide*. Winnipeg: Scirocco Drama.

Laughlin, Robert M., and Sna Jtz'ibajom. 2008. *Monkey Business Theater*. Austin: University of Texas Press.

Lenze, Christine. 2001. "The Whole Thing You're Doing Is White Man's Ways": *fareWel*'s Northern Tour. *Canadian Theatre Review* 108 (Fall): 48–51.

León Portilla, Miguel. 2006. *The Broken Spears: The Aztec Account of the Conquest of Mexico*, translated from Náhuatl into Spanish by Angel María Garibay K., English translation by Lysander Kemp. Boston: Beacon Press.

Lings, Martin. 1998. *The Sacred Art of Shakespeare: To Take Upon Us the Mystery of Things*. Rochester, VT: Inner Traditions.

Luna-Firebaugh, Eileen M. 2002. The Border Crossed Us: Border Crossing Issues of the Indigenous Peoples of the Americas. *Wicazo Sa Review* 17, no. 1 (Spring): 159–181.

Lutz, Hartmut, ed. 1991. *Contemporary Challenges: Conversations with Canadian Native Authors*. Saskatoon, Saskatchewan: Fifth House Publishers.

————. 2000. Native American Studies in Europe: Caught Between 'Indianthusiasm' and Scholarship. In *ZENAF Arbeits- und Forschungsbericht* 1 (December): 13–25.

Manuel, Vera. 1998. *Strength of Indian Women*. In *Two Plays about Residential School*, 75–119. Vancouver: Living Traditions Writers Group.

Mason, Tina. 1991. *Diva Ojibway*. Excerpt in *Canadian Theatre Review* 68, no. 3 (Fall): 82–85.

Maufort, Marc. 2003. *Transgressive Itineraries: Postcolonial Hybridizations of Dramatic Realism*. Brussels: P.I.E.-Peter Lang.

————. 2010. *Labyrinth of Hybridities: Avatars of O'Neillian Realism in Multiethnic American Drama (1972–2003)*. Brussels: P.I.E.-Peter Lang.

Maufort, Marc, and Dorothy Figueira, eds. 2011. *Theatres in the Round: Multi-ethnic, Indigenous, and Intertextual Dialogues in Drama*. Brussels: P.I.E.-Peter Lang.

McMaster, Gerald, ed. 2005. *New Tribe, New York: The Urban Vision Quest.* Washington, DC: Smithsonian National Museum of the American Indian.

Meinholtz, Rolland R., ed. 1969. *Indian Theater: An Artistic Experiment in Progress.* Santa Fe: Institute of American Indian Arts.

Mignolo, Walter D. 2005. *The Idea of Latin America.* Malden, MA: Blackwell.

Miguel, Muriel. 2009. Director's Notes on Persistence of Memory. In *Performing Worlds Into Being: Native American Women's Theater,* ed. Ann Elizabeth Armstrong, Kelli Lyon Johnson, and William A. Wortman, 42. Oxford, OH: Miami University Press.

Mojica, Monique. 1991a. *Princess Pocahontas and the Blue Spots: Two Plays.* Toronto: Women's Press.

———. 1991b. Theatrical Diversity on Turtle Island: A Tool Towards the Healing. Editorial. *Canadian Theatre Review* 68 (Fall): 3.

Mojica, Monique, and Ric Knowles, eds. 2003. *Staging Coyote's Dream: An Anthology of First Nations Drama in English.* Toronto: Playwrights Canada Press.

———. 2009. *Staging Coyote's Dream: An Anthology of First Nations Drama in English.* Volume 2. Toronto: Playwrights Canada Press.

Momaday, N. Scott. 2007. *Three Plays.* Norman: University of Oklahoma Press.

Montemayor, Carlos, and Donald Frischmann, eds. 2007. *Words of the True Peoples / Palabras de los Seres Verdaderos,* Volume 3: Theater/Teatro. Austin: University of Texas Press.

Moraga, Cherrie. 2001. *The Hungry Woman.* Albuquerque, NM: West End Press.

Morris, Jim. 1991. *Ayash.* Excerpt in *First People, First Voices,* ed. Penny Petrone, 203–12. Toronto: University of Toronto Press.

Moses, Daniel David. 1990. *Coyote City.* Stratford, ON: Williams-Wallace.

———. 1991. Interview with Hartmut Lutz. In *Contemporary Challenges: Conversations with Canadian Native Authors,* ed. Hartmut Lutz, 155–68. Saskatoon, Saskatchewan: Fifth House Publishers.

———. 1992. *Almighty Voice and His Wife.* Stratford, ON: Williams-Wallace.

———. 1995. *The Indian Medicine Shows: Two One-Act Plays.* Toronto: Exile Editions.

Moses, Daniel David, and Terry Goldie, eds. 1991. *An Anthology of Canadian Native Literature in English.* Toronto: Oxford University Press.

Moses, L. G. 2002. Performative Traditions in American Indian History. In *A Companion to American Indian History,* ed. Philip J. Deloria and Neal Salisbury, 193–208. London: Blackwell.

Native Theater Festival. 2009. The Online Journal of the Public Theater's Native Theater Festival. http://thenativetheaterfestival.blogspot.com/ (accessed December 6, 2009).

NAWPA Authors' Roundtable. 1999. Native American Women Playwrights' Archive. staff.lib.muohio.edu/nawpa/roundtable.html (accessed December 6, 2009).

New, Lloyd Kiva. [1969] 2000. A Credo for American Indian Theater. In *Indian Theater: An artistic Experiment in Progress*, ed. Rolland R. Meinholtz. Santa Fe: Institute of American Indian Arts. Repr. in *American Indian Theater in Performance: A Reader*, ed. Hanay Geiogamah and Jaye T. Darby, 3–4. Los Angeles: UCLA American Indian Studies Center.

Nolan, Yvette. 1995. *Blade, Job's Wife and Video*. Toronto: ArtBiz Comm.

———. 1998. *Annie Mae's Movement*. Toronto: Playwrights Canada Press.

———. 2005. *Seeing Things Invisible*. In *First Nations of North America: Politics and Representation*, ed. Hans Bak, 39–48. Amsterdam: Vrije Universiteit Press.

Nothof, Anne F., ed. 2000. *Sharon Pollock: Essays on Her Works*. Toronto: Guernica.

Nunn, Robert, ed. 2008. *Drew Hayden Taylor: Essays on His Works*. Toronto: Guernica.

Osoyoos Museum. 2008. The Inkameep Day School. http://www.osoyoosmuseum.ca/inkameep_index.htm (accessed September 20, 2009).

Phillips, McCandlish. 1972. Indian Theater Group: Strong Beginning. *New York Times*, national edition, November 9: 56.

Pinazzi, Annamaria. 1997. The "Fervent Years" of the American Indian Theatre. *Letterature D'America: Rivista Trimestrale* 18, no. 71–72: 105–31.

Preston, Jennifer. 1992. Weesageechak Begins to Dance: Native Earth Performing Arts Inc. *The Drama Review* 36, no. 1 (Spring): 135–59.

Pulitano, Elvira. 1997. Waiting for Ishi: Gerald Vizenor's Ishi and the Wood Ducks and Samuel Beckett's Waiting for Godot. *Studies in American Indian Literatures* 9, no. 1 (Spring): 73–92.

———. 1998. Telling Stories Through the Stage: A Conversation with William Yellow Robe. *Studies in American Indian Literatures* 10, no.1 (Spring): 19–44.

Rathbun, Paul. 2000a. Native Playwrights' Newsletter Interview: Bruce King. In *American Indian Theater in Performance: A Reader*, ed. Hanay Geiogamah and Jaye T. Darby, 303–19. Los Angeles: UCLA American Indian Studies Center Press.

———. 2000b. Native Playwrights' Newsletter Interview: William Yellow Robe, Jr. In *American Indian Theater in Performance: A Reader*, ed. Hanay Geiogamah and Jaye T. Darby, 342–58. Los Angeles: UCLA American Indian Studies Center Press.

Reaney, James. 1979. *Wacousta! A Melodrama in Three Acts with a Description of Its Development in Workshops*. Toronto: Porcépic.

Rimbaud, Arthur. 1873. Mauvais Sang. *Une Saison en Enfer*. Brussels: Alliance Typographique.

Roach, Joseph. 1996. *Cities of the Dead: Circum-Atlantic Performance*. New York: Columbia University Press.

Ross, Ian. 1997. *fareWel*. Winnipeg: J. Gordon Shillingford.

———. 2005. *Bereav'd of Light*. Winnipeg: Scirocco Drama.

Ruffo, Armand Garnet. 1993. Inside Looking Out: Reading Tracks from a Native Perspective. In *Looking at the Words of Our People: First Nations Analysis of Literature*, ed. Jeannette Armstrong, 161–76. Penticton, BC: Theytus Books.

———. 2005. A Windigo Tale: Contemporizing and Mythologizing the Residential School Experience. In *Aboriginal Drama and Theatre*, ed. Robert Appleford, 166–80. Toronto: Playwrights Canada Press.

Ryga, George. 1970. *The Ecstasy of Rita Joe*. Vancouver: Talonbooks.

Sarkowsky, Katja. 2007. *AlterNative Spaces: Constructions of Space in Contemporary Native American and First Nations' Literatures. Heidelberg: Winter.*

Schele, Linda, and Peter Mathews. 1998. *The Code of Kings: The Language of Seven Sacred Maya Temples and Tombs*. New York: Scribner.

Schneider, Rebecca. 1997. *The Explicit Body in Performance*. New York: Routledge.

Scott, James D. 1992. *Domination and the Arts of Resistance*. New Haven: Yale University Press.

Scott, Jill. 2004. Translating Myth: The Task of Speaking Time and Place. In *Translation and Culture*, ed. Katherine M. Farell, 58–72. Lewisburg: Bucknell University Press.

Slemon, Stephen. 1995. Magic Realism as Postcolonial Discourse. In *Magical Realism: Theory, History, Community*, ed. Lois Parkinson Zamora and Wendy B. Faris, 407–26. Durham: Duke University Press.

Smith, Paul Chaat, and Robert A. Warrior. 1997. *Like a Hurricane: The Indian Movement from Alcatraz to Wounded Knee*. New York: New Press.

Spiderwoman Theater. 1976. Women in Violence. Unpublished manuscript.

———. 1992. *Reverb-ber-ber-rations. Women and Performance: A Journal of Feminist Theory* 5, no. 2: 184–212.

———. 2003. *Winnetou's Snake Oil Show from Wigwam City*. In *Keepers of the Morning Star: An Anthology of Native Women's Theater*, ed. Jaye T. Darby and Stephanie Fitzgerald, 229–62. Los Angeles: UCLA American Indian Studies Center Press.

———. 2009. *Persistence of Memory*. In *Performing Worlds Into Being: Native American Women's Theater*, ed. Ann Elizabeth Armstrong, Kelli Lyon Johnson, and William A. Wortman, 42–56. Oxford, OH: Miami University Press.

Stanlake, Christy Lee. 2001. Native American Theatre. In *Introducing Theatre*, ed. Joy H. Reilly and M. Scott Phillips, 74–75. 9th ed. New York: Alliance Press.

———, ed. 2007. *Nations Speaking: Indigenous Performances Across the Americas*. Special issue of *Baylor Journal of Theatre and Performance* 4, no. 1 (Spring).

———. 2010. *Native American Drama: A Critical Perspective*. Cambridge: Cambridge University Press.

Swann, Brian, ed. 1992. *On the Translation of Native American Literatures*. Washington: Smithsonian Institute.

Taylor, Diana. 2003. *The Archive and the Repertoire*. Durham: Duke University Press, 2003.

Taylor, Diana, and Rosalyn Costantino. 2003. *Holy Terrors: Latin American Women Perform*. Durham: Duke University Press.

Taylor, Diana, and Sarah J. Townsend, eds. 2008. *Stages of Conflict: A Critical Anthology of Latin American Theater and Performance*. Ann Arbor: University of Michigan Press.

Taylor, Drew Hayden. 1990. *Toronto at Dreamer's Rock and Education Is Our Right*. Saskatoon: Fifth House.

———. 1991. *The Bootlegger Blues*. Saskatoon: Fifth House.

———. 1993. *Someday*. Saskatoon: Fifth House.

———. 1996a. Alive and Well: Native Theatre in Canada. *Journal of Canadian Studies* 31 (Fall): 29–37.

———. 1996b. The Re-Appearance of the Trickster: Native Theatre in Canada. In *On-Stage and Off-Stage: English Canadian Drama in Discourse*, ed. Albert-Reiner Glaap and Rolf Althof, 51–59. St. John's, NL: Breakwater.

———. 1997. Storytelling to Stage: The Growth of Native Theatre in Canada. *The Drama Review* 41, no. 3 (Fall): 140–52.

———. 1998. *Only Drunks and Children Tell the Truth*. Burnaby, BC: Talonbooks.

———. 2000. *alterNatives*. Burnaby, BC: Talon Books.

———. 2003. Canoeing the Rivers of Canadian Aboriginal Theatre: The Portages and the Pitfalls. In *Crucible of Cultures: Anglophone Drama at the Dawn of a New Millennium*, ed. Marc Maufort and Franca Bellarsi, 25–29. Brussels: P.I.E.-Peter Lang.

———. 2006. *In a World Created by a Drunken God*. Vancouver: Talonbooks.

Te Ata World Premiere. 2005. http://www.usao.edu/teata/ (accessed August 18, 2009).

Tedlock, Dennis. 2003. *Rabinal Achi: A Mayan Drama of War and Sacrifice*. Oxford, UK: Oxford University Press.

Tozzer, Alfred M. 1941. *Landa's Relación de las cosas de Yucatán, a Translation*. Cambridge, MA: The Museum.

———. *Caracol*: Transcontinental Substantiations in the Recent Work of Coatlicue Theater Company. *Baylor Journal of Theatre and Performance*, special issue "Nations Speaking: Indigenous Performance Across the Americas" 4, no.1 (Spring): 55–72.

Traditional Elders' Circle. 1980. Resolution of the Fifth Annual Meeting of the Traditional Elders' Circle. Fourth World Documentation Project. October 5. www.cwis.org/fwdp/Resolutions/Other/elders.txt (accessed December 17, 2003).

Tunooniq Theatre. 1992a. *Changes*. In *Canadian Theatre Review* 73 (Winter): 54–57.

———. 1992b. *In Search of a Friend*. In *Canadian Theatre Review* 73 (Winter): 57–59.

Underiner, Tamara L. 2004. *Contemporary Theatre in Mayan Mexico: Death-Defying Acts*. Austin: University of Texas Press.

———. 2007. Caracol: Transcontinental Substantiations in the Recent Work of Coatlicue Theatre Company. *Baylor Journal of Theatre and Performance* 4, no. 1 (Spring): 55–72.

Valdez, Luis. 1992. *Zoot Suit and Other Plays*. Houston: Arte Público Press.

———. 2005. *Mummified Deer and Other Plays*. Houston: Arte Público Press.

Valgemae, Mardi. 1972. *Accelerated Grimace: Expressionism in the American Drama of the 1920s*. Carbondale and Edwardsville: Southern Illinois University Press.

Van Fossen, Rachael, and Darrell Wildcat. 1997. Ka'Ma'Mo'Pi Cik / The Gathering. *Canadian Theatre Review* 90 (Spring): 40–77.

Venuti, Lawrence. 1998. *The Scandals of Translation: Towards an Ethics of Difference*. New York: Routledge.

Versényi, Adam. 1989. Getting Under the Aztec's Skin: Evangelical Theatre in the New World. *New Theatre Quarterly* 19, no. 5 (August): 217–226.

Vizenor, Gerald. 1998. *Fugitive Poses: Native American Indian Scenes of Absence and Presence*. Lincoln: University of Nebraska Press.

Wakiknabe Theatre Company American Theatre website. www.american theaterweb.com/TheaterDetail.asp?ID=1486 (accessed September 15, 2003).

Whittaker, Robin C. 2009. Fusing the Nuclear Community: Intercultural Memory, Hiroshima 1945 and the Chronotopic Dramaturgy of Marie Clements' *Burning Vision*. *Theatre Research in Canada / Recherches théâtrales au Canada* 30, no. 1–2: 129–51.

Wilmer, Steven E., ed. 2009. *Native American Performance and Representation*. Tucson: University of Arizona Press.

Wilmeth, Don B. 2000. Noble or Ruthless Savage? The American Indian on Stage and in the Drama. In *American Indian Theater in Performance: A Reader*, ed. Hanay Geiogamah and Jaye T. Darby, 127–56. Los Angeles: UCLA American Indian Studies Center.

Zamora, Lois Parkinson, and Wendy B. Faris, eds. 1995. *Magical Realism: Theory, History, Community*. Durham and London: Duke University Press.

Contributors

Günter Beck studied American and German literature at the University of Augsburg, Germany, and at Brandeis University. He received his PhD from the University of Augsburg in 2006 with a thesis on the role and function of history in contemporary Native Drama in the USA and Canada. He taught American literature at the University of Augsburg and German studies as a DAAD lecturer at the Haifa Center for German and European Studies at the University of Haifa, Israel. Teaching and research interests include, among others, German and American drama.

Birgit Däwes is a junior professor of American studies at the Johannes Gutenberg University of Mainz, Germany. Her study on *Native North American Theater in a Global Age* (Heidelberg: Winter, 2007) was the first comprehensive analysis published in the field of indigenous North American drama; it won the Bavarian American Academy's Annual Book Award (2007) and the University of Würzburg's Award for Excellent Research by Women (2008). Her second book, *Ground Zero Fiction: History, Memory, and Representation in the American 9/11 Novel* (Heidelberg: Winter, 2011) just won the American Studies Network's biennial book award in 2012, a prize presented by a group of seventeen European American studies centers. Other grants and awards include a Fulbright fellowship in 2003 and the DGfA's Best Article Award in 2008 (for an exploration of literature and transnational memory). Her work has been published in *Contemporary Literature*, the *Columbia Encyclopedia of Modern Drama* (2007), *Amerikastudien / American Studies*, *ZAA*, *LWU*, *Canadian Literature*, and the Methuen Drama series. As a fellow at Mainz University's Center for Comparative Native and Indigenous Studies, Birgit Däwes currently works on the thematic and methodological intersections between indigenous literatures, life writing, and ecocriticism.

Floyd Favel (Cree) is a theatre and dance (contemporary and native traditional) director, performer, film producer and writer, journalist and teacher. His ethos and style is informed by the dynamic relationship between performance/process/tradition entitled Native Performance Culture, and he is working on a book of essays. He received his education from the Native Theatre School in Toronto, the Tukak Teatret in Fjaltring, Denmark (a school for Greenlandic Inuit, Sami, and Native Americans), and the Centro di Lavoro di Grotowski, Pontedera, Italy. His published dramas include *The House of Sonya* (1997), *Lady of Silences* (1992), and *Governor of the Dew / Le Maître de la Rosée* (2004). His essays have been published in *The Navajo Times*, *Native Peoples Magazine*, *Lakota Country Times*, *The Globe and Mail*, Kluwer Academic Publishers, *Alt Theatre Magazine on Culturally Diverse Theatre*, and *Canadian Theatre Review*. His work has been presented at the Santa Fe Institute of American Indian Arts, the Denver Art Museum, and the National Museum of the American Indian.

Diane Glancy's last play, *Salvage*, was produced in 2008 at the Autry National Center in Los Angeles and traveled to the 2009 Indigenous Festival at Riverside Studios in London. Glancy is professor emeritus at Macalester College in St. Paul, Minnesota, where she has taught Native American Literature and Creative Writing. She held the Richard Thomas Chair at Kenyon College in the spring semesters of 2008 and 2009. She will be a professor at Azusa Pacific University near Los Angeles in 2011–2012. Glancy received her MFA from the University of Iowa. She has published two books of plays, *American Gypsy*, a collection of six plays (University of Oklahoma Press, 2002), and *War Cries*, a collection of nine plays (Holy Cow! Press, 1998). A group of shorter plays, *The Sum of Winter*, and an introduction to factional theatre appear online at www.alexander-street.com. Her new play, *The Bird House*, will be performed at the Autry in 2013.

Ann Haugo holds a PhD in theatre history with a graduate minor in women's studies from the University of Illinois at Urbana-Champaign. For the School of Theatre at Illinois State University, she teaches courses in theatre history, dramatic literature, and theory and criticism. Haugo is also an affiliated faculty member of the women's studies program and the minors in ethnic studies and Native American studies. Haugo coedited with Scott Magelssen (Bowling Green State University) *Querying Difference in Theatre His-*

tory (Cambridge Scholars Publishing). Her publications on American Indian and First Nations theatre have appeared in books such as *The Color of Theatre: A Critical Sourcebook in Race and Performance*, *American Indian Theatre: A Reader*, *The Cambridge Companion to Native American Literature*, and Blackwell's *A Companion to Twenti-eth-Century American Drama*, as well as various academic journals and periodicals.

Tomson Highway was born in a snow bank on the Manitoba/Nunavut border to a family of nomadic caribou hunters. He had the great privilege of growing up in two languages, neither of which was French or English; they were Cree, his mother tongue, and Dene, the language of the neighboring "nation," a people with whom they roamed and hunted. Today, he enjoys an international career as playwright, novelist, and pianist/songwriter. His best known works are the plays *The Rez Sisters*, *Dry Lips Oughta Move to Kapuskasing*, *Rose*, *Ernestine Shuswap Gets Her Trout*, and the best-selling novel *Kiss of the Fur Queen*. For many years, he ran Canada's premiere Native theater company, Native Earth Performing Arts (based in Toronto), out of which has emerged an entire generation of professional Native playwrights, actors, and, more indirectly, the many other Native theatre companies that now dot the country. He divides his year equally between a cottage in northern Ontario (near Sudbury, from whence comes his partner of twenty-five years) and a seaside apartment in the south of France, at both of which locales he is currently at work on his second novel.

Klára Kolinská teaches at the Department of Anglophone Studies at Metropolitan University, Prague, Czech Republic, and at the Department of Anglophone Literatures and Cultures at Charles University, Prague. Her main areas of teaching and research include early and contemporary Canadian fiction, theatre and drama, multiculturalism, and Aboriginal literature and theatre. She has published mainly on Canadian Aboriginal literature and theatre, Canadian prose fiction, and theory and practice of narrative and storytelling. Her main publications and coeditions include: *Women in Dialogue: (M)Uses of Culture* (Cambridge Scholars Publishing, 2008); *Waiting for Coyote: Contemporary Canadian Aboriginal Drama and Theatre* (V trné mlýny, 2007); *Contemporary Aboriginal Literature in North America*: special issue of *Litteraria Pragensia: Studies in Literature and Culture* (Charles University, Prague, 2005); and *Shakespeare and His Collaborators Over the Centuries* (Cambridge Scholars Publishing, 2008).

Marc Maufort is a professor of English, American, and postcolonial literature at the Université Libre de Bruxelles (Belgium). He is the current European secretary of the International Comparative Literature Association (ICLA). Maufort has authored three monographs: *Songs of American Experience: The Vision of O'Neill and Melville* (1990), *Transgressive Itineraries: Postcolonial Hybridizations of Dramatic Realism* (2003), and *Labyrinth of Hybridities: Avatars of O'Neillian Realism in Multi-ethnic American Drama, 1972–2003* (2010). He has coedited a number of critical anthologies, including *Performing Aotearoa: New Zealand Theatre and Drama in an Age of Transition* (2007) and *Signatures of the Past: Cultural Memory in Contemporary Anglophone North American Drama* (2008).

Rolland Meinholtz (Cherokee, Scottish/Irish), educator, dramatist, director, and actor/singer holds degrees from Northwestern University and the University of Washington. Drama instructor at the Institute of American Indian Arts, Santa Fe, New Mexico 1964–1970, he was charged with training theatre students and leading them in the creation of Native American Theatre. Working with students, plays and theatre events were produced that arose directly out of the history and culture of Native Americans; plays performed, and toured nationally. Meinholtz was artistic director of both the First and Second Festivals of Indian Performing Arts, sponsored by the Interior Department and performed in Washington, D.C., 1965 and 1966. Students of Meinholtz have since formed the core of theatre artists attempting to create a commercial Native American Theatre. In 1970, Meinholtz joined the faculty of the Theatre Department at the University of Montana. He was head of the directing program, retiring in 1992. He has authored plays, directed over 200 productions, and performed in more than 150 productions. Professional credits include the Festivals, the Santa Fe Opera, and the Montana Rep.

Monique Mojica is an actor and playwright from the Kuna and Rappahannock nations. Based in Toronto, she was spun directly from the web of New York's Spiderwoman Theater. Her first play *Princess Pocahontas and the Blue Spots* was produced in 1990. She is the coeditor, with Ric Knowles, of *Staging Coyote's Dream: An Anthology of First Nations Drama in English*, Volumes 1 and 2. She appeared as Grandma Builds-the-Fire in Sherman Alexie's film *Smoke Signals*, and was a cofounder of Turtle Gals Performance Ensemble, with whom she cocreated *The Scrubbing Project* and *The Triple Truth*.

Monique was last seen as Caesar in *Death of a Chief*, Native Earth's adaptation of Shakespeare's *Julius Caesar*. A longtime collaborator with Floyd Favel in Native Performance Culture research, she was the artist in residence for American Indian studies at the University of Illinois in Spring 2008. Currently she is creating a collaborative, interdisciplinary performance project, *Chocolate Woman Dreams the Milky Way*, with Floyd Favel, Oswaldo De León Kantule, Erika Iserhoff, Gloria Miguel, and other collaborators of the Chocolate Woman Collective. Monique continues to explore theatre as healing, as an act of reclaiming historical/cultural memory and as an act of resistance.

Daniel David Moses calls the Six Nations lands along the Grand River in southern Ontario, Canada, home. He is registered there as a Delaware Indian. His poems are collected in *Delicate Bodies, The White Line, Sixteen Jesuses*, and *A Small Essay on the Largeness of Light and Other Poems* (2012). Other publications include, most recently, as author, *Kyotopolis*, a play in two acts (2008), and, as editor, *The Exile Book of Native Canadian Fiction and Drama* (2010), both from Exile Editions, *River Range Poems* (2009), a self-produced CD with music by David Deleary, and a new edition of his best-known play *Almighty Voice and His Wife* (2009) from Playwrights Canada Press. He is also coeditor of Oxford University Press's *An Anthology of Canadian Native Literature in English*, the fourth- and twentieth-anniversary edition of which appeared in 2012. He holds an Honors BA in General Fine Arts from York University, an MFA in Creative Writing from the University of British Columbia, and teaches playwrighting in the Department of Drama at Queen's University in Kingston, Ontario.

Henning Schäfer graduated from the University of Hannover, Germany, in 1990. From 2001 to 2004 he was a member and scholarship-holder of the graduate program Cultural Hermeneutics in a World of Difference and Transdifference at the University of Erlangen, Germany. He has taught at the universities of Braunschweig and Hannover and works on his PhD project entitled "Native Canadian Theatre: An Analysis of Its History and Contemporary Scene." He has published several articles on Native theatre, and his research has led him to Canada several times. At the moment, he is the head of the department for the accreditation of study programs at the Central Evaluation and Accreditation Agency Hannover. His main areas of interest are postcolonial studies and drama.

Tamara L. Underiner is associate professor and director of graduate studies at Arizona State University, directs the PhD concentration in Theatre and Performance of the Americas, and teaches in the general areas of theatre history and culture studies. She is the author of *Contemporary Theatre in Mayan Mexico: Death-Defying Acts* (University of Texas Press, 2004) and has also published on indigenous and Latina/o theatre and critical pedagogy in *Theatre Journal*, *Signs*, the *Baylor Journal of Theatre and Performance*, and critical anthologies from the University of Arizona and Routledge Presses. Her current research focuses on performances of indigeneity and Nativism in border contexts. She is active in the Association for Theatre in Higher Education, the Latin American Studies Association, and the American Society for Theatre Research, and serves on the Board of the Hemispheric Institute for Performance and Politics.

Index